HUMANE
EDUCATION
IN HIGHER
EDUCATION

ADVANCING INCLUSIVE
SOCIAL JUSTICE STUDIES IN A
POSTSECONDARY ENVIRONMENT

EDITED BY STEPHANIE ITLE-CLARK

WCY
HUMANE PRESS

WCY

HUMANE PRESS

Published by WCY Humane Press
an imprint of Who Chains You Publishing
P.O. Box 581
Amissville, VA 20106

www.WCYhumanepress.com
www.whochainsyou.com

Book cover and interior design by Tamira Thayne
www.tamirathayne.com

ISBN: 978-1-946044-86-0

Printed in the United States of America

First Edition

DEDICATION AND
Acknowledgments

All of us, the editor and the authors, would like to thank postsecondary educators who strive to make collegiate courses memorable and impactful. With strong models in academia standing for equal justice and inclusivity toward all people, animals, and the planet, we will support generations of humane literate societies.

Thank you to Dr. Sean Kelly, who had the foresight to organize thought leaders in humane and higher education and who daily works to bring inclusive social justice into the university through classes, coaching, and his personal model.

TABLE OF
CONTENTS

PART THREE: BUILDING THE HUMANE INSTITUTION

PART FOUR: COURSE DESIGN AND SYLLABUS SAMPLES

AUTHOR BIOGRAPHIES

FOREWORD

Moving Postsecondary Practice Toward Truly Inclusive Social Justice

Stephanie Itle-Clark and Erin Comaskey

Education and schooling are often the avenues through which the values, norms, and knowledge of a society transfer from one generation to the next. Higher education is traditionally thought of as an institution aligned with socially conscious development and it plays an important part in preparing society for the future and instilling or solidifying values. At the heart of the liberal education is its duty to democracy and within that its service to its citizens. In this way, education links to social justice issues, not just in its functionality but also in its purpose. Considering Dewey's proposal that democracy and in turn a democratic education is one that must involve participatory action to achieve the Good Society, it follows that an education is more than books and rigor; it takes place when the individual participates in social activities and relationships with others (Dewey, 2011; Dewey, 1990). Indeed, those thinkers who have shaped the present state of higher education saw the need for the university setting to pursue the new, to culminate in innovation, and to challenge the antidemocratic political philosophy. Similarly, Freire imagined that education would be "… the means by which men and women deal critically and creatively with reality and discover how to participate in the transformation of their world" (2000, p.34). In many ways, the university determines the character of the overall schooling system. "Through the school system … every family in this entire broad land of ours is brought into touch with the university; for from it proceeds the teachers, or the teacher's teachers" (Harper, 1905: 25). The state of the university is a reflection of the state of the democracy.

So, what does this say about the state of higher education right now? Certainly, within education the focus is increasingly on curricular content, performance goals, and student completion rates. We must ask ourselves if we are content with this being the norm and philosophical underpinning of education. Are these norms those that allow democratic principles of learning and compassionate actions to be both integrated into higher education and to trickle into all levels of education through graduates?

Evidence exists to show that institutional support of service or civic engagement at the collegiate level has a major influence on patterns of future behavior (Franklin, 2004). If an entity of higher learning shares only in language, and not in action, the goals of prosocial living toward people, animals, and the planet, we will continue to replicate a population of morally illiterate individuals. If schooling is the "leading societal subsystem" (Harper, 1905) then it must develop in ways that build capacity to expand the human experience through what can only be a humane education. A humane education initiates learning that activates the head, heart, and hands by encouraging cognitive, affective, and behavioral growth. A truly humane education revolves around inclusive social justice and supports personal development of "critical thinking, problem solving, perspective-taking, and empathy as it relates to people, animals, the planet, and the intersections among them" (Itle-Clark, 2016). The theory and practice of this education, or the humane pedagogy, "allows learners to process personal values and choose prosocial behaviors aligned with those values" (Itle-Clark, 2016).

The manifestation of the Greater Society is to prompt the evolution of the learner through building connections and creating transformation. Consequently, higher education cannot ignore the intersections among people, animals, and the planet, but instead decide this is the foundation of its purpose. In other words, institutions of higher education should commit to building a humane institution which serves as a model that can be replicated within all systems. Schooling is in many ways a model of the Greater Society and the early model provided by higher education allows students to practice feelings and behaviors they will replicate in the larger world upon graduation. The college level is a formative time when future leaders learn and live the things they will teach, model, and in the long run, reproduce in society.

Therefore, the creation of a humane institution views teaching, learning, cognitive evolution and the culmination of the human experience through a humane lens. This lens places humane pedagogy as a core value in education and helps learners to become literate in inclusive social justice and to see both positive and negative systems related to people, animals, and the planet. "Within a humane approach to education (a humane pedagogy), species is an intersecting identity in the same way that other forms of stratification such as race, class, age, and gender are. The privileges or disadvantages inherent of each intersecting component become equally valid.... The providence of human-kind is linked to humane work and the development of the prosocial traits that create a world in which all living beings are afforded the ability to live as they were meant to, in a fair and comfortable way." (Itle-Clark & Comaskey, in press, p.10). It further creates the opportunity for fulfilling the concept of democratic participation, as students and teachers prepare not for the theoretical, but the real opportunity to take action for the good of all (see Figure 1). The danger in removing any one of these topics from studies in higher education is that decisions can become focused only on the human need. Worse yet, it can become focused on the need of only some humans. This book emphasizes the need to bring animals equally into the discussion of these social systems. Each paper presents ideas for new courses, areas of study, and professional practice that allow academic discourse and reflection based on true equity.

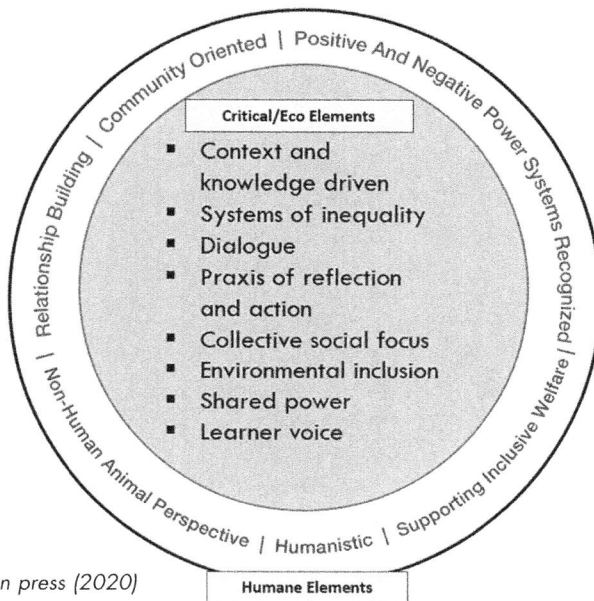

Figure 1.
Itle-Clark &
Comaskey, in press (2020)

References

Dewey, J. (2011) *Democracy and Education.* Milton Keynes: Simon and Brown.

Dewey, J. (1990) *The School and Society* (ed. by P. W. Jackson). Chicago, IL: University of Chicago Press.

Franklin, Mark N. 2004. *Voter Turnout and the Dynamics of Electoral Competition in Established Democracies since 1945.* Cambridge: Cambridge University Press.

Freire, P. (2000). Pedagogy of the oppressed. New York: Continuum

Harper, W. R. (1905) The university and democracy. In the Trend in Higher Education. Chicago, IL: University of Chicago Press.

Itle-Clark, S. What is humane education? Retrieved May 25, 2020, from www. prosocialacademy.org.

Itle-Clark, S. & Comaskey, E. (in press). A proposal for a humane pedagogy. *International Journal of Humane Education, 1*(1).

PART ONE

PROSOCIAL DEVELOPMENT
IN THE FIELD OF EDUCATION

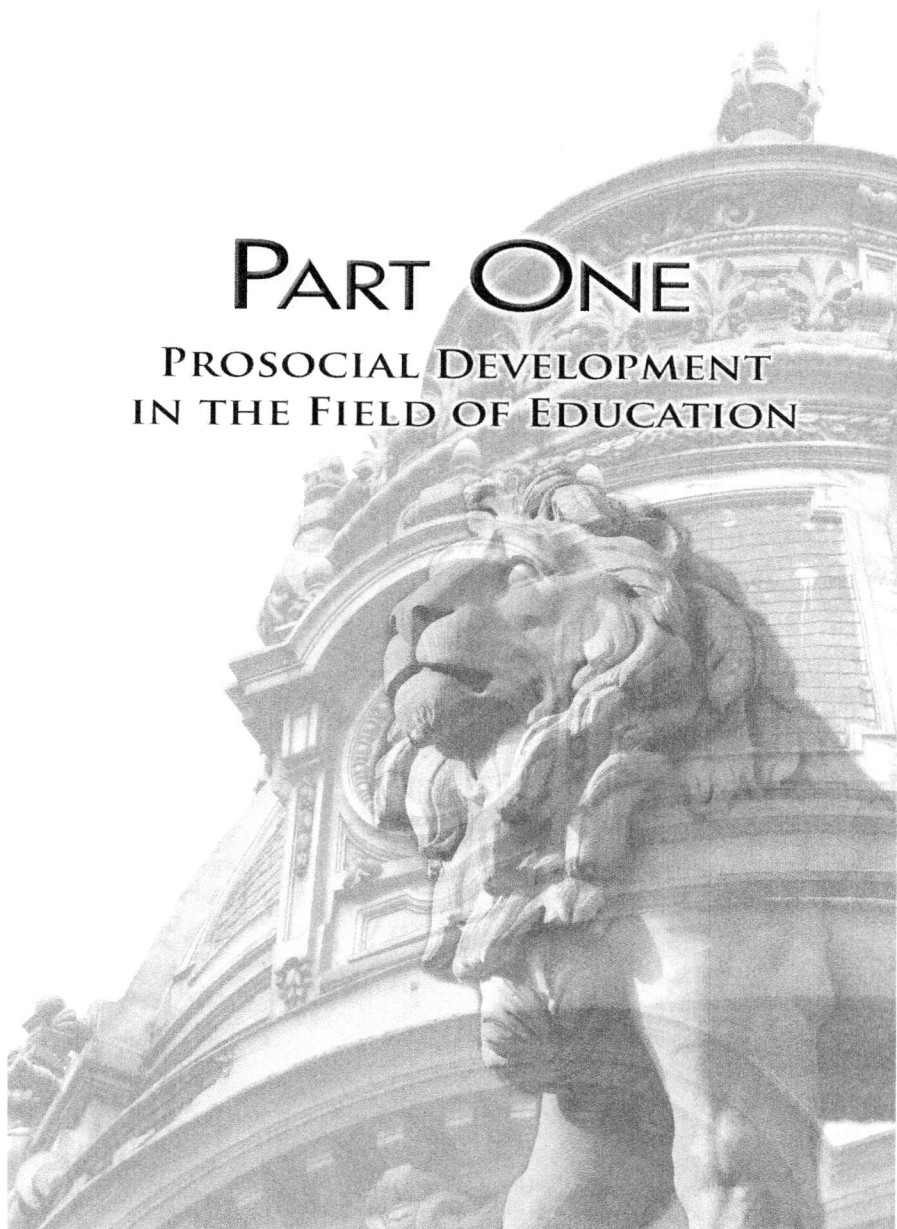

CHAPTER ONE

LOOKING FORWARD:
HUMANE EDUCATION
AND A HUMANE SOCIETY

Bernard Unti, The Humane Society of the United States

The notion that teaching and communicating the lesson of kindness to animals to children and other audiences has broad social benefits and has been one of deep and longstanding promise, and it has had special appeal to the movement for organized animal protection over the last 150 years. Today, however, it remains an arena of uncertain results and unsteady support. Within the context of our global ecological crisis, humane education continues to command the interest of some within higher education, the field of pedagogy, and organized animal protection work for its potential value to encourage a caring attitude toward non-human life. But what is that value, exactly, and how can it be realized? Does it have a role to play in making individuals more sensitive and caring toward nature, to non-human animals, or to other human beings? Can it help to promote and instill a duty of care toward animals and the environment in a society that needs such sensibility? Is there a humane literacy that environmental and prosocial education efforts should cultivate in young and old alike?

As a discipline, humane education centers on inculcating the ethic of kindness through formal or informal instruction of children in the schools or in other contexts such as clubs, church groups, and the like. The term is also sometimes used to describe efforts to reach people of all ages with messages concerning kindness to animals. Over time,

lucation has broadened its scope, from instruction on the
ᴊɪ kindness and the basic prevention of cruelty to animals to
ᵖromotion of the affirmative duty of encouraging environmental awareness as well as a deeper sensitivity to others, human and non-human,
and conscientious behavior and conduct toward all.

Humane education was the third leg of the stool of the pre-20th
century humane movement, along with enforcement action and institution building. Humanitarians placed a high priority on the socialization
of children and emphasized the lessons of kindness to animals as crucial
to the development of a well-adjusted individual (Unti, 2001). They also
placed a premium on humane education targeting those adults who
worked with animals, believing that this outreach would have immediate effects in mitigating the most common forms of cruelty associated
with animal use.

One might think that with respect to our schools, the push for
humane education would be a third rail of humane work, today and
always. But to judge from the low priority it has enjoyed in recent years
with national humane organizations like the American Society for the
Prevention of Cruelty to Animals (ASPCA), The Humane Society of
the United States (HSUS), and the American Humane Association
(AHA), it appears to be in danger of disappearing as a national goal of
the animal protection movement. In recent years, these organizations
have curtailed or eliminated their commitment to humane education
and related programs.

In some respects, this reflects the attitudes of a broader society that
does not value education as a channel of investment, mostly preferring
to pay it lip service instead (DeLisle, 2013; Zawistowski, 2014). The difficulty of integrating humane education into an already crowded and
frequently politicized curriculum has also been a significant factor. The
perception of animal protection as a special interest may have played a
role as well, making the barriers to integration hard to overcome.

It is probable, too, that the acceptance of performance metrics in
the non-profit sector has played a role in the erosion of the humane
movement's commitment to education efforts. Contemporary grantors
and philanthropic donors look for evidence that their investments will
result in measurable changes, and education programs are difficult to
measure. As a colleague observed, "We don't even agree on how best to
measure how effective we are in math education, [and] humane educa-

tion is even more difficult. How do we document the children who do not beat their dogs or starve their cats? We can document changes in live release rate from shelters, laws passed, puppy mills busted and dog fighters arrested. How should we count the number of hearts in which we have kindled the flame of kindness" (Zawistowski, 2014)?

The modern animal movement has also chosen to advance its educational mission in other ways via social marketing campaigns targeting the adult population, public awareness activities, and other work. These initiatives do not fall within the classic definition of humane education as a school- and youth-focused effort, but they do represent a substantial commitment to public education focusing on humane and prosocial values and ideals.

Naturally, the advent of social media has also transformed the approaches that organizations and other moral entrepreneurs take to both youth and public outreach. There are many channels outside of the classroom context through which they can communicate with their audiences, especially with young people. The school remains important, but the Internet, social networking, mobile communication, and many other technological channels have expanded the landscape of opportunity for reaching audiences.

Whatever the commitment of national organizations, at the local level many societies for the prevention of cruelty to animals and humane societies do continue to provide and often expand programs for schools and young people. Moreover, there are a few specialized organizations working to promote humane education by various means, to generate useful resources, and to train teachers. This is an important function and service, with the national animal protection groups, once the source of prepared curriculum and materials, having largely exited the field.

There is much room for improvement in the development and assessment of educational programs in this area. One of the few broad-ranging studies of shelter-based humane education surveyed 600 animal shelters selected at random and revealed that while humane education has remained widespread, it survives mainly as a peripheral issue for humane societies trying to meet other organizational priorities and needs in their communities. Societies rated humane education highly important but generally did not fund it well or staff it accordingly (Olin, 2002).

A BRIEF HISTORY

Humane education emerged in the 17th century, took hold in the 18th, and became central to 19th and 20th century humane work. It has had many advocates. Its modern origins trace back to John Locke's environmentalist theory of mind and his observations in *Some Thoughts Concerning Education* (1693). The concept that a virtuous character could be formed through the ideas, impressions, and experiences of youth prompted the emergence of an entire publishing industry for children's literature in the 18th century. The kindness-to-animals ethic was a prominent theme in such works and had special resonance in the 19th century as a means for inculcating standards of bourgeois gentility and middle-class life, like empathy and moral sensitivity. Humane education was an established instrument of youth socialization by the time animal protection societies formed in England, Europe, and North America. Women were especially strong champions of humane education as authors, lecturers, and organizers (Grier, 2006; Unti, 2002; Unti & DeRosa, 2003).

During the post-Civil War period, American moral reformers, including humane advocates, viewed the formation of character as a dynamic driver for social change. The era's liberal evangelicalism, with its emphasis on individual perfection that could lead to a broader social perfection, helped to fuel enthusiasm for humane education. Importantly, the movement's promotion of humane education as a solution to numerous social ills drew animal protection into close alignment with other reform causes, especially child protection and temperance. Temperance in particular had a strong educational outreach program targeting schools and other institutions. Significant expressions of the era's social feminism, animal protection, and temperance shared a deep concern about the implications of cruelty and violence – particularly male cruelty and violence – for individuals, the family, and the social order. The educational work of humane societies and temperance organizations sustained an ongoing discourse about the proper behavior of men and the threat that poorly socialized boys could pose to animals, people, and social institutions (Unti, 2002).

In the late 19th century, it was much easier for elite advocates of humane education to approach and to penetrate institutions of learning with their ideas, their agendas, and their programs. Temperance advocates, nature study advocates, and other interest groups were all actively seeking to promote their values and views in the nation's public schools. During the first two decades of the 20th century, taking advantage of increased attention to children's character and moral development, typical of the Progressive era, humane advocates successfully passed compulsory humane education requirements in a number of states—23 of them by 1925, in fact. They reinforced this achievement with the production of humane anthologies and textbooks. This was the era of the first films, the first poster contests, and the first professional humane educators, usually employees of local societies for the prevention of cruelty to animals (DeLisle, 2013; Unti, 1999; Unti, 2002; Unti & DeRosa, 2003).

The compulsory humane education laws ended up becoming what today would be called "unfunded mandates"; they were usually dead letters where approved and did not lead to consistent efforts or activities toward the incorporation of humane education into the school curriculum. Moreover, as local societies became bogged down with the substantial challenges of municipal animal control, humane education became a lower priority. Given limited resources, such organizations had a hard time fielding good humane education programs, and it was at most an adjunct function. The humane movement's declining social influence in the early 20th century also contributed to the failure of its efforts to institutionalize humane education within teacher-training institutions and school systems. Humane education was not taken up by institutions of higher learning, and it did not become integrated into American educational theory or pedagogy (Unti, 1999; Unti, 2002).

What might have been the result had humane education found a purchase within higher education, or within the philanthropic sector, from which funding support might have emerged? In 1907, a onetime Columbia University trustee gave $100,000 to the university for humane education work. Columbia's president appointed a committee that concluded that "the improvement of the instruction of young children in the primary schools in the sentiment of kindliness and consideration for each other and in their duty towards the lower animals would be one means of carrying out the wish of the donor" (Unti, 2002). But there were other suggested means, and Columbia decided to fund a program of study and reports on legislative affairs concerning the protection of animals and children. Advocates saw this approach as having limited value, but Samuel Lindsay, the program's director, responded with the argument that the university was not fitted to carry on propaganda. Lindsay's program never addressed humane education, and it disappeared entirely a few decades later (Unti, 1999; Unti, 2002).

Of course, on the campus was the Columbia Teachers College, and not far away were the ASPCA, the New York Humane Society, and the Women's League for Animals. With a little ingenuity, the university might have pioneered in the formal study of humane education in theory and in practice. Had the money been differently allocated, it could have made possible the review and validation of teaching methods and content; the examination of differences between nature study, science education, and other disciplines; and assessments of the feasibility of introducing humane education into the nation's schools.

Even then, it was clear that both humane education and research concerning children's interactions with animals could have been subjects of proper attention from academic investigators. At Clark University, G. Stanley Hall and his associates studied children and animals, and Clifton Fremont Hodge, along with other nature-study advocates, not only viewed animal abuse by children as an important topic, but believed that there was tremendous potential to the study of animals in children's lives both within and outside of the classroom (Ascione, 2005). There were also examples like that of Susan Isaacs in the 1930s, who undertook pioneering research that treated seriously the role of animals in children's moral development. (Isaacs, 1930; Unti, 1999; Unti, 2002).

In the middle decades of the 20th century, both humane education and the role of animals in childhood and human development languished as subjects of study, with just the occasional flash of interest. In 1944, sociologist James Bossard proposed a more serious focus on the role that pets play in family life and particularly in the mental health of family members, a concern he pursued for several decades. Beginning in the late 1960s, psychiatrist Boris Levinson took a more comprehensive approach and argued for a framework of study that went beyond human relations alone to include the whole ecology of children's experience with institutions, family relationships, communities, and non-human animals. Levinson's contribution anticipates the modern ecological approach, which considers the importance of all the varied contexts in which children develop, from the intimacy of their family relationships to schools, church, neighborhood, society, and culture (Ascione, 2005; Bossard, 1944; Bossard, 1950; Bossard & Boll, 1966; Levinson, 1969; Levinson, 1972).

There would also have been possibilities in this era for the study of humane education's effect on compliance with animal control work being carried out by major SPCAs. In the early decades of the 20th century, in New York, young people supported the ASPCA by bringing stray animals to its shelters as the organization's humane education officials were asking them to do. In addition, humane education both within and outside of schools may have played its part in raising awareness of the importance of spaying and neutering. The data on shelter intake and euthanasia (pet overpopulation) suggests that the numbers were starting to go down (certainly in New York City) before aggressive spay/neuter programs emerged in the 1970s. The period between 1920 and 1960 was a high point for humane education programs at the local level. There was strong interest and activity in the form of essay contests, poster contests, and clubs (Unti, 2002; Zawistowski, 2014).

Humane education could also have been studied to assess its part in helping to normalize kindness to animals as the sign of a well-balanced person and shaped a broader understanding of the social value of the humane ethic. By the middle decades of the 20th century, wanton acts of cruelty to animals by individuals had come to be seen as signs of a maladapted and sick personality. Conversely, a kind disposition toward animals was by then viewed as an important attribute of a well-rounded and mentally healthy individual. These things were true even before the appearance of empirical studies confirming the link between cruelty to animals and interpersonal violence (Unti, 1999; Unti & DeRosa, 2003).

HUMANE EDUCATION IN THE POST-WORLD WAR II ERA

When the post-World War II animal organizations like The HSUS and the Animal Welfare Institute (AWI) formed, partly reactive to dramatic changes in animal use and partly responsive to the perception that leading animal organizations were not fulfilling their charge properly, they had other priorities, and with limited resources they could not attend to humane education work although they recognized its importance. This was true of The HSUS, which made humane slaughter and laboratory animal welfare legislation its earliest focus in the 1950s (Unti & Rowan, 2001).

In 1964, The HSUS launched formal efforts in humane education research, commissioning a study by Stuart Westlerlund of George Washington University to identify what was already going on in schools with respect to humane education, to assess the feasibility of development and implementation of coordinated programs, to determine essential needs, and to sample humane attitudes. The study identified key stakeholders including universities, other educational institutions, government agencies, publishers, professional organizations, private groups and entities, research institutions, and foundations (Westerlund, n.d.)

The Westerlund study suggested that humane education materials had not greatly evolved since the early 20th century, that available materials were mostly ad hoc in nature and reflecting little continuity, that their presentation required a separate allocation of time in the school day, that there was a serious challenge with respect to training of teachers and educators, and that little or no validation of effectiveness and impact was taking place (Westerlund, n.d.; Westerlund, 1976).

Subsequent to the Westerlund study, The HSUS and the University of Tulsa (which had since hired Westerlund) launched a joint initiative, the Humane Education Development and Evaluation Project (HEDEP). In succeeding years, The HSUS launched the National Association for the Advancement of Humane Education (NAAHE), which registered some remarkable achievements under the leadership of Kathleen Savesky and others. NAAHE developed the first comprehensive blended curriculum, People and Animals; carried out and sponsored a handful of validation and other academic studies; launched a journal; challenged the biased or inaccurate materials produced for the conservation/environmental education curriculum Project Wild in the 1980s; and sought to build and serve a community of those interested in humane education (Ascione, 2005; Savesky, 1981; Vockell & Hodal, 1980; Unti, 2004).

During the same period, groups like the Animal Welfare Institute, The HSUS, and the Scientists' Center for Animal Welfare achieved beneficial reforms concerning classroom and science fair uses that involved cruelty and in promoting practices and codes of conduct for keeping animals in the classroom setting. In addition, the last quarter of the 20th century saw the broad promotion of alternatives to dissection and vivisection in classroom instruction, criticized in many quarters as an animal welfare problem, a violation of individual conscience, and an exercise of questionable educational value (Balcombe, 2000; McGiffin & Brownley, 1980; Orlans, 1991; Orlans, 1993).

There have also been synergies between the humane education movement and the most recent cycles of attention to character education in our schools. As at other times in the past, the emphasis on character education, in the form of core or consensus values that transcend political, cultural, and religious differences, promises to increase opportunities for the expansion of humane education teaching. Character education has been popular with educators and parents alike, but is itself bedeviled by questions of effectiveness. The largest federal study to date of school-wide character education programs found that they don't produce any improvements in student behavior or academic performance (U.S. Department of Education, 2010).

THE FUTURE LANDSCAPE OF HUMANE EDUCATION

In recent decades, the locus of humane education continues to be the animal care and control community, and more specifically the private animal shelters, SPCAs, and humane societies sponsoring such work across the country. Many organizations and agencies offer programs at the municipal or county level, sometimes involving partnerships with schools or other youth-oriented institutions. Companion animal issues predominate in program content for reasons having to do with agency mission, institutional sensitivities, interest group politics, and the view that certain issues are not age-appropriate for young people. Within SPCAs and humane societies at the local level, humane education must compete for resources with other functions, including the most basic ones associated with operating a shelter, finding homes for animals, and keeping humane agents on duty. This is a limiting factor in its funding.

Moreover, humane education suffers from a disadvantage in the lack of sufficient proof to demonstrate its effectiveness. There is relatively little existing research or evidence to show that humane education programs actually improve children's attitudes and behavior toward animals and none to show that such gains carry into adulthood. Intuition, anecdotal evidence, the stronger empirical case that underpins the value and effectiveness of contemporary environmental education, and a few formal studies continue to suggest its promise, but there is an urgent, ongoing need for formal evaluation and assessment of humane education with respect both to content and methodology.

There are some new areas of opportunity in the era of mass communication, the Internet, and our thriving social media. Now, more than ever, children can be reached directly, without the mediation of their schools, their teachers, or their parents. In addition, the values of animal protection have more deeply permeated our world, so that children's literature, children's television programming, and other elements of popular culture tend to reinforce humane values as the norm. There are people espousing and promoting these values who are not themselves part of the humane movement. The emergence of social marketing as a feature of humane work at all levels means that local societies can communicate messages that shape and reshape behavior more immediately, with increasing understanding how such behavioral change can lead people toward humane attitudes and better conduct toward animals overall.

How might humane education fit into our future, our future as a society, our future institutions, and our future lives? It is a question deeply imbricated in discussions of the moral development of children and adults, the challenge of global sustainability, the preservation of natural lands, the human relationship with other species, and much more. The case for humane education today rests upon a few persistent themes, including a continuing focus on the nexus between cruelty to animals and interpersonal violence; concern over the spiritual fragmentation that accompanies loss of wilderness space and pristine nature; the perception of humane education's value as a bridge to caring about the natural world; in helping children in their understanding of how to think and reason about environmental problems (Kahn, 2011); and its potential contributions to healthy human social development, sensitivity to the needs of others, and willingness to assume responsibility for them (Myers & Saunders, 2005).

An increasing number of influential thinkers on the environment and our global future have singled out the education and engagement of young people as an urgent priority. David Orr (1992, 2005) has spoken of ecological literacy; Richard Louv (2005) of nature-deficit disorder; and Stephen Kellert and E.O. Wilson (1993), Kellert (2007, 2012), and others of biophilia, the notion that humans have an innate desire and need to commune with nature.

Together, these thinkers are the anchors of a movement to connect children with nature and to do so deeply. Their argument is that we do not have just an environmental crisis on our hands but a social crisis, a public health crisis, and perhaps a psychical crisis, tied to the idea that humans are spiritually fragmented as a result of the increasing environmental degradation and fragmented experiences (Pyle, 2005). Advancing the more positive idea of useful knowledge, Richard Louv (2012) has suggested that our global future will be shaped by the "Nature Principle," which holds that "in an age of environmental, economic and social transformation, the future will belong to the nature-smart—those individuals who develop a deeper understanding of nature and balance the virtual with the real."

The biocentric view, as variously defined, is a threshold concept for the future of humane education and its relationship to other forms of knowledge, especially environmental education. We have had this kind of consciousness since at least the advent of Earth Day in the last decades of the 20th century. It is the idea that "the perception of a common fate that humans and animals share … is considered an integral part of identification with others, either humans or animals, of empathy with them, and of an attitude of respect toward nature in general" (Pagani, 2000).

There is another threshold concept in play now too, however, which is prosocial education. This umbrella concept refers to the processes and methods that help to create the right learning environment for children; acknowledge and nurture the nonacademic, emotional, moral and civic capacities that comprise character; and cultivate autonomy, responsibility, sense of self, sense of connectedness to others, and sense of purpose (Brown et al, 2011). Prosocial education configures both social and moral development as they are tied together in the demonstration of empathy for others. Humane education, with its goals of reinforcing compassion, nurturance, and kindness toward others, is a form of prosocial education supporting behavior change (Itle-Clark, 2013).

If it cares about such things, the animal protection movement needs to revalue humane education and to reclaim its value. The challenge of helping local societies to fund and to deliver humane education in a modern world is substantial, but there is so much our national organizations can do to help to guide its spread within the local and regional societies. Why not strive to have an education specialist at every one of the thousands of animal care and control entities in this country? Why not support new and expanded studies assessing the strength, quality, and prevalence of humane education in our nation's shelters and the communities they serve? Why not explore the relationship between early exposure to the lessons of kindness to animals and humane education in schools and subsequent stages of the lifetime learning cycle?

The entire infrastructure and function of the humane movement in the United States will undergo significant transformation over the course of the next few decades. Shelters will necessarily reinvent themselves, as the population of homeless animals continues to decline and additional resources allow shelters to do more as community centers or magnets for animals and those who care about them. Shelters could be even stronger anchors for the development and delivery of humane education programs in every community. This is consistent with the determination of some practiced hands and observers within the humane education field that the shelter-offered, school-visit focused approaches are reaching their limit and that non-school options might provide a more productive avenue and use of resources (Savesky, 2002; Savesky, 2014; Unti & DeRosa, 2003).

There is also a strong emerging need for global programming in humane education, and, with very few shelters and animal care centers operating in the developing world, we must necessarily look to innovative approaches that are community-wide and community-based. Most people think of "humane education" as something that happens in the classroom via dissemination of documents and other education materials. However, a broader conception of action as education may help us to imagine the future of humane education in the fullest way, especially outside of the U.S. In India and other places where Humane Society International's veterinary rescue teams enter a community and launch a dog sterilization program, their activity if completed with an educational component is a far more powerful "educator" than any amount of classroom instruction or an advertising campaign. The actual delivery of dog sterilization and vaccination in a community is the educational prompt, best paired with outreach and teaching about how the result is positive impact for the community–this is part of the Humane Education Framework of Social Change (Itle-Clark & Comaskey, 2014.)

Within higher education, there is so much that can be done with respect to humane education. For many reasons, colleges of education have yet to integrate humane education into their curricula. This is such a deficit given our urgent and universal need for a widespread environmental intelligence that encompasses greater sensitivity toward the natural world and all of its inhabitants. More effort is needed within schools of social work and criminal justice studies to integrate professional training on the issue of animal abuse and its overlap with other forms of family and community violence and to add the positive values of humane education to youth violence prevention and intervention programs.

It is essential that more be done to close the assessment gap with advanced evaluation studies of humane education, and this is an area in which academic institutions can play a leading role. Most local humane society programs in this area are considered successful by those who run them and, in the 1980s, The HSUS and the Massachusetts SPCA carried out several validation studies (Unti & DeRosa, 2003). But Olin's 2002 survey showed that only 7% of the animal care entities providing humane education were involved in evaluation of their own programs (Olin, 2002). This is an area of great opportunity, both to develop a body of empirical evidence necessary to refine pedagogical strategies and to fortify attitudes toward humane education as a proper and productive focus of study and activity. University researchers would be able to work with local shelters to gain the needed qualitative and quantitative data and information, marrying social science off to community-level experience and practice.

Remarkably, there is not a single general Animal Studies text that features a chapter or serious discussion about humane education, animals and the moral development of children, or the place of animals within scholarship concerning the sociology of childhood. This suggests a relative lack of focus on humane education, and the relationships of children with animals, in comparison with other topics within animal studies. Within specialized journals like *Anthrozoos* and *Society and Animals*, the situation is more encouraging, and these two publications have featured a considerable amount of relevant scholarship. Finally, a recent work focused on promoting a duty of care among children shows just how rich a synoptic essay could be in helping to give shape and focus to the field (Muldoon et al., 2009).

There are so many areas of potential investigation, as a quick survey of such studies suggests. What do children think about animals, and how do they think about animals (Wells & Hepper, 1995)? How do they relate to their pets (Berjke, Kaltenborn, & Ødegårdstuen, 2001; Bjerke, Ødegårdstuen, & Kaltenborn, 1998; Filiatre, Millot, Montagner, Eckerlin, & Gagnon, 1988)? How do children make sense of animals' needs (Myers, Saunders, & Garrett, 2004)? How does caring for animals in childhood shape children's grasp of basic biological concepts (Inagaki, 1990; Inagaki, 2001; Williams & Smith, 2006)? Does petkeeping shape future professional choices (Vizek-Vidovic, Arambasic, Kerestes, Kuterovac-Jagodic, & Valhovic-Stetic, 2001)? Is there a case for keeping animals in the classroom (Morrow, 1998; Rost & Hartmann, 1994; Rud & Beck, 2003)? What is the impact on children's biological knowledge and capacity to care of education delivered at zoos, sanctuaries, visiting farms, and other facilities (Altman, 1998; Tunnicliffe, Lucas, & Osbourne, 1997)?

It is also the case that we still know so very little about why and how people come to the animal protection movement. To have a social movement of any size and to lack real insights as to what draws people into its ranks is surprising (Jasper, 1997). What if it turns out that the answer lies in the developmental stages in which we encounter animals, first as children in our earliest years and then in various contexts through our adolescent years and adulthood as we face the question of animal treatment, from time to time, as an issue of social, cultural, and political importance? Do we even know or agree upon the outcomes we seek? Is it "the humane person," and what does that phrase mean?

Environmental education and animal welfare education are sometimes viewed as indistinguishable, but there are important differences. To a degree, the animal welfare component of humane education challenges the reigning paradigms in environmental education, starting with the clear premise that there is a difference between animate and inanimate nature, making the point that animals are not merely part of the environment and that the environment doesn't end with trees, rivers, and forests. While both fields incorporate the idea that human life is not all the life there is, humane education is more likely to insist on the point that learning to care for the environment involves learning to understand and to care for the needs of animals as part of that environment.

The absence of such awareness will leave us confused in a world in which we are but a fraction of all there is, and it certainly limits the soundness of the decisions we can make when it comes to the management of wild space and wild animal populations. The need to understand and make such decisions involving animals and their well-being will become more important and more frequent in the world we leave to our descendants, as increasing population and other factors threaten to place our interests into conflict with those of nonhuman animals in a variety of settings.

In that world to come, a world beset by serious ecological challenges, society's concern with the kindness-to-animals ethic goes beyond the traditional character development focus that typified humane education in its earlier manifestations. In a world that is humane, we would find such values being discussed across the entire curriculum in every field of study and within every institution across the whole of society. Many people frame humane education as part of a broader social justice agenda that includes non-human animals and, together with older frames based on compassionate concern, mercy, or welfare, this perspective has generated steadily mounting moral pressure concerning the status and treatment of nonhuman animals. Some would cast animals as an emerging "diversity" challenge for human society, and without question there is a growing social agenda that incorporates their interests. Our duties of care and responsibility toward them will become an ever-increasing focus of public, corporate, social, and cultural concern. As citizens, increasingly, we will vote on matters concerning animals and nature. As decision-makers, we will have to analyze and rule on policy and practices that affect animals within a host of institutions. *A broader humane literacy will be needed to meet these challenges.* There are so many institutions we must hold accountable for such efforts. It is not just animal shelters and schools that are responsible for educating people about animals, obviously. We need more studies assessing the educational impact of institutions like zoos, natural history museums, aquariums, and the like. The value of their educational work is not clear, but these are permanent institutions with tremendous potential for shaping popular opinion and behavior toward animals and nature (DeRosa, 1985).

We should view humane education and its relationship to the broader humane society as one of tremendous potential for philanthropy. With some exceptions, as in the 1970s when the Geraldine R. Dodge Foundation supported programming and curriculum work undertaken by The HSUS, animal protection in general and humane education in particular have suffered from terrible underinvestment from the philanthropy sector. There has been a continuing prejudice manifest in the disregard and overthrow of testators' wishes by the trustees of the Brach Foundation, the Doris Duke Foundation, the Leona Helmsley Trust, and others. In these and other cases, the original donors' clear intent to help animals was cast aside by trustees more interested in other causes. This bias has hurt the prospects for stronger commitment to the study of the human-animal bond, humane education, and related topics, starving the field of funds and reinforcing a view that these are not worthwhile matters for investment and inquiry.

It is interesting that, after 150 years, humane education continues to carry a sense of "reform" with it. Humane education is caught up in the fundamental question of whether our schools should direct social change or be directed by it. While humane education has been unevenly adopted into our legal and educational systems over the years, there is always a sense of unfinished business. And there is unfinished business. Certain problems identified long ago still exist. Above all, humane education remains incidental in our schools, and those who believe in it are still somewhat removed from the formal processes and structures of our educational institutions (Wallace, 1974; Westerlund, 1976).

In most respects, the challenges of school-based humane education today are not much different than those of a few decades ago—chronic underfunding, insufficient commitment to evaluation, and poor consensus concerning measures of effectiveness. Humane education needs a revitalization strategy to address the standing five lacks that have long limited its growth: lack of awareness, lack of commitment, lack of training, lack of resources, and lack of research. That strategy would seek to bring individual educators closer to concern for nature and animals, enhance their abilities to teach and encourage such concern, and reinforce society's understanding of the true dangers posed by indifference, unchecked cruelty, and lack of thought toward animals. It could be built around educator workshops, service-learning opportunities, and other services tailored to the needs of our institutions of higher learning and our school systems (Clark, 2011). It would also involve the shelter, as it evolves from its traditional role as the last stop for society's unwanted animals toward becoming a center for learning, being, thinking, and doing when it comes to animals. Still, in the absence of a stronger programmatic and financial commitment from the animal protection movement, acknowledgment and backing from philanthropy, and better efforts to establish humane education within institutions of higher learning, progress cannot be assumed.

"Tomorrow's humanitarians are in today's classrooms" read the phrase used as a one-time headline in a humane education magazine issued forty years ago by The Humane Society of the United States (Dommers, 1974). I hope that it is true. But I now believe that it may not be sufficient, and I hope that we will see a broader effort within and outside of higher education to focus attention and energy on the value of learning about animals and their needs and greater support and momentum toward the creation of a society in which all of us, human and nonhuman alike, can flourish. Humane education, with its focus on personal and global responsibility, is highly compatible with other prosocial educational theories and practices, such as service-learning, character education, and democratic education (Clark, 2011).

The humane movement should value its educational outreach as something that helps to lay the social, cultural, and psychological foundations for a humane society, and it should certainly continue to care about and to help investigate the idea that people come to humane values through developmental stages that include those of childhood and early education in our schools. But our institutions of higher learning should also take a leading role as a champion of the proposition that humane education is central, not marginal, to the emergence of a just, sustainable, and humane society.

References

Altman, J. D. (1998). Animal activity and visitor learning at the zoo. *Anthrozoos, 11*(1), 12-21.

Antoncic, L. (2003). A new era in humane education: How troubling youth trends and a call for character education are breathing new life into efforts to educate our youth about the value of all life. *Animal Law, 9,* 183-213.

Armitage, K. (2009). *The nature study movement: The forgotten popularizer of America's conservation ethic.* Lawrence: University Press of Kansas.

Ascione, F. R. (1992). Enhancing children's attitudes about the humane treatment of animals: Generalization to human-directed empathy. *Anthrozoos, 5*(3), 176-191.

Ascione, F. R. (1996). The abuse of animals and human interpersonal violence: Making the connection. In F. R. Ascione & P. Arkow (Eds.), *Child abuse, domestic violence, and animal abuse: Linking the circles of compassion for prevention and intervention* (pp. 50-61). West Lafayette, IN: Purdue University Press.

Ascione, F. R. (2005). *Children and animals: Exploring the roots of kindness and cruelty.* West Lafayette, IN: Purdue University Press.

Balcombe, J. (2000). *The use of animals in higher education: Problems, alternatives, and recommendations.* Washington, DC: Humane Society Press.

Bjerke, T., Kaltenborn, B. P., & Ødegårdstuen, T. S. (2001). Animal-related activities and appreciation of animals among children and adolescents. *Anthrozoos, 14*(2), 86-94.

Bjerke, T., Ødegårdstuen, T. S., & Kaltenborn, B. P. (1998). Attitudes toward animals among Norwegian adolescents. *Anthrozoos, 11*(2), 79-86.

Bossard, J. (1944). The mental hygiene of owning a dog. *Mental Hygiene, 28,* 408.

Bossard, J. (1950). I wrote about dogs. *Mental Hygiene, 34*(3), 385-390.

Bossard, J., & Boll, E. S. (1966). *The sociology of child development.* New York, NY: Harper and Row.

Brown, P. H., Corrigan, M. W., & Higgins-D'Allesandro, A. (Eds.). (2012). *Handbook of prosocial education* (Vols. 1 & 2). Plymouth, United Kingdom: Rowman and Littlefield.

Clark, S, (2011). Humane education beyond the shelter: Developing humane pedagogy. *The Packrat, 4*(98), 4-6.

DeLisle, S. (2013). A look back on humane education: An interview with Dr. Bernard Unti. *Humane Education Quarterly, 4,* 8-9.

DeRosa, B. (1985). Assessing the educational impact of zoos. *Children and Animals, 9*(4), 22-43.

Dommers, J. J. (1974, Fall). Tomorrow's humanitarians are in our school classrooms today. *NAAHE Journal, 1,* 27.

Eisenberg, Nancy. (1992). *The caring child.* Cambridge, MA: Harvard University Press.

Filiatre J. C., Millot J. L., Montagner H., Eckerlin A., & Gagnon, A. C. (1988). Advances in the study of the relationship between children and their pet dogs. *Anthrozöos, 2*(1), 22–32.

Grier, K. C. (1999). Childhood socialization and companion animals: United States, 1820-1920. *Society and Animals, 7*(2), 95-120.

Grier, K. C. (2006). *Pets in America: A history.* Chapel Hill: University of North Carolina Press.

Inagaki, K. (1990). The effects of raising animals on children's biological knowledge. *British Journal of Developmental Psychology, 8*(2), 119-129.

Inagaki, K. (2001). *Effects of raising mammals on young children's biological inference.* Paper presented at the SRCD Conference, Minneapolis, MN.

Isaacs, S. (1930). *Intellectual growth in young children.* London, United Kingdom: Routledge.

Itle-Clark, S. (2013). *In-service teachers understanding and teaching of humane education before and after a standards-based intervention* (Doctoral dissertation). Retrieved from http://animalstudiesrepository.org/acwp_he/1

Itle-Clark, S. & Comaskey, E. (2014). *Humane education frameworks of social change.* Animal Care EXPO Humane Society International Track, Daytona, FL.

Jasper, J. (1997). *The art of moral protest: Culture, biography, and creativity in social movements.* Chicago, IL: University of Chicago Press.

Kahn, P. H., & Kellert, S. R. (Eds.). (2002). *Children and nature: Psychological, sociocultural, and evolutionary investigations.* Cambridge, MA: MIT Press.

Kellert, S. R. (1997). *Kinship to mastery: Biophilia in human evolution and development.* Washington, DC: Island Press.

Kellert, S. R. (2012). *Birthright: People and nature in the modern world.* New Haven, CT: Yale University Press.

Kellert, S. R., Heerwagen, J., & Mador, M. (Eds.). (2008). *Biophilic design: The theory, science and practice of bringing buildings to life.* Hoboken, NJ: Wiley.

Kellert, S. R. & Wilson, E.O. (Eds.). (1993). *The biophilia hypothesis.* Washington, DC: Shearwater Books.

Levinson B.M. (1962). The dog as a "co-therapist." *Mental Hygiene, 46,* 59-65.

Levinson, B. M. (1969). *Pet-oriented child psychotherapy.* Springfield, IL: Thomas.

Levinson, B.M. (1972). *Pets and human development.* Springfield, IL: Thomas.

Louv, R. (2005). *Last child in the woods: Saving our children from Nature-Deficit Disorder.* Chapel Hill, NC: Algonquin Books.

Louv, R. (2011). *The nature principle: Reconnecting with life in a virtual age.* Chapel Hill, NC: Algonquin Books

Locke, J. (1989). *The Clarendon edition of the works of John Locke: Some thoughts concerning education*. J. W. Yolton & J. S. Yolton (Eds.). Oxford, United Kingdom: Oxford University Press.

Malcarne, V. (1981). *The effects of role-play and maximization of perceived similarity on children's empathy with other children and animals* (Unpublished honors thesis). Stanford University, Stanford, CA.

Malcarne, V. (1983). Evaluating humane education: The Boston study. *Humane Education, 3*(1), 12-13.

McGiffin, H. & Brownley, N. (Eds.). (1980). *Animals in education: The use of animals in high school biology classes and science fairs*. Washington, DC: Institute for the Study of Animal Problems.

Melson, G. (2013). Children's ideas about the moral standing and social welfare of nonhuman species. *Journal of Sociology and Social Welfare, 40*(4), 4.

Morrow, V. (1998). My animals and other family: Children's perspectives on their relationships with companion animals. *Anthrozoös, 11*(4), 218-226.

Muldoon, J., Williams, J., Lawrence, A., Lakestani, N, & Currie, C. (2009). *Promoting a 'duty of care' toward animals among children and young people: A literature review and findings from initial research to inform the development of interventions.* Child and Adolescent Health Research Unit, University of Edinburgh, Defra.

Myers, E. O. (1998). *Children and animals: Social development and our connection to other species*. West Lafayette, IN: Purdue University Press.

Myers, E. O., & Saunders, C. (2002). Animals as links toward developing caring relationships with the natural world. In P. Kahn & S. Kellert (Eds.), *Children and nature: Psychological, sociocultural, and evolutionary investigations* (pp. 153-178). Cambridge, United Kingdom: MIT Press.

Nabhan, G. P., & Trimble, S. (1995). *The geography of childhood: Why children need wild places*. Boston, MA: Beacon Press.

Olin, J. (2002). *Humane education in the 21st century: A survey of animal shelters in the United States* (Master's thesis). Tufts University, Boston, MA.

Orlans, F. B. (1991). Use of animals in education: Policy and practice in the United States. *Journal of Biological Education, 25*(1), 27-32.

Orlans, F. B. (1993). *In the name of science: Issues in responsible animal experimentation*. New York, NY: Oxford University Press.

Orr, D. (1992). *Ecological literacy: Education and the transition to a postmodern world*. Albany: State University of New York Press.

Orr, D. (2005). *Ecological literacy: Educating our children for a sustainable world*. San Francisco, CA: Sierra Club Book

Pagani, C. (2000). Perception of a common fate in human-animal relations and its relevance to our concern for animals. *Anthrozoos, 13*(2), 66-73.

Pyle, R. (2002). Eden in a vacant lot: Special places, species, and kids in the neighborhood of life. In P. H. Kahn & S.R. Kellert (Eds.), *Children and nature: Psychological, sociocultural, and evolutionary investigations* (pp. 305-328). Cambridge, MA: MIT Press.

Rost, D. H., & Hartmann, A. (1994). Children and their Pets. *Anthrozoos, 7*(4), 242-254.

Rud, A. G., Jr., & Beck, A. M. (2003). Companion animals in Indiana elementary schools. *Anthrozoös, 16*(3), 241-250.

Savesky, K. (1981). *People and animals: A humane education curriculum.* Washington, DC: National Association for Humane & Environmental Education

Savesky, K. (2002, April). Presentation delivered at the HSUS Animal Care Expo, Miami, Florida.

Tunnicliffe, S. D., Lucas, A. M., & Osborne, J. (1997). School visits to zoos and museums: A missed educational opportunity? *International Journal of Science Education, 19*(9), 1039-1056.

Unti, B. (1999). *Humane education in the United States, 1866-1945.* Special report for The Humane Society of the United States. Unpublished manuscript, Humane Society of the United States, Washington, DC.

Unti, B. (2002). *The quality of mercy: Organized animal protection in the United States 1865-1930* (Unpublished doctoral dissertation). American University, Washington, DC.

Unti, B. (2004). *Protecting all animals: A fifty-year history of The Humane Society of the United States.* Washington, DC: Humane Society Press.

Unti B., & DeRosa, B. (2003). Humane education: Past, present, and future. In D. J. Salem & A. N. Rowan (Eds.), *The state of the animals II.* Washington, DC: Humane Society Press.

U.S. Department of Education (*2010). Efficacy of schoolwide programs to promote social and character development and reduce problem behavior in elementary school children.* Washington, DC: Author.

Vizek-Vidovic, V., Arambasic, L., Kerestes, G., Kuterovac-Jagodic, G., & Vlahovik-Stetic, V. (2001). Pet ownership in childhood and socio-emotional characteristics, work values and professional choices in early adulthood. *Anthrozoos, 14*(4), 224-231.

Vockell, E. L., & Hodal, F. (1980). Developing humane attitudes: What does research tell us? *Humane Education, 4*(2), 17-21.

Wallace, G. R. (1974). Program Development in Humane Education, *NAAHE Journal,* (4) 27.

Wells, D. L., & Hepper, P. G. (1995). Attitudes to animal use in children. *Anthrozoos, 8*(3), 159-170.

Westerlund, S. R. (n.d.). "Strategies for Improving Humane Education," Unpublished document prepared for The Humane Society of the United States.

Westerlund, S. R. (1976). Keynote Address, *NAAHE Journal (4)*4, 8-11.

Westerlund, S. R. (1983). *Humane education and realms of humaneness: Readings.* Washington, DC: University Press of America.

Whitlock, E. S. (1973). *Humane education: A survey of programs of selected national humane organizations* (Doctoral thesis). University of Tulsa, Tulsa, OK.

Whitlock, E. S., & Westerlund, S. R. (1975). *Humane education: An overview.* Tulsa, OK: National Association for the Advancement of Humane Education.

Williams, J. M., & Smith, L. A. (2006). Social and environmental influences on the development of inheritance concepts during childhood and adolescence. *International Journal of Behavioural Development, 30,* 148-157.

Wilson, E. O. (1984). *Biophilia.* Cambridge, MA: Harvard University Press.

CHAPTER TWO

CHANGING THE EDUCATION SYSTEM: CREATING HUMANE PEDAGOGY AND PROSOCIAL EDUCATION THROUGH TEACHER LEADERSHIP AND ACTION RESEARCH

Stephanie Itle-Clark, Academy of Prosocial Learning

Moral intelligence and compassion of children are shaped by many social dynamics and in countless ways. The amount of time that children spend in schools presents the educational system a chance to incorporate prosocial and moral development into educational concepts. These concepts include "value education, moral development, critical thinking and critical pedagogy" (Veugelers, 2000, p. 38). This chapter first looks at the way educators influence prosocial or moral development and introduces how humane education is a component of this broad spectrum. This comprehensive and inclusive view of prosocial development situates humane education as one piece of a larger tent, and humane pedagogy is introduced as a means of building this comprehensive view. The article introduces systems thinking and the ways that the current educational system is closed to the complete inclusion of humane education and moral pedagogy. Additionally, the article reviews the way university education departments and teacher leadership can guide growth in student values and moral development through the process of instruction and daily student interaction. Educators can drive change and create a system open to humane and prosocial education by embracing humane pedagogy, action research, and teacher-led professional development.

Educators are drawn to the profession for a plethora of reasons. Some teachers have a love of a specific subject area, some wish to become an administrator, and others enjoy working with children. Among these motives, working with youth and helping each student to reach his or her potential and become a strong contributor to society rank among the highest. A 1992 study found that the most frequently provided response concerning why a pre-service teacher candidate entered the field was "to make a difference in the lives of children" (Stiegelbauer, 1992). Additionally, in a 2003-2009 longitudinal study of over 4,300 individuals in teacher training programs, 98% (n = 4,330) reported that they entered their training in order to help young people learn (Hobson et al., 2004). According to the National Education Association (n.d.), most educators "find that teaching is a calling and a gift, which includes a love of children and an ability to engage them in the learning process" (Myths and Facts about Educator Pay, para 21). Student success compels educators to continue.

Being a successful teacher requires more than the knowledge of a subject area; it encompasses the entire ecosystem of the student. According to The Education Trust, the "most significant factor in student achievement" is the teacher (Haycock, 1998, p.2). Educators act as an extension of initial familial relationships experienced by the child and expand the support provided to the student as well as to the family (Edwards & Raikes, 2002). As an extension of the family, the teacher is an important part of both social skill development and socialization (Bredekamp & Copple, 1997). This ecological methodology to education therefore "focuses on the interrelations among and connectedness of organisms, objects, and particles and their contexts" (Wideen et al., 1998, p.168). The interconnectedness among the student, family, and school and the occurrences and activities of each is one example of how educators can support development beyond academics. Knowledge of humane education encompassing moral or prosocial development is a valuable component in the ecological methodology and one an educator can use to facilitate learning and create a healthy and satisfying learning environment. If it is true that "the processes in ... education may be more important than the knowledge that is provided," then the practices modeled by the educator may encourage similar behavior on the part of the students and may be "more important" than the academic content (Wideen et al., 1998, p. 167). In fact, American schools are often the place "where prosocialization takes place" (Brown, 2011, p.1). This prosocialization is a combination of "social and moral development that are inextricably" correlated (Brown, 2011, p. 1). Our moral development forms through the combination of empathy, fairness, and social learning, which is connected self-regulation and responsibility to others (Brown, 2011).

Along with the central duty of subject-matter expertise, effective educators also know how to inspire moral purpose and change through the building of an open classroom system in which communication and reflection are present. In fact, the development of moral and social learning melds well with cognitive learning, as empathy is a reaction involving both affective and cognitive components (Zahn-Waxler & Radke-Yarrow, 1990). Values modeled through the speech and action of teachers impact student development (Bandura, 2002). Through a variety of techniques, including action research, mentoring, and teamwork, educators gather the tools they need to create a "change theme" in their respective institutions (Fellen, 2003, p. 12). Teachers as change agents include four dimensions that allow change capacity: "personal vision-building, inquiry, mastery, and collaboration" (Fellen, 2003, p.12). Critical pedagogy, teacher empowerment, and action research are at the crux of this change-agentry, as knowledge cannot be isolated from the realm of values and "liberating education consists in acts of cognition" (Friere, 1993, p. 79).

LITERATURE REVIEW

PROSOCIAL DEVELOPMENT, HUMANE EDUCATION, AND THE EDUCATOR

The development of prosocial behaviors, or the voluntary actions which benefit others, has gained attention since the 1970s, often in response to anti-social behaviors (Eisenberg, Fabes, & Spinrad, 2006). Prosocial learning describes an area of study involving civic traits and abilities, and it has many similar counterparts (Riley, San Juan,

Klinkner, & Ramminger, 2008). Character education and social and emotional learning are just two of these similar areas. Humane education, a lesser-known model, holds as its tenets the same core as prosocial education—the "teaching of kindness and compassion to people, animals, and the environment" (Itle-Clark & Forsyth, 2012). Prosocial behavior has been studied as a protective factor against the possible harmful effects of aggression or anti-social behaviors (Griese, 2011; Kochenderfer-Ladd, 2004; Riley et al., 2008).

A wide range of literature shows that early aggressive behavior is linked to later anti-social behaviors or criminal actions (Arluke, Arnold, & Lockwood, 1997; Coie & Dodge, 1998; Rutter, Giller, & Hagell, 1998). Of the various anti-social behaviors, there is "growing evidence that animal abuse is correlated to neglect and abuse initiated toward adult partners, the young, and the elderly" (Arluke et al., 1997, p. 26). While the presence of animal abuse does not cause other abuse or interpersonal violence, its presence can make other forms of violence more likely. Abusing animals desensitizes the abuser to violence and suffering and reduces the likelihood that empathy with a human or animal is possible. Animal abuse is one of the earliest indications of a conduct disorder in children and should serve as an early warning sign of a child who may benefit from a mental health intervention (Ascione, 1999).

Prosocial behaviors encompass cognitive and affective, or emotional, skills (Marion, 2003). Of the many subsets of prosocial education, humane education is perched as the component that provides a wide lens of instruction concerning "compassion and empathy toward people, animals, and the environment and the interconnectedness among the three" (De Lisle & Itle-Clark, 2011). According to McAllister (2002), "Empathy involves cognitive, affective, and behavioral components" (p. 433). Empathetic tendencies allow a person to view events through the perspective of another and see events in a non-judgmental way (Goleman, 1998). Altruistic personalities consider the needs and concerns of others and "act in a way that benefits them" (Penner & Finkelstein, 1998, p. 526).

Prosocial moral reasoning, or the "cognitive side of prosocial behavior," drives personal action and falls into "five developmental levels: 1) hedonistic or self-centered, 2) needs of others orientation, 3) approval orientation and stereotyped orientation, 4) empathetic orientation, and 5) internalized orientation" (Bierhoff, 2002). Within the framework of humane education, these five developmental levels apply to all living beings and their habitats. At the highest stage, or the post-conventional level, actions are judged by what constitutes the right moral principle and are judged neither by social norms nor a fear of punishment (Kohlberg, 1973). Moral reasoning develops over a period of time and not every person reaches the post-conventional level. Longitudinal research on prosocial development indicates that unprompted sharing at age 4-5 was significantly related to prosocial behavior at older ages of 15-16 and 17-18 and how friends' report level of sympathy at age 19-20 (Bierhoff, 2002; Eisenberg et al., 1999). Much like moral development, levels of prosocial moral reasoning are broken down into stages or levels beginning with "hedonistic, self-centered orientation" and ending with "internalized orientation" (Eisenberg, 1986, p. 67).

Humane education, as part of teaching and learning programs, incorporates these broad-based human, animal, and environmental educational items following the aforementioned moral levels and provides age-appropriate, high-interest subject areas and builds critical thinking skills. The tenets of humane education, which encourage compassion for all living beings, assist students in moral development and social and emotional growth. A 1997 study of two secondary-level classes suggests that a teacher-led integrated curriculum creates significant growth in moral reasoning and behavior change (DeHaan, Hanford, Kinlaw, Philler, & Snarey, 1997). Scores in both courses, economics-ethics ($p = < 0.05$) and introductory ethics classes ($p = < 0.05$), indicated significant moral reasoning change and moral behavior change (DeHaan et al., 1997). Each educator models action in all three domains of learning.

It is preferable for all teachers to think of themselves as practical ethicists, regardless of their primary field of formal training, and to integrate ethics instruction into their regular courses. Current curriculum designers also seem to favor an integrated or comprehensive approach. (DeHaan et al., p. 16)

Additionally, a 2011 meta-analysis conducted by Durlak et al. of 213 social and emotional learning programs found that student growth was seen only when the programs were led by well-trained classroom teachers as opposed to visiting experts. The day-to-day commitment and modeling of positive social behaviors and attitudes by classroom teachers produced the most significant results: SEL skills [$ES = .62$], Attitudes

[*ES* = .23], Positive social behavior [*ES* = .26], Conduct problems [*ES* = .20], Emotional distress [*ES* = .25], and Academic performance [*ES* = .34] (Durlak et al, 2011).

This holistic approach to teaching and learning can not only support moral development, but also build a positive emotional attachment to the educational process. The attitudes and feelings of the learner play a part in student success and assist in development of cognitive or intellectual skills, and personal emotions assist a learner in being "open-minded rather than close-minded" (Dewey, 1933, p. 28). In other words, the "gateway to learning is the affective domain" (Iozzi, 1989, p. 3). According to Eiss and Harbeck (1969):

> The affective domain is central to every part of the learning and evaluation process. It begins with the threshold of consciousness, where the awareness of the stimulus initiates the learning process. It provides the threshold for evaluation, where willingness to respond is the basis for psychomotor responses without which no evaluation of the learning process can take place. It includes values and value systems that provide the basis for continued learning and for most of an individual's overt behavior. It provides the bridge between the stimulus and the cognitive and psychomotor aspects of an individual's personality. (p.4)

Teachers connect to the affective domain because they know the students, know the issues, and are the local "experts" ("School Leadership," 2001). Communication between teacher and student can build the critical thinking and moral development skills needed to build humane perspectives, analyze values, and communicate about them. All are "cognitive skills-oriented approaches" (Veugelers, 2000, p. 38).

Connection to moral goodness and cognitive learning is not the only reason educators are interested in humane education and prosocial learning. A longitudinal study involving 294 children from varied socioeconomic backgrounds found that third-grade social behavior can be "used to predict their eighth-grade peer preference and academic achievement" (Capara et al., 2000, p. 302). Review of self-reported prosocialness, peer reports of prosocial classmates, and teacher ratings of prosocial behavior in third grade and then again in eighth grade showed an association between academic achievement and prosocial behavior:

The path to academic achievement and social preference among adolescents is robustly predicted by the extent of their earlier prosocial behavior, with impact coefficients of .52 and .62 for social preference. Early academic achievement correlated strongly, $r = .75$, with prosocial behavior and negatively, $r = -.31$, with aggression; aggression and prosocial behavior were also negatively related, $r = -.39$. (Capara et al., 2000, pp. 303-304)

LOOKING AT THE SYSTEM
AND THE HIDDEN CURRICULUM

How can change leaders in education support this ecological approach to learning so that students develop not only humane or prosocial competencies, but also cognitive components of learning? Modifications to teacher education programming are one part of a necessary change to the system in reference to humane education. Education professionals of today, much like those of the recent past, generally receive little formal training, specifically training in how to combine moral development and academics, concerning humane or character education (Gore & Zeichner, 1991). Along with little pre-service teacher training, a 2012 study of 292 educators reported that 57% of participating teachers did not know if their state required humane education (Itle-Clark & Forsyth, 2012).

Reform in the current university and K-12 school environment that ultimately incorporates systems thinking and a vision and plan is also required. Through system change, over time the metacognitive process involves reflection and the impartial clarification of "things that matter" (Senge, 2006, p. 8). Recognizing the hidden curriculum, including recognizing how humane education is or is not present, is a first step toward understanding an existing system. Giroux (2001) defines the hidden curriculum as "those unstated norms, values, and beliefs embedded in and transmitted to students through the underlying rules that structure the routines and social relationships in school and classroom" (p. 59). The "dimensions of the hidden curriculum" include:

1) interactions and classroom structure
2) process operations, which take account of values acquisition and maintenance of classroom structure
3) the level of intentionality (Vallance, 1973)

Each of the three degrees of the hidden curriculum noted by Vallance (1973) directly imply hegemony as a way to elicit a reproduction of culture (Apple, 1982). The educator's authority need not include a purely negative list, and the hidden curriculum can support prosocial and humane development in the school system.

In an educational setting, the hidden curriculum is not the same in each school nor is there a complete list of hidden items. Common positive hidden curriculums in schools include the importance of treating authority figures with respect, assuming teachers have expectations of their students, and that interrupting a speaker is impolite (Myles et al., 2004). Additionally, the hidden supplementary learning such as the modeling behaviors of adults, impacts a student more than intentional teaching of civics or moral education. Students are "taught how to deal with and relate to the structures of authority ... by the patterns of interaction" to which they are exposed during their educational experiences (Apple, 1971, p. 28).

Beyond the hidden curriculum, the school systems are driven by academic requirements such as No Child Left Behind, the Common Core, and the standards-based and test-measured accountability (U.S. Department of Education, 2006).

> With increasing demands for academic accountability, the only outcome measures that really count are achievement test scores. The tests have become the be-all and end all . . . this produces a growing disconnect between the reality of what is needed to enhance academic performance (Adelman & Taylor, 2007, p. 69).

The testing associated with Adequate Yearly Progress in the current system provides academics assessment but does not support the building of formative assessment or insight into long-term change (Amrein-Beardsley, 2008). Long-term systemic change related to humane education and prosocial development would assess how students build efficacy and "social and personal functioning," including "social learning and behavior, character/values, civility," which are all components of humane education (Adelman & Taylor, 2007, p. 70).

Even the schools that incorporate character building and prosocial education often provide a human-centric perspective ("Character Counts," 2013; "Character Education Partnership," n.d.; "The Bullying Project," 2010). This prosocial work is a step toward the greater development of institutionalized humane education and an empathetic and internalized orientation, but does not imply that these prosocial traits will cross into interactions with non-human animals (Bierhoff, 2002). Systems thinking in the university and classroom can support prosocial growth, and critical pedagogy as gradual change to include humane education is introduced. Critical pedagogy introduces the greater relationship among knowledge, the school, and the social world (McLaren, 2006). In the same vein as critical pedagogy, humane pedagogy supports a change in the system of education and learner development. "The prosocial components of humane pedagogy allow for the modeling of important character traits and the increase in the humane narrative of a student who is learning new behaviors" (Itle-Clark, 2013, p. 10). Humane pedagogy considers how the system of education and practice of teaching can provide learners with the tools to build a more compassionate and just society for all human and non-human animals and to deploy education in a process of progressive and transformative social change to generate a humane and prosocial society; a humane economy; and an understanding of intercorrelation of human, animal, and environment. Humane pedagogy provides teachers with the tools to critically analyze social and educational systems and the construct of learning with an understanding of the affective and cognitive impact on learners. Building humane literacy as part of the educational system empowers educators to build a praxis-oriented culture in which learners codify or develop consciousness and the ability to turn consciousness into constructive and compassionate action (Itle-Clark, 2011). Later in the paper, strategies for implementing critical and humane pedagogy are introduced.

TEACHING TOWARD CHANGE

Teachers and administrative leaders at all levels can support the development of curriculums and learning activities that include not only cognitive components, but also affective modules (Smith & Ragan, 1999). Most schools and teachers, whether they intend to or not, do some form of attitude teaching (Miller, 2005). Through both words and action, the values important to an educator and institution are shared with the students through modeling and critical pedagogy (Veugelers, 2000). In fact, a balanced education provides academic instruction as well as skills related to becoming responsible adults (Association for Supervision and Curriculum Development, 2007).

Schools today serve students with wide-ranging socioeconomic and cultural backgrounds as well as varied capabilities and incentives for learning (Learning First Alliance, 2001). Classroom educators must be able to provide optimal academic training to all student populations to drive success; attitudes and moral development is much like the other forms of scholarship and must also be taught (Greenberg et al., 2003). Over 30 years of research indicates the need for educators to teach prosocial education, including all themes of humane education and social and emotional learning, as part of regular practice (Diekstra & Gravesteijn, 2008; Greenberg et al., 2003; Weissberg et al., 2003; Weissberg & O'Brien, 2004). A meta-analysis of 317 studies, involving over 320,000 students in grades K-8, described growth in "knowledge, attitudes, and skills" related to the development of "one or more social-emotional" competency (Payton et al., 2008, p. 4). Growth included an 11-percentile-point gain in academic achievement, a reduction in grade retention, and improved test scores (ES = 0.28) and grades (ES = 0.34) rates, as well as:

- Increased prosocial behavior
- Increased mastery of subject material
- Increased motivation to learn
- Improved attendance and violence-related delinquency
- Fewer suspensions, expulsions, and disciplinary referrals
- More commitment and attachment to school
- Improved prospects for employment (Greenberg et al., 2003; Payton et al., 2008, p. 4).

Results from 82% (n = 260) of the studies indicated that school personnel [including counselors and educators] were effective in conducting moral development programs, and the programs were efficacious for students of varied ages, socio-economic backgrounds, and settings (Payton et al., 2008).

Applications of academic and social development in classrooms are based upon best practices and knowledge about how children learn. Students are engaged through authentic and active learning, and student-centered tasks while classrooms are arranged in a way to build activity—versus the traditional rows. Education for the whole child provides creative and active participants, promotes brain growth, and includes all subject areas (Gardner, 2011; Tomlinson, 2003). Best practices also include using an enriched classroom space, which promotes brain growth (Jensen, 2005).

Strategies for implementation of active humane and prosocial learning consist of four optimal instruction techniques (Payton et al., 2008). Each "letter in the acronym SAFE refers to a ... teaching skill" (Durlak et al., 2011, p. 411):

- *Sequenced:* Does the program apply a planned set of activities to develop skills sequentially in a step-by-step fashion?
- *Active:* Does the program use active forms of learning such as role-plays and behavioral rehearsal with feedback?
- *Focused:* Does the program devote sufficient time exclusively to developing social and emotional skills?
- *Explicit:* Does the program target specific social and emotional skills? (Payton et al., 2008).

Teacher-led activities engage students' higher-order cognitive skills including analysis, synthesis, and evaluation as well as higher-order affective skills such as valuing, organizing, and characterizing (Bloom, 1956). Learning that incorporates the affective domain helps students to gain awareness of the perspective of others and focus on growth of personal attitude and emotional skills (Bloom, 1956; Payton et al., 2008). Programs and lessons similar to the SAFE model infuse humane and prosocial learning into the school and classroom culture, where students can identify social capabilities and recognize why the skills are necessary (Johnson et al, 2000). Incorporation of humane pedagogy and models such as SAFE in the classroom combine the affective and cognitive domain and build empathy for human and non-human animals.

Comprehensive curriculums build affective development opportunities into cognitive work, infusing humane and prosocial learning into the academic and standards-based school day (Clark, 2010). Prospects for infusion can be found in all academic areas (Clark, 2010; Preusse, 2008). Examples include language arts lessons encouraging skills such as verbal discussion and writing, as well as oral or written problem solving, about the connection between habitat protection and the animals on the endangered species list or books that help students to take the perspective of another or deal with personal feelings. Life skills and helping behaviors can be promoted through the creation of dramatic play areas such as a veterinary hospital or wildlife rehabilitation facility. Learning in the classroom utilizing social and emotional skills such as those found in humane pedagogy focus on the increase of self-worth as well as respect for others (Preusse, 2008). Role-plays, observations, simulations, or case studies are other strategies that can be incorporated into almost any subject, and role-taking ability grows with age (Hoffman, 2000, p. 71). Curricula in the proposed humane education-infused system are intentionally designed to promote kindness, caring, and sharing (Bandura, 2002; Herr et al., 2004). The curriculum builds upon academic requirements and emphasizes respect for self and other people, community, animals, and the environment. Through curriculum infused with proactive humane and prosocial education, students model, receive coaching, converse, and play in a way that allows perspective building (Chilampikunnel, 2010).

The learning system open to this ecological methodology includes operative instruction designed to build affective and prosocial skills in which a learner assimilates new information into that which he or she already knows and connects emotionally (Auger & Rich, 2007). The educator plays an important part in both designing the curriculum and modeling prosocial behaviors (Bandura, 1986). Critical and humane pedagogy provides students with the opportunity to practice new feelings, attitudes, and behaviors and receive positive reinforcement (Itle-Clark, 2011; Miller, 2005). Educators who instruct in a way that includes these qualities are likely to see the attitude or behavioral change results they desire (Diekstra & Gravesteijn, 2008; Miller, 2005). McMahon and Washburn (2003) emphasize that programs designed to meet "cultural, developmental, and behavioral" needs of students are most successful (p. 51).

SYSTEMIC CHANGE STRATEGIES:
ACTION RESEARCH AND IN-SERVICE

While research related to educational leadership has traditionally focused on administrative leaders, recent studies are looking at teachers as leaders (Bellon & Beaudry, 1992). Change in schools occurs at all levels. Neither centralized change, including top-down initiatives, nor decentralized change from the bottom-up can work in isolation. Systemic change requires a blend of the two areas (Fullan, 1994; Murphy, 1988). A blended approach to change allows administrators and educators to take an active role in the decisions impacting their classrooms and schools (universities or K-12). This parallel leadership "is a process whereby teacher leaders and their principals engage in collective action to build school capacity" and encourages "mutual trust, shared purpose, and allowance for individual expression" (Crowther, Ferguson, & Hann, 2009, p. 53). Beer et al. (1990) studied 26 companies to learn what best inspired collective action or a culture of change, finding the following:

- Change efforts that begin by creating ... programs to alter the culture of the management of people ... are inherently flawed even when supported by top management.
- Formal organizational structure and systems are the last things an organization should change when seeking renewal.
- Effective changes in the way an organization manages people do not occur by changing the organization's human resource policies and systems.
- Starting ... renewal at the very top is a high-risk revitalization strategy not employed by the most successful companies.
- Organizations should start corporate revitalization by targeting small, isolated, peripheral operations, not large, central, core operations. (p.6)

Change in any organization, a university education program, a K-12 school, or a for-profit institution occurs at the macro-, meso-, and micro-levels, and each piece is managed differently (Pandey, 2011). Educators often have the ability to create an open system and include humane and prosocial learning in their personal classrooms, but how can these visionaries become less isolated and create change to impact the entire institution and provide their students with educational experiences designed for the whole person?

Action research is one way educational institutions can begin to incorporate isolated competencies and build change from within. This reflective approach is compatible with humane education in the way it combines social justice, emancipatory theory, and organizational change (Friere, 1993; Lewin, 1946). When incorporating action research into curriculum, educators are able to design programs that best fit the needs of their students, and educators can use reflection to build better practice (Dewey, 1933). Building on preliminary needs or questions, educators view their work with an "inquiry stance" in which they support standards-based education and student academic success as well as "social justice" within the school and classroom culture (Cochran-Smith & Lytle, 2001, p. 46). The inquiry stance "talks back to, and challenges, many of the assumptions that define teaching and research on teaching in the current era of acute educational accountability" (Cochran-Smith & Lytle, 2009, p. 44). Educators use "systemic questioning ... as a basis for development" and study of personal practice (McNiff & Whitehead, 2006, p. 37). Department heads and principals alike can embrace humane-themed action research as a means to build humane pedagogy in institutions of learning.

Educators initiating action research are looking to make system-wide change using the cycle of inquiry to investigate situations (McLaughlin, 2001). Action research enhances pedagogy and allows educators to integrate student "intelligences, personalities, emotional states, stages of development, and family backgrounds" into curriculum (Stringer, Christensen, & Baldwin, 2010, p. 43). When designing a classroom action research project, Mettaetal (2002) outlines seven steps for educators. Each step provides an example of how humane and prosocial education can fit within the phase:

1. *Identify a question relevant to the classroom:* Do students pay more attention when lessons include humane education themes?

2. *Review the literature:* Review recent relevant literature to learn background information about the question raised in step one. For example, read journals on prosocial and character education and look for other studies about humane

education.

3. *Plan a research strategy:* Research can be gathered in various ways and can be about the whole class or individual students. The school Institutional Review Board should be consulted.

4. *Collect data:* Qualitative and/or quantitative data should be gathered. Utilize items that are readily available, i.e., test scores or assignments and add information from student comments and observations of behavior during the lessons.

5. *Analyze data:* Look for patterns in the data collected.

6. *Take action:* Based on the results of the data, will the inclusion of the new strategy be one that is used again? Did the inclusion of humane themes engage students? And how can this be instituted again in the future?

7. *Share findings:* Share the information with other educators at conferences, in-service workshops, or team meetings. (Mettetal, 2002)

Upon conclusion of the research, faculty-led in-service and mentoring allows educators to share their experience and knowledge and tackle the day-to-day problems they face in schools (Elliot, 1988). Ash and Persall (2000) propose that collaborative and reflective planning provides educators with opportunities to be less isolated and share information, learn together, and plan for student achievement. School leaders must have the ability to create systemic change and pursue ever-higher levels of student achievement. To be effective instructional leaders, school administrators and faculty must think in new patterns and act within new models. (p. 19)

Faculty led in-service and mentoring are effective means for leadership training and change creation, as "researchers emphasize that teachers learn better from their peers than a supervisor" (Schmoker, 2006, p.125). The reflective instruction that practicing educators can provide to one another allows teachers to connect knowledge to personal practice and to receive coaching from other professionals in the discipline (Schon, 1996). According to Ferraro (2000), researchers "recommend that reflective teaching combine John Dewey's philosophy on the moral, situational aspects of teaching with Schon's process" (para. 3). These items combined will provide appropriate instruction in both academics and social learning (Clift et al., 1990). Along with faculty-led in-service, curriculum working groups, department head roles, committee chairpersons, faculty focus groups, and lesson reviews are a handful of peer-based reflective activities or roles leaders can organize (Boles & Troen, 1992; Mooney & Mausbach, 2008). According to Westley and Mintzberg (1989), this parallel visionary leadership is dynamic and "empower[s] those followers so that they can enact the vision" and work toward mastery and collaboration (p. 18).

Visions of educational leaders influence the culture and climate, both of which impact instruction and staff conduct along with student outcomes (SEDL, 2013). In Chrispeels' (1990) report of effective schools, "shared vision [is viewed as] . . . a commitment to change" (p. 39). In schools looking to build prosocial and humane models into the cultural system, in-service and mentoring is led by those who participate in action-research. In research studies on the effects of similar programs, "many of the teachers ... felt a greater sense of control over their work ... [T]hey now looked at their teaching in a more analytic, focused manner, a habit they claimed to have internalized and applied beyond the research experience" (Caro-Bruce et al., 2007, p. 113).

DISCUSSION

Federal mandates are focused more and more on numeracy and literacy, with accountability being driven in these areas only. Ironically, it is not only these subjects which correlate to student success; "social, emotional, academic, and ethical education can help children reach the goals their parents and teachers have for them," and these values do not resonate in the pre-service or in-service development provided to teachers (Cohen, 2006, p. 203). Reform leaders dedicated to redesigning educator development support change through both personal action and by sharing their vision and personal mastery within the learning disciplines (Pearce, 2003; Senge et al., 1999. The possibility of an open system at the university and K-12 levels related to and providing training in humane pedagogy and prosocial learning would allow educators to make the decisions that are best suited to the needs of their community of learners, as well as assist students in affective and cognitive growth. True reform in curriculum will occur when pre-service and in-service educators are able to embrace humane pedagogy through action research.

Beyond the individual pedagogy of educators or lessons that occur in separate classrooms, shared vision, group inquiry, and collaboration commanded by school leadership at all levels is part of building systemic change and humane pedagogy. The proper infrastructure plays an important part in any transformation effort. Establishment of a humane pedagogy steering committee is a first step and builds a "broad-based and potent mechanism for guiding change" (Adelman & Taylor, 2007, p. 65). The steering committee (made up of change-agents) "ensures sustainability" by overseeing planning and increasing participation or buy-in (Adelman & Taylor, 2007, p. 65). This is not a closed group, however, and the steering committee should solicit feedback from others to build leadership and capacity (Fullan, 1993).

Part of capacity building is "training for change agents or those who will be responsible for facilitating change" in the organization (Adelman & Taylor, 2007, p. 65). When introducing a humane pedagogy learning initiative, specially trained staff can "form and train an on-site *team* that includes ... working groups (Adelman & Taylor, 2007, p. 66). The working group is charged with being the promoters of change in the first stage of the process and sustaining the upkeep and vision of the initiative. These chosen groups of change leaders rally interest and develop linkages among resources, facilitate redesign of regular structural mechanisms, and establish other temporary mechanisms. They are also problem solvers ... taking a proactive stance by designing strategies to counter anticipated barriers to change, such as negative reactions and dynamics, common factors interfering with working relationships, and system deficiencies. Their goal is to do all this in ways that enhance empowerment to new approaches. (Adelman & Taylor, 2007, p. 67).

In the example of building humane and prosocial development within the school and learning system, the framework designed by the steering committee will plan and oversee the effort. Committee members may desire to survey existing resources or conduct a needs assessment (Hall & Hord, 2006). The capacity building team will prioritize the pilot program and professional development. Progress should be evaluated regularly and feedback from participants will guide further development and implementation (Fullan, 1993).

Educators bring a variety of personalities, beliefs, and expectations to their classroom work. These beliefs and expectations will not change quickly. Integration of humane education or prosocial learning into the classroom or school culture takes time, and educators need to learn new expectations and practices. Research suggests that system-wide sustainable prosocial development programs may take three to five years (Adelman, 1995; Elmore, 2004; Hall & Hord, 2006). It is imperative, therefore, that "dispositions towards reflective practice and inquiry into practice be supported in the work environment" (Kitchen & Stevens, 2008, p. 26).

CONCLUSIONS AND FUTURE ACTIONS

Adding humane education and prosocial education to traditional education and encouraging use of humane pedagogy by teachers is a way to increase both affective and cognitive student learning:

> When evidence-based social, emotional, and ethical education is integrated into traditional teaching and learning, educators can hone the essential academic and social skills, understanding, and dispositions that support effective participation in a democracy. In doing so they are also laying the foundation for well-being and the pursuit of happiness. (Cohen, 2006, p. 203)

Creating the systemic change in any organization can seem overwhelming, especially when the desire is to introduce a concept that is not integrated into the existing structure. The addition of humane pedagogy and prosocial learning to the training, culture, and curriculum requires readiness development in which the faculty and staff are motivated to create the change. This may require a readiness evaluation and will require professional development for and by the staff. Initial implementation, designed in phases that can be accomplished, will drive the institutionalization of humane education and prosocial frameworks. These foundations will increase youth academic and social achievement (Achenbach & Edelbrock, 1986; Bandura et al., 1996; Capra & Pastorelli, 1993; Levin, 1996; Stringer, Christensen, & Baldwin, 2010).

Beyond academic success, actions on the part of those reforming education must connect "development based on moral purpose and change agentry with the restructuring of schools" (Fullan, 1993, p. 17). The finding that educators influence humane and prosocial growth in youth has implications for the creation of faculty-led in-service trainings and curriculum built around both academics and moral development (Bandura et al., 1996; Capra & Pastorelli, 1993; Capara et al., 2000; Cohen, 2006; Levin, 1996). Educators who know strategies that support academic achievement and prosocial attitudes allow these topics to become part of the classroom and school culture. Considerable effort needs to be put forth to create an educational system in which components of humane pedagogy and prosocial learning permeate the system, but this change can be achieved by empowering the classroom teachers from their pre-service university courses through their on-going education. As the teacher leaders of today become the change agents of tomorrow, schools will include new paradigms built upon the action research and reflection of practitioners.

References

Achenbach, T. M., & Edelbrock, C. (1986). *Manual for the teacher's report form and teacher version of the child behavior profile*. Burlington, VT: University of Vermont Press.

Adelman, H. S., & Taylor,L. (2007). Systemic change for school improvement. *Journal of Educational and Psychological Consultation, 17*(1), 55-77.

Amrein-Beardsley, A. (2008). Methodological concerns about the education value-added assessment system. *Educational Researcher, 37*(2), 65–75.

Apple, M. W. (1971). The hidden curriculum and the nature of conflict. *Interchange, 2*(4), 27-40.

Apple, M. W. (1982). *Education and power*. Boston, MA: Routledge and Kegan Paul.

Arluke, A. & Lockwood, R. (1997). Guest editors' introduction: Understanding cruelty to animals. *Society and Animals: Journal of Human-Animal Studies, 5*(3), 25-33.

Ascione, F. R. (1996). The abuse of animals and human interpersonal violence: Making the connection. In F. R. Ascione & P. Arkow (Eds.), *Child abuse, domestic violence, and animal abuse: Linking the circles of compassion for prevention and intervention* (pp. 50-61). West Layfayette, IN: Purdue University Press.

Ash, R. C., & Persall, J. M. (2000). The principal as chief learning officer: Developing teacher leaders. *NASSP Bulletin, 84*(616), 15-22.

Association for Supervision and Curriculum Development. (2007). *The learning compact redefined: A call to action — A report of the Commission of the Whole Child*. Alexandria, VA: Author.

Auger, W. F., & Rich, S. J. (2007). *Curriculum theory and methods: Perspectives on learning and teaching*. Mississauga, ON: Wiley Canada.

Bandura, A. (1986). *Social foundations of thought and action: A social cognitive theory*. Englewood Cliffs, NJ: Prentice-Hall.

Bandura, A. (2002). Selective moral disengagement in the exercise of moral agency. *Journal of Moral Education, 31*(2), 101–119.

Bandura, A., Barbaranelli, C., Capara, G. V., & Pastorelli, C. (1996). Multifaceted impact of self-efficacy beliefs on academic functioning. *Child Development, 67*(3), 1206-1222.

Beer, M., Eisenstat, R. A., & Spector, B. (1990). *The critical path to corporate renewal*. Boston, MA: Harvard Business School Press.

Bellon, T. & Beaudry, J. (1992). *Teachers' perceptions of their leadership roles in site-based decision making*. Paper presented at the Annual Meeting of the American Educational Research Association, San Francisco, CA.

Bierhoff, H. (2002). *Prosocial behavior*. New York, NY: Taylor & Francis.

Bloom, B. S. (1956). *Taxonomy of educational objectives, handbook I: The cognitive domain.* New York, NY: McKay.

Boles, K. & Troen, V. (1992). How teachers make restructuring happen. *Educational Leadership, 49*(5), 53-56.

Bredekamp, S. & Copple, C. (1997). *Developmentally appropriate practice in early childhood programs.* Washington, DC: National Association for the Education of Young Children.

Brown, P. M. (2011). *Prosocial development: Defining the basis for prosocial education.* Discussant background notes presented at the 2011 Workshop on Transforming Humiliation and Violent Conflict, Columbia University, New York, NY.

The Bullying Project. (2010). *The Bullying Project curriculum.* Retrieved from http://bullyingproject.com/curriculum

Capara, G. V., Barbaranelli, C., Pastorelli, C., Bandura, A., & Zimbardo, P. G. (2000). Prosocial foundations of children's academic achievement. *Psychological Science, 11*(4), 302-306.

Capara, G. V., & Pastorelli, C. (1993). Early emotional instability, prosocial behavior and aggression: Some methodological aspects. *European Journal of Personality, 7*(1), 19-36.

Caro-Bruce, C., Flessner, R., Klehr, M., & Zeichner, K. (2007). *Creating equitable classrooms through action research.* Thousand Oaks, CA: Corwin Press.

Character Counts. (2013). *The six pillars of character.* Retrieved from http://charactercounts.org/sixpillars.html

Character Education Partnership. (n.d.). *Key topics in character education.* Retrieved from http://www.character.org/key-topics

Chilampikunnel, M. A. (2010). *A manual for parents, teachers, and principals on early childhood education.* Bloomington, IN: Xlibris.

Chrispeels, J. A. (1990). Achieving and sustaining school effectiveness: A five year study of change in elementary schools. Paper presented at the Annual Meeting of the American Educational Research Association, Boston, MA.

Clark, S. (2010). Standard practice: Swimming in the pool of educational standards. *The Packrat. 3*(94), 1-3.

Clift, R.T., Houston, W. R., & Pugach, M. C. (Eds.). (1990). *Encouraging reflective practice in education: An analysis of issues and programs.* New York, NY: Teachers College Press.

Coie, J. D., & Dodge, K. A. (1998). Aggression and antisocial behavior. In W. Damon & N. Eisenberg (Eds.), *Handbook of child psychology: Vol. 3. Social, emotional, and personality development* (pp. 779–862). New York, NY: Wiley.

Cochran-Smith, M., & Lytle, S. L. (1993). *Inside/outside: Teacher research and knowledge.* New York, NY: Teachers College Press.

Cochran-Smith, M. & Lytle, S. L. (2001). Beyond certainty: Taking an inquiry stance on practice. In A. Lieberman & L. Miller (Eds.), *Teachers caught in the action: Professional development that matters* (pp. 45-58). New York, NY: Teachers College Press.

Cochran-Smith, M., & Lytle, S. L. (2009). *Inquiry as stance: Practitioner research for the next generation.* New York, NY: Teachers College Press

Cohen, J. (2006). Social, emotional, ethical, and academic education: Creating a climate for learning, participation in democracy, and well-being. *Harvard Educational Review, 76*(2), 201-237.

Crowther, F., Ferguson, M., & Hann, L. (2009). *Developing teacher leaders.* Thousand Oaks, CA: Corwin Press.

DeHaan, R., Hanford, R., Kinlaw, K., Philler, D., & Snarey, J. (1997). Promoting ethical reasoning, affect and behaviour among high school students and evaluation of three teaching strategies. *Journal of Moral Education, 26*(1), 5-20.

DeLisle, S., & Itle-Clark, S. (2011). Humane education: A way to empower youth, enhance humane behaviors, and promote animal welfare. *Silhouettes.* Retrieved from http://www.atriskeducation.net/pdf/Silhouettes-2011-Fall-DeLisle-Humane_Education.pdf.

Dewey, J. (1933) *How we think.* Lexington, MA: Heath.

Diekstra, R. F., & Gravesteijn, C. (2008). Effectiveness of school-based social and emotional education programmes worldwide. *Social and emotional education: An international analysis, 255-312.*

Durlak, J. A., Weissberg, R. P., Dymnicki, A. B., Taylor, R. D., & Schellinger, K. B. (2011). The impact of enhancing students' social and emotional learning: A meta-analysis of school-based universal interventions. *Child Development, 82*(1), 405-432.

Eisenberg, N. (1986). *Altruistic emotion, cognition, and behavior.* Hillsdale, NJ: Erlbaum.

Eisenberg, N., Fabes, R. A., & Spinrad, T. L. (2006). Prosocial behavior. In N. Eisenberg (Vol. Ed.) and W. Damon & R. M. Lerner (Series Eds.), *Handbook of child psychology, vol. 3: Social, emotional, and personality development* (6th ed., pp. 646-718). New York, NY: Wiley.

Eisenberg, N., Guthrie, I. K., Murphy, B. C., Shephard, S. A., Cumberland, A., & Carlo, G. (1999). Consistency and development of prosocial dispositions: A longitudinal study. *Child Development, 70*(6), 1360-1372.

Edwards, C., & Raikes, H. (2002). Extending the dance: Relationship-based approaches to infant/toddler care and education. *Young Children, 57*(4), 10-17.

Elliot, J. (1988). *What is action-research in school?* Victoria, Australia: Deakin University Printery.

Elmore, R.F. (2004). *School reform from the inside out: Policy, practice, and performance.* Cambridge, MA: Harvard Education Press.

Fellen, M. G. (1993). Why teachers must become change agents. *Educational Leadership, 50*(6), 12-17.

Ferraro, J. M. (2004). Reflective practice and professional development. *Cyc-Online, 63*(4). Retrieved from http://cyc-net.org/cyc-online/cycol-0404-reflective.html

Friere, P. (1993). *Pedagogy of the oppressed.* New York, NY: Continuum.

Fullan, M. G. (1994). Coordinating top-down and bottom up strategies for education reform. In R. Anson (Ed.), *Systemic reform: Perspective on personalizing education* (pp. 7-23). Washington, DC: GPO.

Gardner, H. (2011). *Frames of mind: The theory of multiple intelligences.* New York, NY: Basic.

Giroux, H. A. (2001). *Theory and resistance in education.* London, England: Bergin & Garvey.

Goleman, D. (1998). *Working with emotional intelligence.* New York, NY: Bantam.

Gore, J. M., & Zeichner, K. M. (1991). Action research and reflective teaching in preservice teacher education: A case study from the United States. *Teaching and Teacher Education, 7*(2), 119-136.

Greenberg, M. T., Weissberg, R. P., O'Brine, M. U., Zins, J. E., Fredericks, L., Resnik, H., & Elias, M. J. (2003). Enhancing school-based prevention and youth development through coordinated social, emotional, academic learning. *American Psychologist, 58*(6-7), 466-474.

Griese, E. R. (2011). *Prosocial behavior as a protective factor for children's peer victimization* (Master's thesis). Retrieved from http://digitalcommons.unl.edu/cehsdiss/115

Hall, G. & Hord, S. (2006). *Implementing change: Patterns, principles, and potholes* (2nd ed.). Boston, MA: Allyn and Bacon.

Haycock, K. (1998). *Good teaching matters: How well-qualified teachers can close the gap.* Washington, DC: Education Trust.

Herr, J., Lynch, J., Merritt, K., Preusse, K., & Wurzer, R. (2004). *Moozie's kindness curriculum: Preschool.* Breckenridge, CO: Children's Kindness Network.

Hobson, A. J., Tracey, L., Kerr, K., Malderez, A., Pell, G., Simm, C., & Johnson, F. (2004). *Why people choose to become teachers and the factors influencing their choice of initial training route: Early findings from the Becoming a Teacher (BaT) project.* (Research Brief No. RBX08-04). London, England: Department for Education and Skills.

Hoffman, M. I. (2000). *Empathy and moral development: Implications for caring and justice.* Cambridge, NY: Cambridge University Press.

Itle-Clark, S. (2011). Humane education beyond the shelter: Developing humane pedagogy. *The Packrat, 4*(98), 4-6.

Itle-Clark, S. (2013). *In-service teachers understanding and teaching of humane education before and after a standards-based intervention* (Doctoral dissertation). Retrieved from http://animalstudiesrepository.org/acwp_he/1

Itle-Clark, S., & Forsyth, N. (2012). *Humane literacy and formal educators.* Unpublished manuscript.

Iozzi, L.A. (1989). What research says to the educator: Part one: Environmental education and the affective domain. *The Journal of Environmental Education, 20*(3), 3-9.

Jensen, E. (2005). *Teaching with the brain in mind.* Alexandria, VA: Association for Supervision and Curriculum Development.

Johnson, C., Ironsmith, M., Snow, C., & Poteat, G. (2000). Peer acceptance and social adjustment in preschool and kindergarten. *Early Childhood Education Journal, 27*(4), 207-212.

Kitchen, J., & Stevens, D. (2008). Action research in teacher education: Two teacher-educators practice action research as they introduce action research to preservice teachers. *Action Research, 6*(1), 7-28.

Kochenderfer-Ladd, B. (2004). Peer victimization: The role of emotions in adaptive and maladaptive coping. *Social Development, 3*(3), 329-349.

Kohlberg, L. (1973). The claim to moral adequacy of a highest stage of moral judgment. *Journal of Philosophy, 70*(18), 630–646.

Kohlberg, L. (1981). *The psychology of moral development: Moral stages and the idea of justice* (Vol. 1). Essays on moral development. San Francisco, CA: Harper & Row.

Kohlberg, L. (1984). *The psychology of moral development: The nature and validity of moral stages* (Vol. 2). Essays on moral development. San Francisco, CA: Harper & Row.

Learning First Alliance. (2001). *Every child learning: Safe and supportive schools.* Washington, DC: Learning First Alliance.

Levin, H. M. (1996). Accelerated schools after eight years. In R. Glaser & L. Schauble (Eds.). *Innovations in learning: New environments in education* (pp. 329-352). Mahwah, NJ: Erlbaum.

Lewin, K. (1946). Action research and minority problems. *Journal of Social Issues, 2*(4): 34-46.

McAllister, G. (2002). The role of empathy in teaching culturally diverse students: A qualitative study of teachers' beliefs. *Journal of Teacher Education, 53*(5), 433-443.

McLeran, P. (2006). *Life in schools: An introduction to critical pedagogy in the foundations of education.* Washington, DC: Pearson.

McMahon, S. D., & Washburn, J. J. (2003). Violence prevention: An evaluation of program effects with urban African American students. *Journal of Primary Prevention, 24*(1), 43-62.

McNiff, J. & Whitehead, J. (2006) *All you need to know about action research.* London, England: Sage.

Marion, M. (2003). *Guidance of young children*. Columbus, OH: Merrill Prentice Hall.

Mendez-Morse, S. (1992). *Leadership characteristics that facilitate school change*. Austin, TX: Southwest Educational Development Laboratory.

Mettetal, G. (2002). *Improving teaching through classroom action research*. Retrieved from http://academic.udayton.edu/FacDev/Newsletters/EssaysforTeaching-Excellence/PODvol14/tevol14n7.html

Miller, M. (2005). Teaching and learning in affective domain. In M. Orey (Ed.), *Emerging perspectives on learning, teaching, and technology* (pp. 93-103). Retrieved from http://projects.coe.uga.edu/epltt

Mooney, N. J. & Mausbach, A. T. (2008). *Align the design*. Alexandria, VA: ASCD.

Murphy, J.T. (1988). The unheroic side of leadership: Notes from the swamp. *The Phi Delta Kappan, 69*(9), 654-659.

Myles, B.S., Trautman, M., & Shelvan, R. (2004). *Asperger syndrome and the hidden curriculum*. Shawnee Mission, KS: Autism Asperger.

National Education Association. (n.d.). *Myths and facts about educator pay*. Retrieved from http://www.nea.org/home/12661.htm

Pandey, A. (2011). Leading wholesome change in integral ways. *NHRD Journal on Change, 4*(2), 18-23.

Payton, J., Weissberg, R. P., Durlak, J. A., Dymnicki, A. B., Taylor, R. D., Schellinger, K. B., & Pachan, M. (2008). *The positive impact of social and emotional learning for kindergarten to eighth-grade students: Findings from three scientific reviews*. Chicago, IL: Collaborative for Academic, Social, and Emotional Learning.

Penner, L. A. & Finkelstein, M. A. (1998). Dispositional and structural determinants of volunteerism. *Journal of Personality and Social Psychology, 74*(2), 525-537.

Preusse, K. (2008). Fostering prosocial behavior in young children. Retrieved from http://www.earlychildhoodnews.com/earlychildhood/article_view.aspx?ArticleID=566

Riley, D., San Juan, R. R., Klinkner, J., & Ramminger, A. (2008). *Social and emotional development*. St. Paul, MN: RedLeaf.

Rutherford, F. J. & Ahlgren, A. (1990). *Science for all Americans: Project 2061*. New York, NY: Oxford University Press.

Rutter, M., Giller, H., & Hagell, A. (1998). *Antisocial behavior by young people*. Cambridge, NY: Cambridge University Press.

Schmoker, M. (2006). *Results now: How we can achieve unprecedented improvements in teaching and learning*. Alexandria, VA: Association for Supervision and Curriculum Development.

Schon, D.A. (1996). *Educating the reflective practitioner: Toward a new design for teaching and learning in the professions*. San Francisco, CA: Jossey-Bass.

School Leadership for the 21st Century Initiative. (2001). *Leadership for student learning: Redefining the teacher as leader*. Washington, DC: Institute for Educational Leadership.

Senge, P. M. (2006). *The fifth discipline: The art and practice of the learning organization.* New York, NY: Doubleday.

Senge, P. M., Roberts, C., Ross, R., Smith, B., Roth, G., & Kleiner, A. (1999). *The dance of change: The challenge of sustaining momentum in learning organization.* New York, NY: Doubleday.

Smith, P. & Ragan, T. J. (1999). *Instructional design.* New York, NY: Wiley.

Stiegelbauer, S. (1992). *Why we want to be teachers.* Paper presented at the annual meeting of the American Educational Research Association, San Francisco, CA.

Stringer, E. T., Christensen, L. M., & Baldwin, S. C. (2010). *Integrating teaching, learning, and action research.* Thousand Oaks, CA: Sage.

Tomlinson, C. (2003). *Differentiation in practice: A resource guide for differentiating curriculum.* Alexandria, VA: Association for Supervision Curriculum and Development.

U.S. Department of Education. (2006). *Improving data quality for Title I standards, assessments, and accountability reporting: Guidelines for states, LEAs, and schools.* Retrieved from www2.ed.gov/policy/elsec/guid/standardsassessment/nclbdataguidance.doc

Vallance, E. (1973). Hiding the hidden curriculum: An interpretation of the language of justification in nineteenth-century educational reform. *Curriculum Theory Network, 4*(1), 5-21.

Veugelers, W. (2000). Different ways of teaching values. *Educational Review, 52*(1), 37-46.

Weissberg, R. P., Kumpfer, K., Seligman, M. E. (2003). Prevention that works for children and youth: An introduction. *American Psychologist, 58*(1), 425-432.

Weissberg, R. P., & O'Brien, M. U. (2004). What works in school-based social and emotional learning programs for positive youth development. *The Annals of the American Academy, 591*(1), 86-96.

Westley, F. & Mintzberg, H. (1989). Visionary leadership and strategic management. *Strategic Management Journal, 10*(51), 17-32.

Wideen, M. F., Mayer-Smith, J., & Moon, B. (1998). A critical analysis of the research on learning to teach: Making the case for an ecological perspective on inquiry. *Review of Educational Research, 68*(2), 130–178.

Zahn-Waxler, C. & Radke-Yarrow, M. (1990). The origins of empathetic concern. *Motivation and Emotion, 14*(2), 107-130.

CHAPTER THREE

HUMANE EDUCATION AS AN ACADEMIC FIELD: COURSES AND PROGRAMS DEVELOPED AT THE UNIVERSITY LEVEL

Andrew Domzalski and Boguslawa Gatarek, Madonna University

I n this new millennium, two issues have been tied with social justice—environmental conservation and animal protection (Goodall & Bekoff, 2002; Weil, 2004)—thus creating a fertile ground for so-called broad-based humane education. This development is reflected in humane education programs mushrooming across K-12 schools worldwide, most notably Roots and Shoots. In addition, there are now two North American universities that offer graduate programs in the field of broad-based humane education: the pioneer Institute for Humane Education and a recently established program in humane studies at Madonna University. A pivotal course in the latter program is HUS 6010: Pedagogical Strategies in Humane Education (see Appendix 1). This paper discusses the benefits and challenges of establishing and teaching broad-based humane education at the university level, using the aforementioned course as a case study. A special emphasis is given to definitions and conceptual developments in the field, as the authors suggest the Common Ingroup Identity Model as a possible unifying paradigm for the field.

HUMANE EDUCATION IN MODERN NORTH AMERICA AND ITS DEFINITIONS

In the modern era, the focus of humane education was at first solely on children and animal welfare. In the 19th century's America, the field was developing as a corollary to growing humane societies (Antoncic, 2003; Selby, 2000; Unti & DeRosa, 2003). "The golden age" of humane education, which took place in the first two decades of the 20th century (Oakley, 2007), was prompted by its appeal as a tool for character building. The very perception made it possible for humane education to become a part of school curricula across the United States, even if only nominally (Unti & DeRosa, 2003). As any educational field, subject to the twists and turns of the socio-political climate of the day, humane education diminished in the subsequent decades, as world wars and external threats motivated cultural shifts.

The current conceptualization of humane education as a broad-based field encompassing social justice and environmental ethics along with animal welfare comes from the work and activism of several scholars and activists, most notably Jane Goodall, a British primatologist; Mary Gordon, who established the Canadian school program "Roots of Empathy"; David Selby, professor at the International Institute for Global Education, Ontario Institute for Studies in Education at the University of Toronto and author of *Earthkind: A Teacher's Handbook on Humane Education*; and Zoe Weil, the founder of the Institute for Humane Education.

Jane Goodall's conservationist efforts to save chimpanzees and their natural habitat through creating opportunities for local people in the Gombe National Park have been replicated across Africa (The Jane Goodall Institute, 2010). Goodall's international youth action program, Roots and Shoots, which focuses on activities and service-learning projects benefiting local communities, their environments, and animals has inspired educators around the world. The Roots and Shoots (n.d.) mission provides a definition of humane education, "To foster respect and compassion for all living things, to promote understanding of all cultures and beliefs and to inspire each individual to take action to make the world a better place for people, animals and the environment" (para 4).

The above definition is somewhat broader than a succinct conceptualization by Selby (2000), "Humane education focuses on fostering an ethic of care and compassion for all living things, human and non-human."

In Canada, the most internationally acclaimed pioneer of humane education is Mary Gordon. Her program, Roots of Empathy, which focuses on teaching empathy to children and adults, grew from a small Toronto-based kindergarten pilot program in 1996 into an organization that currently has chapters in all Canadian provinces and many countries across the globe. Gordon's approach is based on classroom visits of an infant and parent. The loving interactions between them provide modeling for observing students. As a result, prosocial behaviors increase and aggression decreases in participating students (Roots of Empathy, n.d). In the U.S., also in 1996, Zoe Weil established the Institute for Humane Education (the IHE) which partnered with a local college, becoming the first educational institution that supports university-level humane educators. The IHE (n.d.) website provides a comprehensive definition of humane education:

> Humane education is a lens, body of knowledge, and set of tools and strategies for teaching about human rights, animal protection, environmental stewardship, and cultural issues as interconnected and integral dimensions of a just, healthy society. Humane education not only instills the desire and capacity to live with compassion, integrity, and wisdom, but also provides the knowledge and tools to put our values into action in meaningful, far-reaching ways so that we can find solutions that work for all (para 3).

Weil's ideas are based on providing accurate information to foster the 3Cs (Curiosity, Creativity, and Critical thinking) and instill the 3Rs (Reverence, Respect, Responsibility) (Weil, 2004). Her approach is used by the Institute's graduates and their associates who implement it across K-12 curricula from literacy to foreign languages, social studies, science, and art education. An excellent example of applying humane education as defined by Weil to pedagogical praxis is HEART, which stands for Humane Education Advocates Reaching Teachers. The HEART mission provides another example of humane education definition, "To foster compassion and respect for all living beings and the environment by educating youth and teachers in Humane Education" (HEART, n.d.).

This educational organization promotes humane education through student-centered programs called Humane Living, which is geared toward K-3, 4-6, 7-8, and high-school students. It also offers teacher training and advocacy support.

At the college level, new graduate programs in humane studies are modeled on the combination of the above definitions of humane education. The mission of the Master of Science in Humane Studies at Madonna University echoes the definitions previously quoted while situating them in academic context designed to support professional preparation in areas of social justice, sustainability, and animal protection.

Since both humane education and humane studies are used in reference to the aforementioned programs, it is worthwhile to discern how they relate to each other. While the term humane education has been used for many decades, both in its narrow meaning of teaching kindness to animals and in its broad-based sense as discussed earlier in this section, the term humane studies better describes the program at Madonna University. The reason for the departure from the traditionally employed term humane education was the perceived need for a conceptual distinction between curricula that prepare bona fide humane educators versus those that train a broad spectrum of other professionals in the field, from non-profit leaders to animal cruelty investigators. While a case can be made that all of those professionals are in some sense informal humane educators, as they interact with the public in promoting humane causes, the distinction remains valid in capturing various professional roles.

As humane education seems to be gaining momentum across North American colleges and elsewhere (Howard, 2009; Selby, 2000), likely due to its broader definition uniting under one umbrella animal protection along with social justice concerns and environmental conservation, its future may lie in its successful fusion with a large spectrum of existing fields that at first glance may seem conceptually distant from humane education. One such example is language teaching. As language teachers always strive to identify authentic texts upon which they can base their instruction of such skills as speaking, listening, reading, writing, and grammar, using appropriate readings that promote humane causes may serve two purposes simultaneously: making students aware of social, environmental, and animal protection issues that need our solutions and enhancing language learning through providing engaging topics for discussions (Domzalski & Gatarek, 2011). Another example is interweaving humane education principles with such aspects of the field of criminal justice as inmate rehabilitation and investigative work. The former is well reflected in the programs in which inmates care for rescue dogs, such as The Inmate Dog Alliance Project of Idaho (n.d) or Paws For Life (n.d.) at California State Prison amongst many others. An example of the latter is the creation of Animal Cruelty Investigation Certificate at Madonna University.

INSTITUTIONAL HISTORY: FROM AN UNDERGRADUATE COURSE TO A GRADUATE PROGRAM

Establishing a university course, let alone a degree program, in a field that is quite new to academia requires time, perseverance and, above all, persuasive arguments that satisfy both fellow faculty members and administrators. Starting with one course situated within the existing curriculum and showing success in terms of high student enrollments and satisfaction rates, alongside demonstrating achieved learning outcomes, may prove to be an effective first step in the process. This was the route taken by the faculty members at Madonna University interested in humane education. In the early 2000s an undergraduate course, *Do Animals Matter?*, covering human-animal issues from the perspective of both humanities and social sciences, was created and offered on a rotating basis with other general education options. Due to its instant enrollment success and the fact that it became a platform for a collaboration between the University and the Detroit Zoo in terms of service-learning projects conducted by the students, the course became a regular offering, and its graduate version was developed for students in the Liberal Studies program seeking an elective. At that time, another graduate course, Humane Studies, was created as part of the requirements of a then newly established program in Liberal Studies. The Humane Studies course was a scholarly exploration of relationships among social justice, environmental conservation, and animal protection.

As more students taking the above two courses became interested in a possibility of pursuing a career in humane studies, the faculty teaching the courses conducted a year-long feasibility exploration, including surveying students to gauge the number of potential candidates, researching job market opportunities for graduates, and analyzing curricula of related programs at other institutions. Two other crucial issues regarding the institutional fit of the program were considered: its relation to the mission and values embraced by Madonna University, a Catholic university in the Franciscan tradition, and the existence of a department that could house the program. Regarding the first issue, it was determined that a humane studies program would directly reflect such Franciscan values guiding the University as respect for the dignity of each person, peace and justice, and reverence for all creation. As for the choice of a unit to house the program, while humane studies curriculum is clearly both multidisciplinary and inter-disciplinary, its primary focus on social change warranted its place in the Sociology Department in the College of Social Sciences. Teaching faculty, however, came from humanities, education, and business departments in addition to sociology. Having received the institutional approval, the program started recruiting students in Fall 2011 and has boasted a successful enrollment since.

The term humane studies, as opposed to a more widely used humane education, reflects the program's curriculum and outcomes, which are geared toward preparing professionals for non-profit organizations, churches, governmental agencies, businesses, and educational institutions to work "toward developing practical solutions to current challenges affecting the well-being of people, environment, and animals," as stated in the program's brochure (Madonna University, 2015). The curriculum aims at enhancing students' marketability in conjunction with their undergraduate degrees, regardless of their majors. Thus, its primary focus is not teacher or educator preparation, for which the term *humane education* is customarily reserved.

Yet, in the curriculum including such courses as (a) Humane Studies; (b) Do Animals Matter?; (c) Diversity, Discrimination, and Social Justice; and (d) Environmental Ethics, the course (e) Pedagogical Strategies in Humane Education plays an integrating role, as it aims at giving students practical tools for sharing with various audiences the information gained in other courses.

TEACHING PEDAGOGICAL STRATEGIES IN HUMANE STUDIES

As the course Pedagogical Strategies in Humane Education provides a platform for analyzing relationships among the principles of humane education, critical pedagogy, and the Franciscan values, it does so mostly in the context of pedagogical assignments (Appendix 1). Although the graduates' job titles may not be those of humane educators, the skills of effective sharing of information with different audiences will likely assist them in their future work duties. To this end, the bulk of course assignments are designed for that purpose. Creating a lesson plan, evaluating a classroom activity, and designing and delivering a workshop provide the students with hands-on experiences that make them ready for professional tasks in the field.

While learning both the science and art of designing an audience-appropriate lesson or workshop plan may prove challenging for students without backgrounds in education, it is also a valuable experience in effective communicative strategies. These strategies are easily transferrable to various settings from K-12 classrooms to colleges, universities, and community outreach venues. Just as learning the format of lesson plans requires practice, so does making connections among issues of social justice, environmental conservation, and animal protection and incorporating them into an audience-friendly form of outreach.

The selection of content for a humane education course is of great importance, and modeling of humane education principles throughout the program of instruction is of equal significance. Since "the medium is the message," as Selby (1995) repeats after Marshal McLuhan at the beginning of his discussion of humane learning, the humane education instructor has the responsibility "to walk the talk" (p. 34). Selby lists the following strategies as compatible with humane learning: interactive and cooperative learning, decentralization of teacher power, initiative-taking by students, building self-esteem and group bonding, and real-life opportunities for social action, among others.

All the above strategies help to achieve the overarching goals for HUS 6010 Pedagogical Strategies in Humane Studies and ultimately for the whole program in humane studies. Those goals include empowering students, instilling positive attitudes toward social change, and equipping students with plans, tools, and strategies to manage such change in complex and challenging contexts. In addition, generous scholarship, which includes sharing ideas, materials, and expertise, is modeled across the curriculum.

Teaching humane education calls for interweaving several dimensions into instruction: from personal to social and political, as well as from local to global. The course HUS 6010 encourages making connections among those dimensions through required essay postings. As students learn accurate information about the world, which includes awareness of specific examples of social injustice and inequality, environmental degradation, and institutional animal abuse, they often feel angry, frustrated, and powerless. It is of paramount importance always to accompany such examples with positive solutions for those problems and model how to frame such problems in a positive way, which is ultimately a more effective manner of presenting them to the public.

Humane Education Strategies

There exists a body of research examining various approaches to forming positive attitudes toward animals and how those attitudes apply to a broader context of humane education. With some modification, such approaches can be implemented across grades from kindergarten to college. Sorge (2009) reports that simply exposing young students to animals in positive contexts that allow for bonding improves students' attitudes toward them. The same is true of in-class humane education programs for eighth graders (Nicoll, Trifone, & Samuels, 2008). At the college level, critical pedagogy, understood as the teaching and learning practices designed to develop students' critical consciousness about oppressive social conditions, carries a transformative potential regarding views on animals. Yet, some scholars claim that this potential fails to be realized as critical pedagogy remains solidly anthropocentric and thus renders itself useless outside of the self-imposed boundaries of exclusively human-centered interests (Bell & Russell, 2000; Cavalieri, 2008). A remedy to the above state of affairs may lie in the total liberation pedagogy proposed by Khan and Humes (2009), which approaches holistically not only planetary sustainability and social justice but animal advocacy as well. At a university, it can be accomplished through various venues. One should not underestimate the power of building personal relationships with both faculty and administrators, who in turn may become open to making humane decisions about the use of animals in their classrooms or the treatment of campus wildlife. Another venue could be organizing a speaker series with prominent scholars in the area of human-animal studies. Such campus events tend to attract fellow faculty members and serve as an excellent platform for promoting humane ideas among academics. In the past, Madonna University's humane studies program collaborated with the Animals and Society Institute and the Michigan Humane Society to use the campus as the venue for a speaker series of this kind. Its popularity and impact prompted Madonna University to continue similar events, currently in collaboration with the University's Center for Catholic Studies and Interfaith Dialog. A collaborative character of this enterprise assures its cross-curricular impact, as students attending various courses may be encouraged to attend the lectures. The following strategies embraced at the university level can further integrate humane education into the programs of study.

BUILD EMPATHY

Any successful pedagogy needs to be based on exposure and experience. These two elements play a crucial role in developing empathy. This correlates with the Perception-Action Model (PAM) of empathy postulated by Preston and de Waal (2002). According to the authors, it explains the most robust effects in empathy experiments, such as "familiarity (subject's previous experience with object), similarity (perceived overlap between subject and object, e.g., species, personality, age, gender), learning (explicit or implicit teaching), past experience (with situation of distress), and salience (strength of perceptual signal, e.g., louder, closer, more realistic, etc.)" (Preston & de Waal, 2002, p. 3). The PAM model emphasizes neurobiological roots of perception and links it to action. Selecting the venues best suited for de-objectification of animals must take into account the distinction between cognitive and emotional empathy, with the latter being linked to personal distress (Daly & Morton, 2008).

University curricula can promote de-objectification of animals by eliminating the use of live animals in classroom experiments and by organizing service-learning projects whose beneficiaries are individual animals.

CHANGE ATTITUDES

Some examples of powerful techniques transforming students' attitudes toward animals include storytelling, perspective taking, and service-learning. Storytelling, with its protagonists as multidimensional agents, may be an effective way of depicting animals as complex beings (Fawcett, 2000). The research by Peskin and Astington (2004) supports this contention by showing how implicit mentalistic context of picture storybooks helps children build representational understanding of others' state of mind. The above findings, though, need to be qualified in light of the fact that fantasy relates to cognitive rather than emotional empathy (Daly & Morton, 2008) and as such may not lead to attitude changes.

Perspective taking is another well-researched technique, which seems to improve attitudes toward out-group or non-included members. The Common Ingroup Identity Model (Gaertner, Dovidio, & Bachman, 1996; Gaetner at al., 2000) is built on Allport's idea of social categorization (Allport, 1958). It credits social categorization with both reducing and creating intergroup bias. It postulates decategorization and recategorization as factors changing in-group boundaries so former out-group members can be seen as in-group members. According to Allport (1958), people group others into categories to function more efficiently in a society. This categorization results in creating in-groups and out-groups. People favor in-group members over out-group members and those without group membership even in randomly assigned laboratory conditions (Gaertner, Mann, Murrell, & Dovidio, 1989). Although the studies focus on attitudes toward other humans, animals are often perceived as the ultimate out-group members, so their results may shed light on the discussed topic. Shih, Wang, Bucher, and Stotzer (2009) have shown that, while perspective taking of an out-group member improves attitudes toward that out-group and its individual members, this attitude does not transfer to other out-groups. Since perspective taking is linked to cognitive rather than emotional empathy, the caution with which the previous findings on fantasy are interpreted (Daly et al., 2008) applies here as well. Equally important, the results of the above studies are weakened by the key methodological limitation, which is not accounting for the stability of the change. Eagly and Chaiken (1995) report that attitude change is rarely permanent and subject to reversion. In addition, an attitude change may not impact changes in behavior (Kraus, 1995), as several other factors in addition to attitudes play a role in motivating the latter. Arbuthnott (2008) lists the following additional factors: contextual support, intention specificity, perceived control, feedback about target behavior, social norms, action difficulty, and habits. According to her, effective education in addition to targeting values and attitudes should provide personal action plans that help in translating intentions into actions. This is of paramount importance to the theory and praxis of humane education.

END BIAS THROUGH STUDIES

In addition to the above strategies, other concepts constituting the theoretical framework of the Common In-group Identity Model may be applicable to humane education and, more precisely, to exploring the factors responsible for shaping humane educators. This is true of the pivotal concept of bias. Dovidio & Gaertner (2010) define it as "an unfair evaluative, emotional, cognitive, or behavioral response toward another group in ways that devalue or disadvantage the other group and its members either directly or indirectly by valuing or privileging members of one's group" (p. 1084). Bias can be analyzed through its three dimensions: type, expression, and focus of orientation. The first dimension can be characterized as stereotypes, prejudice, or discrimination. The expression of bias can be either explicit or implicit, and the focus of orientation refers to either out-group derogation or in-group favoritism.

Dovidio and Gaertner (2010) describe stereotypes as a set of shared beliefs about a group, prejudice as an attitude, and discrimination as a type of behavior. Stereotypes, defined as a set of over-generalized beliefs about a group or its members associated by negative feelings are used to simplify complex social environments and allow for quick evaluation and reactions. Many studies indicate that social stereotypes, both individual and collective, are resistant to change (Dovidio, Brigham, Johnson, & Gaertner, 1996; Stangor & Shaller, 1996). The changes that occur are slow and gradual and involve transformations in intensity of central features or in their replacement by new ones (Kurcz, 1995). The fact that stereotypes are difficult to change leads to the question of whether their formation can be at all prevented. While their origin is a subject of debate, most researchers agree that stereotypes pertaining to gender, age, or ethnic minorities form early in life. As stereotypes originate on both individual and social level, the knowledge about the origination of the former may be particularly useful in discerning what personal experiences are crucial to making humane educators. Pettigrew (1970) shows that individual stereotypes are formed through homogenous emotionally charged personal experiences, which affect the individual differences in the cognitive category width. On the other hand, socially formed stereotypes are shaped by social standards, social modeling, language, and by the process of social categorization (Tajfel, 1982). While there is no consensus as to the effect of stereotypes on behavior, the opposite seems to be true of prejudice. Dovidio (2001) defines it as "an unfair negative attitude toward a social group or a person perceived to be a member of that group" (p. 829). There exists strong empirical evidence pointing to the influence of prejudice on behavior, yet its mechanisms are not well understood. Various hypotheses have been proposed, from the generalization of negative personal experiences to such social sources as real intergroup conflicts or displacement of aggression, but none has been empirically supported. Dovidio (2001) argues that the concept of social categorization, after Allport (1958), may provide a better framework to understand prejudice. Social categorization influences our perception leading to exaggerating our similarities with the members of the same category and our differences with those belonging to other categories.

SERVICE-LEARNING

Service-learning–a teaching and learning strategy that integrates meaningful community service with instruction and reflection to enrich the learning experience, teach civic responsibility, and strengthen communities–is another venue for de-objectifying animals. When students plan and carry out projects that aim at benefiting animals, in the process they learn how to assume the perspectives that focus on animal interests rather than human ones. They also look at individual animals as possessing specific needs, preferences, likes, and dislikes, which helps them to become more empathetic. An example of such service-learning is the cooperation between Madonna University; Livonia, Michigan; and the Detroit Zoo, where students enrolled in an undergraduate animal-human studies course enrich the habitats of various animals (Domzalski, 2009; Proctor, 2012).

Although various humane education techniques that are discussed in this section represent a number of theoretical paradigms, all of them are used in Madonna's program, as any educational praxis ultimately requires an open mind and an eclectic approach.

CONCLUSION

The future success of humane education may depend on pursuing two seemingly contradictory trends: on one hand solidifying it as a separate field in its own right with a unifying paradigm that provides a useful platform for research and further conceptual development and, on the other hand, interweaving its principles into a wide spectrum of disparate areas from humanities to social sciences and beyond. With a closer look, those two trends can be seen as complementary rather than contradictory, as a well-defined independent field with its own research-based body of knowledge has a greater chance to influence other areas. To this end, further efforts in establishing humane education as a full-fledged academic field through creating new college and university courses, programs, and research centers is of paramount importance.

References

Allport, G.W. (1958). *The nature of prejudice*. Garden City, NY: Doubleday Anchor Books.

Antoncic, L. (2003). A new era in humane education: How troubling youth trends and a call for character education are breathing new life into efforts to educate our youth about the value of all life. *Journal of Animal Law, 9*, 183-213.

Arbuthnott, K. D. (2008). Education for sustainable development beyond attitude change. *International Journal of Sustainability in Higher Education, 10*(2), 152-163.

Bell, A. C., & Russell, C. L. (2000). Beyond human, beyond words: Antropocentrism, critical pedagogy and the poststructural turn. *Canadian Journal of Education, 25*(3), 188-203.

Cavalieri, P. (2008). A missed opportunity: Humanism, anti-humanism and the animal question. In J. Castricano (Ed.), *Animal subjects: An ethical reader in a posthuman world* (pp. 97-123). Waterloo, ON: Wilfrid University Press.

Daly, B., & Morton, L.L. (2008). Empathic correlates of witnessing the inhumane killings of an animal: An investigation of single and multiple exposures. *Society and Animals, 16*, 243-255.

Domzalski, A. & Gatarek, B. (2011). Introducing humane education to TESOL curricula. *MITESOL Conference Proceedings 2009 and 2010*. Ypsilanti, MI: Eastern Michigan University, 40-55.

Dovidio, J. F. (2001). On the nature of contemporary prejudice: The third wave. *Journal of Social Issues, 57*(4), 829-849.

Dovidio, J. F., Brigham, J. C., Johnson, B. T., & Gaertner, S. L. (1996). Stereotyping, prejudice and discrimination. In C. N. Macrae, C. Stangor, & M. Hewstone (Eds.), *Stereotypes and stereotyping* (pp. 276-322). New York, NY: Guilford.

Dovidio, J. F. & Gaertner, S. L. (2010) Intergroup Bias. In S. T. Fiske, D. T. Gilbert, G. Lindzey (Eds.), *Handbook of Social Psychology* (Vol. 2, pp. 1084-1121). Hoboken, NJ: Wiley.

Eagly, A., & Chaiken, S. (1995). Attitude strength, attitude structure and resistance to change. In R. Petty and J. Kosnik (Eds.), *Attitude Strength* (pp. 413-432). Mahwah, NJ: Erlbaum.

Fawcett, J. (2000). Ethical imagining: Ecofeminist possibilities and environmental learning. *The Canadian Journal of Environmental Education, 5*, 134-147.

Goodall, J., & Bekoff, M. (2002). *The ten trusts: What we must do to care for the animals we love*. San Francisco, CA: Harper Collins

Howard, J. (2009, October 18). Creature Consciousness. *The Chronicle of Higher Education*. Retrieved from http://chronicle.com/article/Creature-Consciousness/48804

Inmate Dog Alliance Project of Idaho. (n.d.). Retrieved from https://idahohumanesociety.org/programs/idapi/

Institute for Humane Education. (n.d.). Humane education definition. Retrieved from http://humaneeducation.org/home

Khan, R., & Humes, B. (2009). Marching out from *ultima Thule*: Critical counterstories of emancipatory educators working at the intersection of human rights, animal rights, and planetary sustainability. *The Canadian Journal of Environmental Education, 14*, 179-195.

Kraus, S. J. (1995). Attitudes and the prediction of behavior: A meta-analysis on the empirical literature. *Personality and Social Psychology Bulletin, 21*(1), 58-75.

Kurcz, I. (1995). *Zmiennosc i nieuchronnosc stereotypow* [Changeability and inevitability of stereotypes]. Warszawa, Poland: PAN.

Madonna University. (2015). *Master of science in humane studies brochure.* Livonia, Michigan: Madonna University.

Nicoll, K., Trifone, C., & Samuels, W. E. (2008). An in-class, humane education program can improve young students' attitudes toward animals. *Society and Animals, 16*(1), 45-60.

Oakley, J. (2007). *Humane education: A genealogical consideration and preliminary literature review* (Unpublished PhD portfolio). Lakehead University, Thunder Bay, ON.

Peskin, J., & Astington, J. W. (2004). The effects of adding metacognitive language to story text. *Cognitive Development, 19*(2), 253-272.

Pettigrew, T. F. (1970). The measurements and correlates of category width as a cognitive variable. In P.B. Warr (Ed.), *Thought and personality* (pp. 127-142). Middlesex, England: Penguin Books.

Paws for Life. (2014). Retrieved from http://myemail.constantcontact.com/Paws-For-Life–Outreach-to-Inmates-in-LA-County-Prison.html?soid=110160920 7998&aid=wUWYBH-_2-o

Preston, S. D., & de Waal, F. B. M. (2002). Empathy: Its ultimate and proximate bases. *Behavioral and Brain Sciences, 25*(1), 1-72.

Roots of Empathy. (n.d.) What is Roots of Empathy? Retrieved from http://www.rootsofempathy.org

Roots and Shoots. (n.d.). Mission statement. Retrieved from http://www.rootsand-shoots.org

Selby, D. (1995). *Earthkind: A teacher's handbook on humane education.* Stoke-on-Trent, United Kingdom: Trentham.

Selby, D. (2000). Humane education: Widening the circle of compassion and justice. In T. Goldstein & D. Selby (Eds.), *Weaving connections: Educating for peace, social and environmental justice* (pp. 268-296). Toronto, ON: Sumach Press.

Shih, M., Wang, E., Bucher, E. T., & Stotzer, R. (2009). Perspective taking: Reducing prejudice towards general outgroups and specific individuals. *Group Processes Intergroup Relations, 12*(5), 565-577.

Sorge, C. (2008). The relationship between bonding with nonhuman animals and students' attitudes toward science. *Society and Animals, 16*(2), 171-184.

Stangor, C. & Shaller, M. (1996). Stereotypes as individual and collective representation. In C. N. Macrae, C. Stangor, & M. Hewstone (Eds.), *Stereotypes and stereotyping* (pp. 3-40). New York, NY: Guilford

The Jane Goodall Institute. (2010). *Conservation & communities.* Retrieved from http://www.janegoodall.org/cc-landing

Tyfel, H. (1982). *Social identity and intergroup relations.* Cambridge, NY: Cambridge University Press.

Unti, B. & DeRosa, B. (2003). Humane education: Past, present and future. In D. J. Salem & A. N. Rowan (Eds.), *The state of the animals II: 2003* (pp. 27-50). Washington, DC: Humane Society Press.

Weil, Z. (2004). *The power and promise of humane education.* Gabriola Island, BC: New Society.

PART TWO

HUMANE ETHICS
IN THE HUMANITIES,
SCIENCES, AND BEYOND

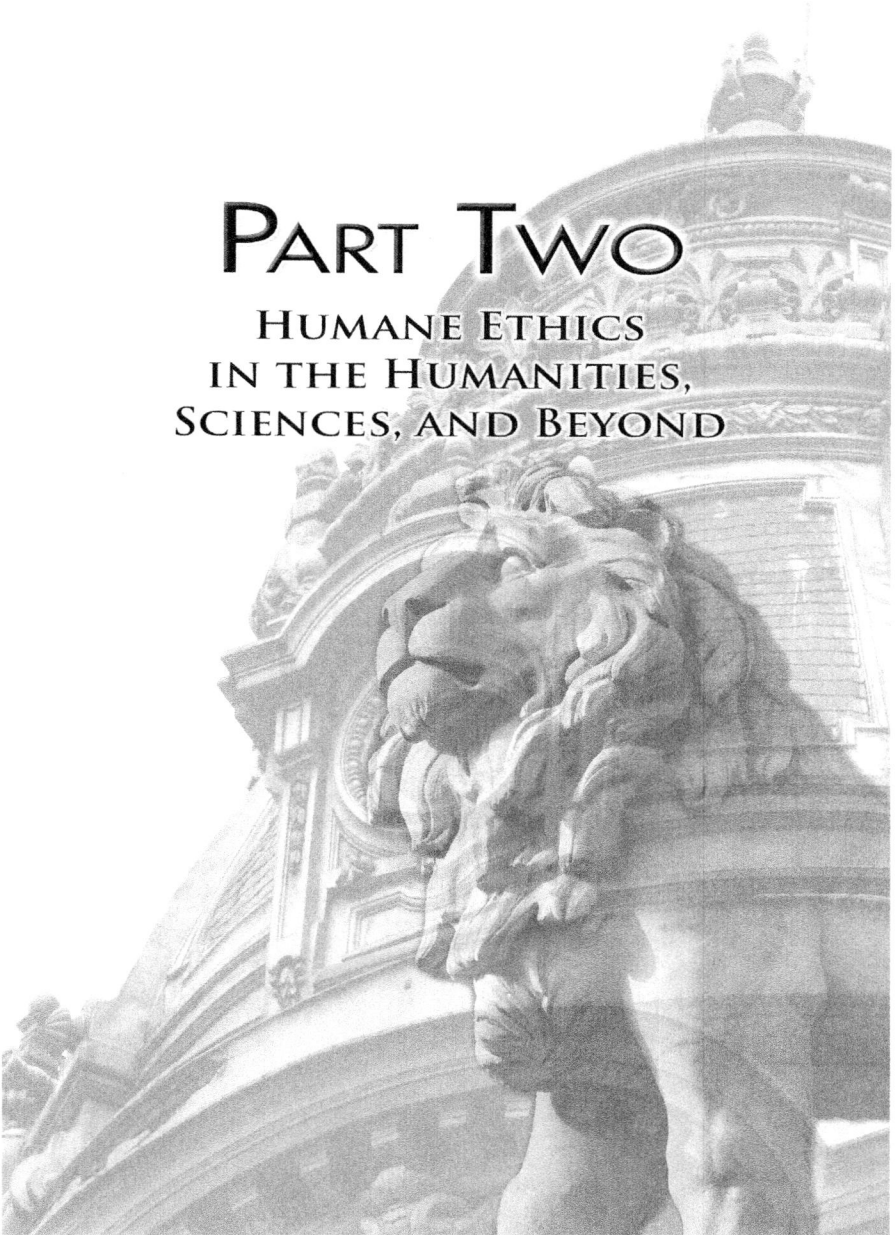

CHAPTER FOUR

REMOVING ETHICAL BLIND SPOTS IN HIGHER EDUCATION: THE NECESSITY OF INCLUDING NON-HUMAN ANIMALS IN SOCIAL JUSTICE DISCOURSE

Kimberly Spanjol, Iona College

I t can be difficult for people to see their connection to non-human animals–or for humans to see themselves as animals at all. Research demonstrates that children from a variety of cultures have difficulty accepting that humans are animals, even when they are taught this explicitly in school (Carey, 1985). Regardless, humans are of course animals and deeply interconnected with other species. This paper advocates for applying Humane Pedagogy (Itle-Clark & Comaskey, in press) in institutions of higher education. Including non-human animal protection issues addresses typical ethical blind spots that obscure people from seeing the commodification, exploitation, and suffering of other species at the hands of humans for what it is–a social justice issue, deeply interconnected with other social justice issues that impact all humans, animals, and the environment we share. This chapter explores why including non-human animal perspectives when educating students of higher education and examining the intersectionality of social justice is imperative for optimal human, animal, and environmental health and wellbeing–as well as maximizing critical thinking, empathy development, and compassionate action in learners. While efforts are typically made to include some form of humane education and prosocial pedagogy in classrooms of younger learners, opportunities to develop systemic problem-solving, attitudinal shifts, and significant behavioral change do not end when learners graduate high school. On the contrary, newly found independence and decision-making around consumer and lifestyle choices provide an opportunity to bring the benefits of conscious and compassionate living to young adults who have the potential to create a more humane, peaceful, healthy and safe world now and in the future.

WHERE WE ARE NOW

The year 2020 has brought global threats to public health not experienced in over a century, continued tragedy and outcries for racial justice, and the intensification of the climate crisis with unprecedented environmental catastrophes. The vulnerability and interconnection of all life is becoming increasingly apparent to a greater number of people. While these events render the importance of addressing past and present relations between human and nonhuman animals (henceforth referred to as "animals") in education and social justice work more pressing than ever, ethical blind spots continue to permeate the dominant culture and obscure the plight of non-human animals as a social justice issue that is interconnected and intertwined with other social justice issues that impact humans, animals, and the environment. Higher education settings contain key drivers for teaching students critical thinking and sustainable prosocial behaviors: supportive learning environments over a sustained period of time (Chatterton & Wilson, 2010; Kasperbauer, 2019). Embedding animal-inclusive social justice discourse within higher education curriculum can effectively raise awareness of the interconnection of all life and cultivate increased empathy and compassion for animals as well as other humans and the earth. Expanding educational discourse to include humane education, and specifically humane pedagogy (Itle-Clark & Comaskey, in press) is crucial for developing perspective-taking and problem-solving skills in learners that can propel individual and systemic level change that benefits all life.

Humane education is defined as learning which is inclusive of compassion and empathy toward people, animals, and the planet and the interconnection among the three (Academy of Prosocial Learning, n.d.; Association of Professional Humane Educators, n.d.; Humane Education Advocates Reaching Teachers, 2019). While ethics, character education, and moral growth and development have long been a focus of educators, and even mandated by law in some cases, clear teaching approaches including the examination of implicit and explicit biases and related behavior have only relatively recently been addressed in educational settings due to successful social justice work and movements (Itle-Clark & Comaskey, in press). Successful social justice activism shapes educational interventions and procedures, and in turn education further shapes and evolves social justice movements. Harmful human-animal relationships, both in and out of educational settings, have largely been ignored and not interpreted as a social justice issue. Including and recognizing the plight of animals as an intrinsic element of social justice conversations that should be addressed accordingly in educational settings has been proposed by humane education models only relatively recently.

As explained by Itle-Clark & Comaskey:

> Within a humane approach to education (a humane pedagogy), species is an intersecting identity in the same way that other forms of stratification such as race, class, age, and gender are. The privileges or disadvantages inherent of each intersecting component become equally valid … The providence of human-kind is linked to humane work and the development of the prosocial traits that create a world in which all living beings are afforded the ability to live as they were meant to, in a fair and comfortable way. In order for this to occur, society must continue to provide humane education and most importantly, to expand the framework of how this education is delivered so the lessons are fair and equitable, without bias toward human or animal-kind, and designed to support each learner (p.10).

Itle-Clark & Comaskey go on to provide a comprehensive account of the evolvement of moral education models and the predominant exclusion of animals. A humane pedagogy empowers learners to identify their values and align their behavior in accordance with them through critical thinking, perspective taking and reflection. Implementing a humane pedagogy can help learners identify the processes of their thinking to reveal implicit and explicit biases behind the creation of their values, attitudes, morality, and ethics. Our educational systems, along with other socially constructed systems, are products of our shared history as well as recent movements in increased privatization and corporate incursions (Urban, Wagoner, Gaither, 2019). All these systems knowingly and unknowingly perpetuate moral blind spots against animals that both maintain and cultivate further implicit and explicit bias against them that almost all humans participate in. This is the case regardless of human status in other violent and oppressive systems that are birthed from fabricated social hierarchies. Examining biases toward animals provides a unique opportunity to practice aware-ness, deep examination, and possible transformation of attitudes and systems that are the products of cultural and structural violence–and the root cause of all social harms perpetrated against other animals, including other humans (Galtung, 1969).

Higher education plays a central role in developing future leaders and developing moral behavior in a complex, rapidly changing, knowl-edge-based society. Moral growth does not always fit neatly into estab-lished disciplines, and educators need essential theory and formative research to support them in creating curriculum and applying methods to effectively expand ethical development, social responsibility, civic engagement and other prosocial behaviors.

Bradenburger and Bowman (2015) explain:

"Higher Education has unique capacities to foster moral mean-ing and to channel students' good will, openness to the world, and developing intellectual abilities for the common good. Each fall, thousands of youths begin a journey of higher learning with a mixture of wonder, trepidation, and trust. Students of traditional college age, while negotiating both new freedoms and challenges, also feel the potentials and callings of young adulthood, and search for something of enduring value worthy of their commitment. Concurrently, college and university mission statements emphasize character development and preparing students for productive roles in society … Whether named or hidden, there is a great deal of moral education taking place in such contexts."

Regardless of this crucial social role, institutions of higher education suffer from the same ethical blind spots as society at large. Otherwise compassionate, ethical people turn a blind eye to the everyday commodification and exploitation of animals. These widely held implicit biases against animals prevent educators from including their concerns in the vast majority of higher education classrooms. This systemic and predictable blind spot of compassion toward animals is a driving force of social harm that directly and indirectly supports and sustains interconnected violent systems of oppression that impact all humans, animals and the environment–and is a sorely missed opportunity to cultivate compassion and empathy in learners (Malahy & Monin, 2014). Instead, our individual and collective empathy is dampened on a daily basis as we ignore the exploitation of animals that maintains, reinforces, and expands oppressive power structures that occur with most of our consent and collaboration (Joy, 2011; 2019). It is morally imperative for institutions of higher learning to recognize and illuminate this ethical blind spot to the plight of widespread and systemic human-caused suffering inflicted on animals.

SHAPING PROSOCIAL BEHAVIORS

Assistance in developing awareness, giving space for cognitive processing, and providing opportunities to take helpful action with support and feedback over time are key factors toward shaping prosocial human behavior (Hatfield & Wallace, 2004). Educational environments can, and have, provided successful settings to foster pro-social behavior change incrementally with guided and supportive inquiry to inspire critical thinking, awareness of values, and subsequent behavioral alignment with acknowledged values. While many education systems and curricula have evolved to include traditionally marginalized groups based on race, class, and gender, species bias is rarely included in educational discourse and is a missed opportunity to foster critical thinking, compassion, and kindness. Education systems and all social justice movements can benefit from including the examination of animal oppression and domination in their intersectional inquiries to more effectively foster deeper understanding of biases and sustained pro-social behavioral change.

As humanitarian anthropologist and physician Paul Farmer said, the idea that some lives matter less than others is the root of all injustice. Maintaining the belief that animal lives matter less than human lives, resulting in the subsequent participation in individual and systematic behavior that harms and oppresses animals, dampens human empathy and perpetuates injustice toward all marginalized groups (Ko, 2019; Joy, 2011). Including animal issues when educating learners and addressing the intersectionality of social justice issues is imperative for the continued development of a more equitable world and optimal human, animal, and environmental health and wellbeing, because nearly all modern humans cause harm to animals in some way through widespread and systematic victimization, exploitation, and oppression. Becoming aware of our participation in sustaining these hidden systems of structural and cultural violence provides endless opportunities to develop critical thinking skills, examine choices regarding alternatives to harmful behavior, and engage in meaningful and manageable compassionate action leading to individual and systemic prosocial change.

However, including animals in these inquiries and accepting in some form the role of harmful perpetrator can be difficult for learners to bear. Relevant research examined here can aid educators and social justice activists in effectively cultivating pro-social attitudes and behaviors. Enabling awareness of biases and barriers to increased empathy and compassion regarding animals–in educators, learners, and the systems we live, teach, and learn in–can be helpful in overcoming them when including animals in higher education dialectic. Teaching learners the psychological processes of how these biases and barriers develop and why, in addition to teaching content topics around issues that impact animals, are important elements of an effective humane pedagogy, in all levels of education.

An abundance of seminal work has transformed and advanced education systems and social justice reform for humans and the environment (eg.,Friere (1970); Zajda,Majhanovich & Rust (2006). The intention here is to provide methods to address and overcome barriers to pro-social behavior change in learners by also including animals in educational discourse and action. It is important to examine why animals are so often disregarded in education systems and intersectional social justice work in order to overcome this tendency that is rooted in speciesist thought and beliefs.

ADDRESSING, EXPLORING, AND ACKNOWLEDGING IMPLICIT BIAS INCLUDING ANIMALS: THE IMPACT OF SPECIESISM

Many, while not all, modern humans have privilege that allows them to access choices that either harm or help others, including animals. As choices are based on beliefs, it is necessary to examine the underlying beliefs that guide otherwise compassionate, kind, and caring people to make conditioned yet unnecessary choices that exploit, harm, and otherwise victimize animals (Joy, 2011). While these choices include harmful acts, they also encompass harmful omissions. These acts and omissions may be explained by understanding the effects of speciesism.

The term speciesism was introduced in 1970 by British psychologist Richard Ryder and was further popularized in 1975 by Australian philosopher Peter Singer in his influential book, Animal Liberation (Ryder, 2004; Singer, 1975). Speciesism is the belief in human supremacy and that the interests of one species are inherently more important than members of another species. Speciesist thought is represented and embedded in human behavior, and therefore expressed in public policy and social institutions on all levels, including education systems. This belief system is also responsible for animals being largely neglected in intersectional social justice work, research, and activism. While this is obviously problematic for animals, this additionally leads to missed opportunities for connection, transformation and advocacy in all populations impacted by social injustice.

Research indicates that people who have speciesist attitudes are less empathic, more prejudiced, and closed-minded toward humans who are different from themselves. Caviola, Everett, & Faber (2018) found significant, sizeable correlations between speciesism and three other major forms of prejudice: sexism, racism, and homophobia. Park and Valentino (2019) found that people who are expansive in their view of human rights and welfare are more likely to support animal rights. This correlation between support for animal rights and human rights and welfare exists on both an individual and a state level, even when controlling for state economic dependency on animal agriculture, political ideology, per capita wealth, and religion and race of residents.

These results suggest that the belief that animals have rights reflects a person's understanding of expanded rights and equality for themselves and others. Educators can teach learners to be more mindful of the ways our thoughts and behaviors maintain the status quo, precluding us from thinking and behaving in more expansive and equitable ways in individual and systemic levels when we include animals in our inquiry. To teach learners to value equality, they can be invited to become curious about the ways they may already be indoctrinated into excluding and harming others themselves–both human and animal.

RAISING THE STATUS OF ANIMALS AND ILLUMINATING BLIND SPOTS: INCLUDING ANIMALS AND ADDRESSING THE INTERSECTIONALITY OF SPECIESISM AND OTHER OPPRESSIONS IN HIGHER EDUCATION DISCOURSE

Kimberlé Crenshaw, civil rights advocate, attorney, and critical race theory scholar, first applied the concept of intersectionality to feminist theory to describe marginalization at the intersection of race and gender in 1989. It is now common to apply the concept to describe and study ways in which overlapping or intersecting fabricated social identities relate to systems of oppression, domination, or discrimination that target the most vulnerable members of society through structures such as racism, sexism, homophobia, transphobia, ableism, xenophobia, classism, etc. These forms of oppression do not exist separately from each other, but rather overlap. For example, Crenshaw demonstrates that the independent realities of being black and a woman must be considered when referring to the experience of black women, and any analysis must include these reinforcing interactions (Crenshaw, 2006).

Speciesism continues to be a pervasive oppression that is mostly overlooked by many social justice scholars, activists, and educators. While the concept of speciesism may allow understanding of how humans often rationalize pain and suffering inflicted upon animals, most of humanity is frequently offended by the suggestion that the moral and ethical considerations we give to members of our own species could or should be extended to nonhumans. For example, when comparisons of animals suffering in factory farms have been made to victims of human slavery and the Holocaust, many people feel outraged, expressing that this comparison trivializes human suffering (Kim, 2011). While this comparison may offend people, and is therefore not always conjured by animal advocates, it does not make it incorrect. Consider that historically black and Jewish people have been targeted for discrimination, exploited, and murdered through systems of oppression, and victimized because they were considered inferior by others who then benefitted or somehow derived pleasure from their use and "othering." Animals are victims of these same systems of oppression and thought. Their species type, as well as cultural perceptions and traditions, defines the ways humans benefit or derive pleasure from their use. For example, billions of animals identified and labeled by humans as "farmed" or "livestock" are killed globally because the animal agriculture industry has tremendous resources to market their products to many people who like the taste and can consume them for a very low direct cost. Other costs of the industry, such as human health, violation of workers' rights, environmental degradation, and heinous animal cruelty are intentionally hidden from public view and consideration, driving profits for an industry that is further supported and subsidized by government through tax dollars (Hidjo, 2013). Killing and using animals for a variety of other reasons is supported by human social systems and relatively easy from both a brute force and legal perspective. While an estimated 53 billion chickens, pigs, cows, and other animals are bred and killed every year for consumption in the United States alone, zero federal laws exist to protect animals raised on factory farms, where 99% of the meat that most people consume comes from (see animalclock.org). Despite this daunting number and lack of legal protection, speciesism runs so deep, and animals are so oppressed, that many people have difficulty even theoretically talking about them as sentient beings capable of fear, pain, distress, joy, and a plethora of other feelings, even when scientific evidence informs us that they do. *Marc Bekoff, Emeritus Professor at the University of Colorado, Boulder and a pioneering cognitive ethologist, wrote in his 2013 op-ed "After 2,500 Studies, It's Time to Declare Animal Sentience Proven"* in response to the continued skepticism of the sentience of non-human beings. Systems of oppression take on a life of their own, churning profit for the benefit of a few at the expense of many, defying logic and rationality. This weaves its way into all systems of education and creates a disconnect between all animals, human included, and nature.

THE ROLE OF PRIOR VICTIMIZATION
IN THE UNDERSTANDING OF VICTIMHOOD
THROUGH "OTHERING"

Some people who have experienced direct victimization of dominant violent ideologies themselves often have an easier time seeing that all oppression is deeply intertwined, including oppression toward animals. There has been a large body of seminal work that scholars and intersectional activists have produced over the years that advocates for connecting and ending all forms of subjugation at the mercy of violent, dominant power structures that victimize humans and animals. Carol Adams, feminist-vegan advocate and activist wrote *The Sexual Politics of Meat: A Feminist-Vegetarian Critical Theory* more than 25 years ago. Marjorie Spiegel published *The Dreaded Comparison* in 1989, where she examined the similarities between the violence and subjugation humans have inflicted against both enslaved humans and enslaved animals. More recently, Aph Ko, founder of Aphro-ism and Black Vegans Rock, articulates how systems of anti-black racism and class discrimination are related to animal cruelty (Ko, 2019). Dr. Amie "Breeze" Harper, the founder of the Sistah Vegan Project, emphasizes the intersection of racialized consciousness, anti-racism, and ethical consumption (2010). Christopher Sebastian is a lecturer, author and researcher who focuses on how violence against animals is related to anti-black racism, queer antagonism, and class discrimination (https://www.christophersebastian.info/). This work is just a small handful of examples from authors who understand and advocate for the examination and acknowledgement of animal victimization as an integral piece of transforming human victimization as well.

Alex Hershaft, Ph.D., the founding president of Farm Animal Rights Movement (FARM), characterizes how his experience surviving extreme systematic oppression, violence, and trauma sparked his focus on advocating for eliminating oppression of animals:

"Once World War II was over and my life was no longer in constant danger, I began to reflect on what meaningful lessons could be drawn from my people's supreme sacrifice in the Holocaust and what my own role should be. In the early 1970s, I had two revelations: I visited a slaughterhouse and I came across a statement by Jewish Nobel Laureate Isaac Bashevis Singer: 'To the animals, all people are Nazis. To the animals, life is an eternal Holocaust.' This is when I knew that there was a lesson to be drawn from the Holocaust and that the rest of my life would be devoted to fighting all forms of oppression, starting with oppression of animals. Why animals? Because animals are the most vulnerable, and therefore, the most oppressed sentient living beings on earth. Once we stop oppressing animals, we will stop oppressing one another."

Many other scholars, writers, and activists have contributed to this conversation, understanding the importance of including animals in their intersectional social justice work. While important work continues to be done to address the intersectionality of violent, dominant systems that oppress humans and animals, we must systematically include and apply this critical body of work in higher education in order to advance social justice for all humans, animals and the environment.

CONNECTING THE DISCONNECT: CULTIVATING EMPATHY AND COMPASSION BY INCLUDING ANIMALS IN HIGHER EDUCATION DISCOURSE

Humans have difficulty seeing animals as science and research informs us they are: sentient beings, worthy of human empathy, concern, and protection that should be included in social justice and pro-social educational work (Carey, 1985). Systems of oppression and the people who contribute to maintaining them must see animals as unworthy of consideration and existing to serve no other purpose than human need and pleasure in order to exploit them without guilt or regret. In order to do this, people must become disconnected from animals emotionally and spiritually. Similar to subjugated human groups, the animals' status must remain low in order for humans to benefit from their domination and oppression. Human behavior exhibits tremendous inconsistency in common attitudes and behaviors toward animals (Joy, 2011). In many countries, children are read books with messages of kindness toward animals, have animal-themed toys and comfort items, pets they live with as family members, and are generally taught to treat animals with compassion. When children are cruel to animals, it is generally seen as an indicator of a disturbed and dangerous personality (Ascione, 2001). Simultaneously youth are taught, both formally and informally, that animals exist solely for our use and pleasure. Indoctrinating children to consume animals, hunt for sport, or attend circuses, zoos, and other forms of entertainment geared for youth that are documented to exploit animals is normalized in most cultures. These extremely mixed messages and inconsistent behaviors lead people to dampen their empathy toward animals to relieve the cognitive dissonance this inconsistency creates (Joy, 2011, Lang 2019).

People seek consistency among their cognitions for psychological wellbeing (i.e. thoughts, beliefs, opinions). When conflict exists between attitudes, beliefs, and behaviors, something must change to eliminate the dissonance. For example, when people wear and eat animals (behavior) but also have affection for animals and know that they suffer for their consumption (cognition), they are in a state of cognitive dissonance. Dissonance can be resolved in one of three basic ways: changing beliefs, changing actions, and changing perceptions of actions (Joy, 2011; Kasperbauer, 2019). Changing beliefs may be the simplest way to resolve dissonance between actions and beliefs. Many people choose to believe that animals exist to serve humans, that this is simply the natural cycle of life and survival of the fittest. These beliefs are even applied when considering the myriad of industries that commodify and exploit animals bred for some type of human consumption through fashion, food, entertainment, sport, and more–even though, when people learn more about them, many would agree there is nothing natural about most of these systems that cause tremendous suffering and no fair chance of escaping extreme victimization. Others choose to believe that animals don't suffer to provide their meat, skin, or any number of animal-derived products. Still others may choose to avoid evidence that they do, or just choose not to think about it (Kasperbauer, 2019).

Because of prolific images and exposés on the extreme violence and suffering of animals at the hands of humans through the internet and social media, a growing number of people cannot avoid images of evidence any longer and are changing their behavior, no longer wanting to support and participate in systems that exploit and torture animals for human use. This highlights the second option for resolving dissonance–for example, to change actions by no longer eating or wearing animals (Kasperbauer, 2019). A third way to alleviate dissonance is to change perception of action. An example of changing perception of action could be choosing to purchase meat from purveyors who promise "humane" meat. This option upon further research would be problematic, as it is documented that these methods of killing animals for consumption could not process and produce their bodies in sustainable quantities to satisfy the masses demanding them at a price most consumers could afford.

It is important for educators to consider and address cognitive dissonance toward animals in themselves, their learners, systems of education, and public policy. While people also justify their behaviors through psychological defenses that hurt and exploit other humans, the process and pervasiveness of this practice toward animals is unique. This is because regardless of real or imagined status relative to other people, every person–no matter how oppressed, targeted, or invisible–typically enjoys at least some privileges that animals do not have access to, simply because they are human. Examining human privilege is an opportunity to acknowledge and reconsider indoctrination and widespread participation in the perpetration of oppression that most people participate in, including people who are also the victims of these systems themselves.

HUMAN IDENTITY AND ATTITUDES TOWARD ANIMALS: ELEVATING OUR OWN HUMANITY TO AVOID OUR ANIMALITY

Typically, people differentiate themselves from animals in order to exploit and use them, but also as a way to provide a sense of place for themselves in the world that is above animals in a socially created hierarchy of status. This benefits all humans, regardless of where they may fall on the spectrum of privilege compared to other humans, and can be considered an adaptive need to elevate one's humanity (Kasperbauer, 2019). Human moral evaluations of animals are also determined by this need. Kasperbauer (2019) explored the role of animals as a contrast class to humans, drawing from the literature on the dehumanization process. He reminds us that dehumanization was used throughout history to justify cruel treatment of certain groups–Nazis compared Jews to rats; black American slaves were compared to apes. "The processes at work when we demean other human beings by comparing them to animals are also at work in our everyday evaluations of animals. This can explain some of the contradictions we see in human treatment of other animals. Dehumanization suggests that we are fundamentally motivated to compare ourselves to animals to create opportunities to see ourselves as superior" (p. 2).

Dehumanization is the process of attributing non-human qualities to an animal or another person, and any entity that is seen as sharing attributes with humans can also have those attributes removed (Kasperbauer, 2019). We can understand human psychological thought and attitudes toward animals when we can look at how animal comparisons are used to demean other human beings by identifying them as non-human and labeling them as inferior (Kasperbauer, 2019; Leyans et.al 2001). Dehumanization utilizes the psychology of ingroup/outgroup relations. Kasperbauer notes that a particular type of ingroup/outgroup psychology characterizes how dehumanization processes are applied to animals in two closely related processes (p.3).

1) identifying other people (or groups of other people) as non-human.
2) identifying other people (or groups of other people) as inferior (infrahumanization).

Labeling people as inferior is the process of infrahumanization–when people are attributed some human qualities but treated as inferior to other humans by comparison. This is often accomplished by denying that they have certain complex emotions that are thought to be distinctly human (Kasperbauer, 2019). The purpose is to create a clear hierarchy regarding who is superior and who is inferior. This is the process found in behavior patterns that subtly dehumanize animals. People can attribute characteristics to animals that establish superiority over them, while not always completely demeaning them. This process allows humans to treat animals as inferior but not entirely worthless–so humans can continue to view them as inferior while simultaneously attributing positive qualities to them (Kasperbauer, 2019).

Negative qualities are attributed to animals when they are viewed as an outgroup to be avoided. The strength of the aversion will be dependent on species as an adaptation to evolutionary pressures, such as predator-prey relationships. Additionally, all animals pose some degree of threat–including domesticated animals we share spaces with–for example, through the transmission of zoonotic diseases. Finally, animals remind us of aspects of our humanity that cause existential anxiety, particularly human fears of death. This is referred to as the "animal reminder" or "mortality salience" (Kasperbauer, 2019; Rozin and Fallon, 1987). Animals' relatively short lives, dangers experienced living in the wild, existence in nature, and abuse and exploitation by humans all contribute to the human desire to see ourselves as possessing higher status than other animals.

Some animals are dehumanized by people in overtly negative ways. This is typically necessary when killing them for a human-derived pleasure, such as eating or wearing them (Joy, 2011). This can also happen when some conflict or hostility exists, perhaps in the wild competing for natural resources, or when domesticated animals behave in ways that people find undesirable or punishable (Kasperbauer, 2019). Animals' different physical features and behaviors, like other groups that are placed in an outgroup category, causes the feeling that they cannot be identified with and can be exploited, denying them ingroup status. Animals may also illicit emotional responses of disgust and fear, or psychological threats in people. Kasperbauer (2019) explains how Terror Management Theory enables us to untangle and understand these human responses to animals. The theory posits that humans are emotionally averse to reminders of their own mortality, a psychological threat known as mortality science. Kasperbauer notes that this stems from animal threats to human physical wellbeing, as well as a core belief that many humans hold that they are somehow special and superior to other animals.

Terror threat management research supports that when humans are reminded of their world view and important ideals, they hold they are enabled to resist thinking about death. Animals often have shorter life spans than humans, domesticated and in the wild, because of their vulnerability and victimization by humans. Viewing other animals as significantly different from humans alleviates and suppresses uncomfortable thoughts and truths that humans are vulnerable and at risk for death, too (Kasperbauer, 2019). A remedy to this is bringing awareness to learners that this is a function of human psychology for self-protection. Increasing self-esteem and self-compassion–and helping learners identify their values and live in alignment with them–can help humans relieve mortality salience by making them feel that they have value and meaning in their lives, even though they will eventually die (Kasperbauer, 2019).

To reduce this perceived threat, the process of infrahumanization helps people attribute qualities to animals that makes it easier to live among them. If animals are seen as having some redeeming qualities, humans can keep interacting with them and deriving benefits from them without feeling threatened. The animals can be subtly treated as an outgroup that can include positive attributions but still allows justifications to abuse, victimize and exploit them. This process allows humans to feel they are ranked above animals on an imagined social hierarchy that has its roots in Colonialism. Again, the burden of the effects of this process is cultural and species dependent. Typically, animals that physically resemble–or are more physically appealing to–humans will be attributed more positive mental states and be treated relatively well. So anthropocentric bias influences human mental states and the placement of animals on a hierarchy of worth. Fewer emotions can be attributed to animals that humans eat, wear, test on and otherwise use to allow for the relief of cognitive dissonance. Placing animals in an outgroup makes their victimization and exploitation easier to accept and allows people to justify and participate in individual and systemic behaviors that harm them.

While negative qualities are attributed to animals that drive the human need to differentiate ourselves from them, positive qualities are also attributed to them by humans. Many people believe that animals deserve care and concern, particularly domesticated animals and any animal humans consider to be physically appealing, or "cute." We are partial to the companion animals we select to allow into our homes, and we transition them to human "ingroup" from "outgroup" status. These positive attributes and attitudes toward animals likely evolved to help humans cope with the biologically innate discomfort of being around them (Kasperbauer, 2019). While we evolved from being as vulnerable to the predatory and disease risks animals can pose for humans, our ancestors could never avoid them because they benefited from their presence–as modern humans continue to do today. Any positive human attitudes toward animals likely evolved from our need to tolerate them for human advancement (Kasperbauer, 2019).

Teaching educators and earners about these biologically driven tendencies could go a long way in evaluating the harm humans cause our own species, as well as when we systematically use and oppress other animals.

THE BENEFITS OF EXAMINING ETHICAL BLIND SPOTS TOWARD NON-HUMANS IN HIGHER EDUCATION

Taking into account cognitive dissonance and the human need for cognitive distortions such as denial, suppression, justification, and compartmentalization to preserve mental health, as well as the evolutionary adaptations discussed that impact human neurobiology and shape human moral attitudes toward animals, how can we use this information most effectively to guide ethical behavior and decision making regarding animals in higher education? To attain achievable and measurable results, we must examine the human psychological limitations mentioned as well as the role of social and political systems to assess human ability to behave ethically toward animals. Teaching educators and learners about the neurobiology of how human negativity bias toward animals contributes to the process of their marginalization, as well as the infrahumanization of animals, can help both groups make choices beyond reactive, adaptive responses toward animals (Siegal, 2012; Smith, Marsh, & Mendoza-Denton, 2010).

Teaching educators and learners that, while these responses served an evolutionary purpose, current harmful attitudes and behaviors toward animals are not necessary for human survival and are actually causing the opposite effect. Our treatment of other species is creating threats to human survival. We must modify and counteract these adaptive neurobiological tendencies to allow for more evolved responses to animals, as these reactions are at the core of our oldest relationships with animals and stem from our reptilian brains rather than more developed, higher level thinking.

We can remind educators and learners that fears of other humans are also rooted in evolutionary adaptations. Humans identified as strangers due to differences in appearance such as skin color or social practices were potentially threatening to life, possibly transmitting novel diseases due to maintaining different levels of hygiene or differential adaptation to biological threats (Kasperbauer, 2019; Smith, Marsh, & Mendoza-Denton, 2010). While these innate biases may still exist, they no longer serve a protective function for human survival. In fact, we must overcome them to progress toward humanity, peace and inclusion of all oppressed groups (Kasperbauer, 2019; Smith, Marsh, & Mendoza-Denton, 2010).

Educators and learners can be taught that petkeeping and agriculture required humans to attend to animals' well-being for the first time–and also increased the tendency to control, dominate and exploit them (Kasperbauer, 2019; Larson and Fuller, 2014). One reason animals may have begun to be kept as pets is because they provide various health benefits to humans. They reduce stress, anxiety, and blood pressure, and improve recovery time from illnesses and overall well-being (Tedeschi, Jenkins & Perry, 2019). These positive consequences of relationships with animals worked to counteract human implicit biases against them (Kasperbauer, 2019). It is thought that anthropomorphism, the tendency to attribute human qualities to animal, may have developed as a strategy to predict animal behavior that could have enhanced human survival (Bartlett, 2005; Kasperbauer, 2019). According to Kasperbauer (2019), this may be what led the human tendency to attribute social needs to animals–such as wanting or needing to spend time with humans to be comforted. We can teach educators and learners to understand that, from an evolutionary perspective, humans have had pressures to care for animals alongside simultaneous pressures to avoid them. These shared evolutionary adaptations are supported by research that demonstrates children from diverse cultures engage in rigid ways of thinking about animal identity and development (Kasperbauer, 2019). Children typically learn that humans are animals only through formal education, and even then some are reluctant to view humans as animals (Carey, 1985; Kasperbauer, 2019). Evolutionary adaptations that shape human attitudes toward animals can be modified once we are made aware of them, which then creates space for the capacity of choice.

Human psychology has evolved, impacting the creation of laws and public policy that limit morally objectionable biases against human groups that are marginalized. While these changes are slow and still painfully necessary for human equity and justice, it is not a surprise that progress for animals has lagged far behind. However, we have seen some progress in this realm and some animals now enjoy variable protections through public policies and laws (Kasperbauer 2019; Animal Legal Defense Fund, 2019, World Animal Protection, 2019). Institutions of higher education are morally obligated to reflect this limited progress more widely to accurately reflect scientific progress made in animal sentience and to contribute toward the evolution of fair and equitable treatment of all sentient beings.

THE ROLE OF LAWS AND PUBLIC POLICY IN SHAPING HUMAN ATTITUDES TOWARD ANIMALS

The treatment of animals is thought to have steadily improved, particularly in recent decades (Kasperbauer 2019; Animal Legal Defense Fund, 2019, World Animal Protection, 2019). However, great variation in human behavior and attitudes toward animals is pervasive, indicating that psychological barriers that occur and influences that exist must be examined. While select animals may be receiving improved treatment in some ways, this more likely reflects the improved ability of some concerned groups to lobby for stronger laws and legal protections of animals rather than some deeper widespread moral evolvement among humans (Kasperbauer, 2019).

Behavioral momentum, awareness and precedent should attract more consideration and increased protection of other species. Addressing barriers in human psychology that limit empathy and compassion toward animals will help to meet moral goals concerning them, which will in turn impact the human ability to expand empathy toward and advocacy for other groups that continue to be marginalized in law and public policy. Examining and becoming aware of the process of ingroup/outgroup psychology and how people dehumanize animals can help learners understand the importance of overcoming these tendencies in moving toward a more equitable world through advocating for changes in laws and public policy.

Equipping learners with psychological resources and awareness regarding these subtle threats instigated by other animals and coping mechanisms to deal with these threats, such as infrahumanization, can increase psychological resources to deal with these biologically driven feelings of threat. Teaching learners that the human tendency to elevate themselves above other animals to find meaning in our lives and suppress fears around our own animality is important when learning about and framing our treatment of animals as the socio-political issue it is. The human drive to conquer nature as a survival mechanism has gone too far and has backfired. Indoctrinated thought that animals can and should be used by humans in systematic ways benefits all human groups through profit, pleasure, elevated status, etc., regardless of race, class, gender identification, or religion.

Participating in socially accepted and encouraged behaviors that harm animals drives humans to harm them more. For example, people who eat animals and animal products and identify them as food attribute fewer secondary emotions to all animals than those who do not, in order to relieve cognitive dissonance. So, eating some animals generally reduces concern for all animals (Kasperbauer, 2019). Even consistent vegetarians pose a psychological threat to meat eaters if their diet is chosen for moral and health reasons (Kasperbauer, 2019). This may be a reason that vegans, who choose to not use or exploit animals based on ethical and moral concerns, are one of the few identifiable groups that have widespread social support to be mocked (Manjoo, 2019). While companion animals, with whom humans live, are often granted honorary ingroup status, this status often depends on their neotenous features and the level to which human emotions are projected onto them. Regardless, the human need for infrahumanization of animals impacts companion animals, as evidenced by their widespread mistreatment in the form of abuse, neglect, abandonment, and euthanasia. Companion animals are victimized in large numbers even in countries like the United States that tend to have overall positive attitudes toward them (Kasperbauer, 2019). It is worth noting that U.S. law and public policy generally provides weak protection for companion animals because of animal agriculture's interest and the "slippery slope" argument. If law and public policy protects companion animals, these protections could potentially widen to encompass animals seen as food and limit the profit the industry could gain if they have to consider their welfare or wellbeing in any way before they are killed.

These power imbalances reflected and maintained by law and public policy reduces empathy for animals. Research demonstrates that feeling empathy for another being typically fails to motivate prosocial behavior toward them when there is a discrepancy between two parties in terms of status and power (Kasperbauer, 2019; Zaki & Cikara, 2015). This is obviously highly relevant to interactions between humans and animals. The psychology of dehumanization indicates that we overlook or minimize the suffering of outgroup members, particularly animals, as their status deems them less important (Kasperbauer, 2019).

While laws have been changing to increasingly protect animals, courts likely will not do this proactively without pressure. Legislation is limited because the exploitation of animals is seen as an instrument to improve human quality of life and support human cultural traditions (Kasperbauer, 2019; Leiter, 2013). While human attitudes toward animals are changing in some parts of the world, we need to build on this behavioral momentum by including relevant topics in educational systems, including higher education (Kasperbauer, 2019).

Government and corporate behavior motivated by goals of economic growth and profit has contributed to support for intensive exploitation of animals such as factory farms, animal testing, and fashion. However, state-sanctioned laws and policies can, and have, influenced human attitudes toward animals for the better through regulating behavior with consequences. This is a necessary part of changing underlying psychological dispositions, but not enough on their own (Kasperbauer, 2019). Progress in societal prosocial behavior and thought will always require individuals to act outside of the larger dominant society and demand change (Kasperbauer, 2019). Teaching learners the relationship between laws, public policy, and social and psychological processes that shape–and are shaped by–them are important factors to examine. Learners can then become curious and explore the human ability to act or change on an individual and societal level. If humans continue to expand their empathy and compassion toward animals, we may see more citizen and consumer demand for justice not only through education, but also through the creation and enforcement of ethical laws, practices, and products that protect animals and their interests. This expansion of empathy can be taught, supported, and cultivated in the classroom to benefit all life.

RAISING AWARENESS AND ENCOURAGING CONSCIOUS CHOICE IN LEARNERS

Psychological processes that pose obstacles to moral attitudes and behavior toward animals are the same that generally affect human ability to act or change in any realm. The main obstacle is that most of human thinking lies outside of conscious awareness (Kasperbauer, 2019, Kornfield, 2008). An example of this is implicit bias. As previously discussed, humans need to alter our beliefs, actions, or perceptions of actions to relieve cognitive dissonance. This impacts large and small choices regarding how people live, think, eat, dress, entertain themselves, etc. A shift away from belief, action, and perception shaped by a speciesist worldview can emerge from how humans become aware of and experience themselves interacting with the natural world. Learners can consider if they believe that other species and the earth exist purely for human use and pleasure, or if they believe that humans are intimately interconnected with other animals, with an inherent duty to protect other species as well as their own. Humans exist and make choices in varying spaces on this "spectrum of use."

Human moral reasoning and thought regarding how we could and should use other species and the natural world runs deep, influenced by biology as well as historical, cultural, philosophical and religious indoctrination. Speciesist thought has its roots in Imperialism and Colonialism, when nations reaping the spoils derived from exploiting and victimizing indigenous people, animals, and natural resources was perceived as an inherent right and rewarded (Kasperbauer, 2019; Ko, 2019). How do we effectively acknowledge and address these influences in human evolution when becoming aware of our own beliefs and how they are intertwined with other oppressions and expressed in our educational systems? Why should we? In addition to contributing to harm and prejudice in law and public policy, education, and all social systems that harm animals, humans, and the environment, speciesist belief systems also cause harm to individual mental health and well-being.

Practices and Procedures to Include Animal Protection Issues in Higher Education Social Justice Discourse

The Contact Hypothesis and Shared Goals

The contact hypothesis and shared goals states that increased physical contact with information presented about the other group, between groups, will reduce negative attitudes (Allport, 1954; Kasperbauer, 2019). Information about animals without focused and directed physical contact with animals has been shown to be ineffective for reducing bias toward them (Hazel, Signal & Taylor, 2011; Heleski & Zanella, 2006; Kasperbauer, 2019). An important aspect of the contact hypothesis is known as the intergroup identity model (Gaertner et. al, 1993). To create favorable attitudes toward each other, the groups must have a shared identity or see themselves working toward a common goal. Acknowledging the intersectionality of systems that perpetrate human and animal oppressions, aided by ethical animal-assisted interactions and service-learning activities involving animals, can move people to see their interconnected well-being with them and move toward seeing a shared identity. It is important that there is equal status between groups, that they are cooperative and self-revealing, and that there are supportive norms by authorities within and outside the contact situation (Kasperbauer, 2019). Training educators and people involved with facilitating human-animal interactions can be taught to conduct lessons and interactions properly so they lead to prosocial attitudes and behaviors toward animals, and not have opposite consequences than intended. This can be accomplished through imagined and simulated contact, as well—such as an experience using virtual reality to bear witness to animal suffering and exploitation. The invisibility of many systems of violence is a key factor that allows them to thrive. The more visible these systems become through social media, discussion, self-reflection and education, the less likely it is that people will tolerate them (Kasperbauer, 2019). When the invisible becomes visible, one can clearly see how these systems of oppression and violence toward humans and animals work together, without distinction. Bearing witness to, and acknowledging, causal systems of suffering and harm through reflection supports awareness and allows space for the expansion of human compassion to include more humans and non-humans.

Acknowledge Shared Animality and Shared Humanity

Educators can extend Martha Nussbaum's *"politics of humanity"* to a *"politics of animality"* to notice shared features of humans and animals, like sentience (Kasperbauer, 2019; Nussbaum 2004, 2013). There is evidence that this approach can reduce dehumanization of human outgroups, and focusing on the humanness of animals—as opposed to the animality of humans—has been found to improve attitudes toward animals (Bastian, Costello, Loughnan, and Hodson, 2012; Kasperbauer, 2019). This still requires strong guidance, such as interventions that can be conducted in a classroom setting. Appealing to people's underlying moral values, such as duties to animals in terms of harm, fairness, loyalty and purity in the protection of animals is important to create prosocial attitudes and behaviors toward them. Educators must also bring attention to human implicit and explicit attitudes toward animals, including the harmful effects of subtle implicit bias, and explicitly teach how attitudes toward animals are influenced by the psychology of dehumanization.

Social Emotional Learning, Emotional Literacy, and Speciesism

Human emotions have been studied deeply over time (see e.g., Johnson, 1999). Emotions are largely processed unconsciously and greatly impact human psychology, moral judgments, and ethical behavior. Emotions can be difficult to detect, making them difficult to change and often resistant to rational control. Emotions drive people to become cognitively rigid and defend their initial reactions rather than revisiting them in light of new information (Kasperbauer, 2019; Haidt, 2001). Attitudes toward animal suffering are influenced by factors we are not always aware of, including situational factors that impact our emotional judgments and biases. However, these unconscious cognitive experiences can be brought to the surface of awareness, influence attitudes, and improve critical thinking with vast resources such as time, support, motivation, and attention that educational settings can provide. Educators can impact these situational factors that subtly influence emotions and have students notice and practice critically thinking about the impact of emotions and how they can influence behavior that hurts or helps others, including animals.

Research on racist attitudes demonstrates that moral change has many emotional and situational obstacles that are the main drivers of attitudes (Kasperbauer, 2019; Wang & Liao, 2011). Typically, learners must be put into situations that are very different from what they would normally experience in order to demonstrate a shift in their biases and judgments. While emotions can be modified with effort and support, the desire to change an emotional response and even making an effort to do so is often insufficient in creating sustained attitudinal and behavioral change. Some form of properly informed external support, such as support that can be offered by an educator or mentor, is required to deal with the challenge of external pressures humans experience when shifting behaviors. This is particularly true when a desired behavior does not conform with dominant social norms, such as viewing animals as someone rather than something (Kasperbauer, 2019). Even learners with innate higher intelligence cannot consistently control automatic emotional processes without some form of external assistance (Kasperbauer, 2019). Self-regulation and goal setting that is required for behavioral change is also more difficult to achieve when human mental resources are depleted. Teaching mindfulness techniques and self-compassion, expecting obstacles to changing behavior, identifying personal values and creating meaningful, attainable goals attached to them helps to shape prosocial behaviors incrementally over time and build on them. Measuring progress and providing resources needed to make continued progress is essential. Without this assistance and support, people are limited in their ability to meet their goals, including individual behavioral and social moral goals.

As the world changes through social justice work and influence, dominant attitudes are influenced and may match prosocial goals, making meeting individual goals easier to accomplish (Kasperbauer, 2019). Social and political change support individual change and vice versa. However, psychological limitations apply to social institutions–including institutions of higher education–as they are simply a collective of humans and their inherent limitations (Kasperbauer, 2019). Working together with like-minded people is helpful to create prosocial behavioral thought and change, as resources such as time and emotional resilience can be combined, making change more likely than individuals acting on their own. Individuals can combine their strengths to pursue specific moral goals and share decision-making procedures over time (Kasperbauer, 2019). The more we know about the capabilities and limitations of human psychology and how humans operate, the more we can use these findings to understand how this shapes public policy regarding marginalized groups like animals and inform curriculum, policies and procedures in higher education. We must also address real-world conditions and barriers to prosocial behavior such as corruption, poverty, greed, self-interest, apathy, bureaucracy and uncertainty when examining issues that impact animals–which simultaneously exist and can be examined in institutions of higher education (Kasperbauer, 2019; Lawford-Smith, 2012).

Service-Learning and Creating Opportunities for Compassionate Action

Students must be given opportunities to engage in activities that can help to raise the status of animals, including working toward regulating behavior through law and public policy, as this influences how people think about and treat animals. It is important to teach learners how policies can be informed by behavior, such as behavioral economics, boycotting certain business, divesting from harmful industries, and findings in the field of cognitive science to help develop critical thinking and reduce impulsive thought and behavior. Teaching students about these psychological processes, such as developing and outlining plans for psychological change, the psychology of dehumanization, implicit bias, and legislation and public policy procedure, are all important to address when shaping prosocial behavior and attitudes toward animals in learners. They can be given manageable and abundant opportunities to be successful and make a difference in the lives of animals, and share and reflect on their work within their communities.

Teaching and Acknowledging the Privilege of Choice

Humans, at least humans with means, have choice. Science and technology have given and will continue to give us an array of choices that will give us the option to choose products, meals, entertainment, and clothing that either cause animals to be dominated, tortured, and exploited, or do not. If and when humans alter our choices and the systems in place that cater to them, we may see a shift away from the pain and torture inflicted on animals by humans in staggering numbers. Moving toward this, some feel, is the greatest social movement of our time. Teaching students how to create space between their thoughts, feelings and actions can help them to expand their ability to exercise choice.

Can humans learn to consider animals as worthy of our attention, compassion, and kindness in larger numbers? It is, after all, humans who create animal suffering. Only we can stop it with our choices in consumption, how we vote at the polls and every day with our dollars, and our activism. But first we have to experience a shift in the way we see other animals. If we value compassion and kindness, then we can live in alignment with those values and stop supporting industries and systems that exploit, torture and kill non-human animals. It requires us to learn about and examine our own indoctrinations into how we came to believe and accept that other animals exist for human use and pleasure. Once humans change thoughts and minds, hearts will ultimately follow.

Addressing Speciesism in Higher Education

Civic engagement goals for higher education are defined as assuring that students develop the combination of knowledge, skills, values, and motivation to make a difference in the civic life of their communities through both political and non-political processes (Ehrlich, 2000). This process should begin early in learners' educational careers to foster success of these goals, and meaningfully continue in their higher education experience. We all learn beliefs through our experiences in formal and informal systems of education. Attending to and transforming speciesist beliefs and practices in institutions of higher education can help accelerate pro-social individual and cultural transformation by developing increased empathy and compassion demonstrated in thought and behavior in the classroom, on campus, and beyond. This requires an examination of human learning and development in our morality and behavior patterns. An informed approach can forge a path forward into shaping an educational system that applies the depth of knowledge from the social sciences regarding optimal human growth, development, morality, and transformation into consideration when developing curriculum and effective teaching in the field of humane pedagogy.

Teaching the Underlying Psychological Processes to Expand Compassion Bandwidth and Prosocial Behaviors: Process Over Content

When promoting prosocial outcomes, it is important to teach the underlying psychological processes that drive human attitudes, emotion, and behavior toward animals in addition to any specific content or facts regarding ways humans oppress and exploit animals. We can teach learners skills to regulate their emotions to get them past fears of being overwhelmed. We can teach strategies for staying with rather than avoiding compassion. We can increase the sense that helping will make a difference, and streamline helping opportunities, providing learners with low effort ways to show compassion and help. Mind training techniques, such as mindfulness practices, will help learners attend to the present moment and accept internal experiences without judging them. Austrian psychologist and Holocaust survivor and Viktor E. Frankl said "Between stimulus and response there is a space. In that space is our power to choose our response. In our response lies our growth and our freedom" (Frankl, Boyne, & Winslade, 2017). We can teach learners how to create space to grow and make choices that help, rather than harm, animals, other humans, and the environment.

In order to do this, educators can rely on well-researched mindfulness and therapeutic techniques to support humane education and humane pedagogy work to most effectively:

- Increase students' psychological flexibility by practicing to move away from the human tendency to perceive thoughts, images, emotions, and memories as real and unchangeable truths.
- Guide and support students to accept and allow unwanted and uncomfortable private experiences (thoughts, feelings, and urges) to come and go without struggling with them. Teach self-compassion practices and allowing students and educators alike the opportunity to make thoughtful, empowering choices without being led around the nose by impulses and emotions.
- Teach students to connect to the present moment, staying aware of the here and now. Lead and practice having experiences with openness, curiosity, interest, and receptiveness. Leave behind former indoctrinated teachings, regrets from the past, or fears of the future that do not serve them or others and get in the way of respectful communication and effective perspective taking.
- Practice and teach having access to an observing self. Experience and cultivate a learning environment that has a more transcendent view of self as a continuity of consciousness, deeply intertwined and interconnected with other humans, animals, and the environment we share.

- Identify and clarify our own values and assist students to do the same. Dedicate time to explore and discover what is most important to yourself and others in a supportive environment. For example, peace, justice, and freedom are core values that many people may believe all beings are entitled to. Once identified, learners can consider how to act and behave accordingly to that held belief.
- Take committed action and model your message. Embodied teaching is vital to delivering effective humane education programs and pedagogy.
- Set teaching goals according to your values and carry them out responsibly, in the service of a meaningful life, and share your experiences with your learners and community, helping students to do the same.
- Practice and teach methods of self-care to carry you and your learners through the inevitable struggles that come with being on the forefront of creating positive social change. Forgive yourself and teach students to do the same when they inevitably fail at times. Teach strategies to move on, correct and continue with compassion for yourself and others.
- Practice and teach being kind and listen with an open heart and mind in communications, rather than perpetrate further disconnect and violence. We are all a work in progress, educators and students alike. We all need support over time and need to create equitable systems we can rely on.

Solving systemic social problems and creating cultural change takes resources, scope of vision and the ability to mediate conflict over different perspectives. Participatory models bring people together from different groups and skill sets to increase perspective exchanges and communication. While we do not have large-scale social support for this because of powerful actors and resources, we have the ability to create this in our classrooms and campuses. Educators can provide a larger framework and help students engage in advocacy, policy change, and leadership. Even conflicting groups can come together when looking at long-term interests that relate to animal protection–for example, less violence in the world, less oppression and "othering," and reducing factors that drive climate change.

Diversity of group members can bring solutions to social problems and oppressive systems by facing each other, processing disagreements, and effectively communicating. It is difficult to demonstrate empathy and perspective-taking once conflict begins. Bring students into an emotionally safe environment, establish common values in the group, create space for all students to have the time to talk with no interruptions, and establish guidelines and ways of behaving to reduce conflict that inevitably surface when solving the social problems we want learners to tackle. Promote respectful sharing of a diversity of opinions, have contingencies when rules aren't followed, and rotate roles frequently to equalize power dynamics. This creates opportunities to reflect on our own behaviors, reinforces pro-social behavior in others, and leads students to come to common understandings while educating them, rather than indoctrinating them.

Practices that encourage empathy, such as mutual introductions, active listening, sharing values, and life experiences that brought them to where they are while establishing higher goals and discovering what learners have in common are motivating for students. Rules that value supportive hierarchicals, such as being part of a group and bringing people together, increase the likelihood of empathic responses as the group feels their role in problem solving. Practices that encourage acceptance and commitment, such as hearing and accepting others' values; clarifying and committing to the group's core values; and exploring emotional discomfort such as shame, conflict, and anxiety, rather than escaping or avoiding it, will be maximizing opportunities for recognizing positive exchanges (Guildford Publications, 1970). Teaching practices to respect and encourage difference, and having everyone speak respectfully and listen actively, keeps learners on track. Learning how to listen, manage disagreements with honesty and prevent avoidance will encourage students to speak up and give them a willingness to hear new ideas. This allows for the reinforcement of innovation and brings diverse perspectives together to prevent impulsive reactions. Instead, learners can develop critical thinking, decrease group polarization and create and reinforce alternate behaviors when problem-solving around behaviors that cause harm. It is important to help group members view others from a behavioral standpoint–not that others are "ignorant," but to perspective-take and see that everyone is behaving in response to their own history and context.

Teaching students to take more of an observer role rather than just listening to the words or seeing the behaviors that are right in front of them is helpful. Create common and interlocking practices that can be sustained outside the learning environment to promote generalization of behavior. For instance, take the interpersonal process that has led to more effective behaviors inside the classroom to outside the classroom by demonstrating work done to the larger community. Continue to tease out the most effective processes. Humans tend to be divorced from contingencies that matter, as we often do not see the consequences of our behavior. We must keep this in our own and our learners' consciousness as we forge ahead toward creating real and sustained equitable change for all animals–including humans.

Acknowledge the Discomfort of "Seeing" Non-Human Animals

The process of moving away from seeing certain humans, animals, and the environment as merely existing primarily for use and exploitation can be very difficult. For example, many people who live a vegan lifestyle and refrain from eating or using animal products credit this to their moral consideration for other living beings and their rejection of systemic cruelty and exploitation of animals–they see their suffering clearly. As vegan therapist Beth Levine states, ethical vegans see the "individual behind the hamburger, cheese, eggs, or leather couch" (Levine, 2013). According to a recent online survey conducted by vegan psychologist Clare Mann, 83% of vegans suffer or have suffered at some point from what she calls "vystopia," the existential crisis experienced by humans who see the participation and complacency of others in the rampant exploitation of animals (2018). According to Mann, symptoms of vystopia include, but are not limited to:

1. Anger, grief, and an intolerance of non-vegans
2. Despair about living in a dark and cruel world of institutionalized animal abuse
3. Angst about living in a world where people collude with the violence toward and exploitation of animals and don't seem to care
4. Traumatized by knowing what happens behind closed doors for the consumption of animal products, whether for food, clothing, furniture, or other products
5. Traumatized by the resistance, ridicule, and criticism that people

respond with when faced with the truth of their choices

6. Loss of connection with society, as the mainstream is causing, either directly or by proxy, institutionalized violence toward non-humans

7. Traumatized by helplessness to save victims of speciesism

Awareness of extensive animal suffering can be extremely traumatic in a world where it is invisible to most. Some people are moving away from using certain animals in some forms because of other concerns. For example, the detrimental effects of some forms of modern animal agriculture on humans, animals, and the environment are becoming widely known. Even when a primary concern may not be animal suffering, other issues such as human health concerns, environmental degradation, worker exploitation, and other forms of human suffering related to factory farming and deforestation are enough reasons for some to withhold their support of the meat, dairy, and palm oil industries. But for the masses, these reasons–even when there is awareness of them–have not proven to be enough motivation to consistently or predictably enact significant or long-term changes in behavior.

Technology, as throughout history, will continue to offer alternative solutions to social problems and harms. When the problem of dead horse carcasses and piles of manure riddled cities, with no solution in sight, the creation of the automobile put an end to these issues as well as the extreme exploitation and suffering of horses used for transportation. While the invention of automobiles created a new set of concerns, innovations will alleviate some animal suffering in various realms, such as food science innovations in clean meat and plant-based proteins (Good Food Institute, 2017). These innovations and alternative systems that cause less harm simultaneously provide some degree of hope, solutions, and opportunities to students in higher education.

Transitioning Animals from "Outgroup" to "Ingroup"

Educators and students can make the effort required to break through the human tendency to believe that we are dominant over other species and disconnected from them. This is necessary for people to survive and thrive in our bio-diverse, interconnected, and cooperative world. However, the need and suffering of animals is so great, we are at risk of turning off our feelings of empathy and compassion, fearing exhaustion and overwhelm. Empirical research in the science of compassion gives us tools we can rely on to expand our compassion toward others while warding off burnout by simultaneously maintaining self-care and compassion toward ourselves. When we do this, humans have the capacity to increase our understanding and emotional connection toward other human and animal beings and build our ability to alleviate suffering.

Daryl Cameron, director of the Empathy and Moral Psychology (EMP) Lab at Penn State University, studies the affective and motivational mechanisms involved in empathy and moral decision-making. His research demonstrates that people's capacity for compassion is not limited. Rather, people control their emotions by shutting that capacity off intentionally for self-protection. Demonstrating to people that their compassionate actions can, and do, have a meaningful impact can alter this. When people turn off their compassion, it is because they can skillfully regulate their emotions. This indicates people have the capacity of choice to feel compassion. We can therefore motivate people to use their skills for emotional regulation to expand compassion rather than avoid and decrease it.

Educators and learners can be taught to get past their fears and discover strategies for being with compassionate emotions rather than avoiding them. This includes increasing the sense that people can make a difference and streamlining helping opportunities to make them less costly from a time and money perspective. Mindfulness work is extremely important in helping people cultivate and expand empathy and compassion (Siegal, 2012). These techniques have been empirically shown to increase compassion toward self, family, friends, enemies, and strangers (Kzarnic, 2015). Mindfulness practices also increase social support and positive emotions, and reduce distress and fear (Siegal, 2012). Helping educators and learners to stay present, focus their attention, and accept and be comfortable with their myriad of internal experiences without distress or judgment are key to increasing the human ability to not only sustain, but also savor the work and ability to see animals as worthy of their care and efforts. If humans continue to expand their empathy and compassion toward non-human animals, we may see more citizen and consumer demand for justice through the creation and enforcement of ethical laws, practices and products that protect animals and their interests.

BEING HUMANE HUMANS: OUR RESPONSIBILITY TO ELEVATE THE STATUS OF ANIMALS IN INSTITUTIONS OF HIGHER EDUCATION

Shifts in belief and action around how humans see animals and their level of tolerance for how they are used and exploited to benefit people will take time. The human experience and eternal quest for an elusive definition of happiness plays a role in this. Citizens in consumer societies are trained to think consumption is the pathway to joy and fulfillment. The belief that humans are superior and disconnected from other animals and the environment we share will continue our path of dampened empathy and limited compassion toward all. When we recognize the interconnectedness of each human with all life, we can all begin a healing process of mind, body, and soul. Without deep recognition of our interconnectedness, justice and freedom will be elusive for all humans, animals, and the environment we share. Humans must move away from an egotistical, dominant perspective of their place on this earth and instead move toward a reverence in our relationships with other creatures and an appreciation of our interdependence with them (Scully, 2011). The ideal place to do this is in institutions of higher education.

Naturalist author Henry Beston writes in the Outermost House:

We need another and a wiser and perhaps a more mystical concept of animals ... For the animals shall not be measured by man. In a world older and more complete than ours, they move finished and complete, gifted with extensions of the senses we have lost or never attained, living by voices we shall never hear. They are not brethren, they are not underlings; they are other nations, caught with ourselves in the net of life and time, fellow prisoners of the splendour and travail of the earth.

Breaking through beliefs of separateness and domination for use requires brutal honesty, awareness and clear seeing. Buddhist psychologist Jack Kornfield writes:

In Ancient Greek the word for awakening is 'alethe.
ing's opposite is not evil or ignorance, but 'lethe,' sle
after some experience of inner awakening, we car
asleep to the consequences of our modern way of living
interdependence is not explicitly taught in schools or a vuiued
part of our political conversation. With compassion we can
educate ourselves to see the invisible benefits and costs of our
actions, until our outer life is in harmony with our heart's true
values.

Solving problems in social systems and creating cultural change takes resources, scope of vision and the ability to mediate conflict over different perspectives. Participatory models bring people together from different groups and skill sets to increase perspective exchanges and communication. While we do not have large-scale social support for this because of powerful actors and resources, we have the ability to create this in our classrooms and campuses.

STUDENT INTEREST IN NON-HUMAN ANIMAL PROTECTION AND STUDIES

Perhaps the most compelling argument for including and expanding Humane Education and Pedagogy in institutions of higher education comes from students themselves. In an ongoing study by the author, a survey administered to a random sample of students (N=156) attending a Catholic college in the northeastern United States that serves approximately 4,000 undergraduate and graduate students from diverse backgrounds representing 35 states and 47 countries of origin asked the following question:

How important is it for society to address animal protection issues? Students could choose answer from the following options:

1) Not at all important
2) Somewhat Important
3) Important
4) Very Important
5) Extremely Important

Eighty-two percent (n=128) of students responded that it is extremely important for society to address animal protection issues. Fourteen percent (n=22) students responded that it is very important for society to address animal protection issues. Six students (3.8%) said it was important for society to address animal protection issues. None of the students from the sample responded that addressing animal protection issues was somewhat or not at all important. Finally, a subsample (n=55), were asked the following question:

Would you be interested in taking classes that teach about issues and topics in animal protection and animal studies?

Eighty-two percent (n=44) of students in the subsample said they would be interested in taking classes that teach about issues and topics in animal protection and animal studies.

Student Feedback

Examples of comments from college students immersed in learning guided by humane pedagogical principles and the above guidelines are shared here to illustrate the potential for shifting attitudes and behaviors regarding issues that impact animals as well as other humans and the environment. Students reported "What I liked best about the class" on a college-wide survey after taking a semester-long class titled "Species Justice" that teaches learners about issues in animal protection, law, and public policy.

- "I thought that the topics we learned were really interesting. It was a class I wasn't really interested in initially taking and I ended up learning so much! I can't wait to recommend it to others."
- "This course discusses such important and relevant topics that I never would have thought I'd have the opportunity to study in college. It was so eye opening and I think every student should have to take it."
- "This course really taught me a lot of things I never knew about and got me thinking differently about things."
- "I strongly believe that this class should be part of the core classes

because of the impact it has on the world and our education as a whole."

- "...Inspiring and makes you want to get involved."
- "You have changed my perspective on an immense amount of things, and I'm truly grateful you teach these topics."
- "...(The professor) had a clear command of the material without forcing her ideas on anyone, rather the objective was to present the ideas to everyone so that they could make decisions for themselves, which I think is the goal of education. All in all, this class has made a huge impact on my (college) career."
- "(The course) opened my eyes to the issues currently occurring in the world, those of which people need to know about before they interact with certain groups and people in the world."
- "(T)he class was great and taught me a lot about a subject that doesn't get a lot of attention, and for that I am thankful."
- "This course really made me want to go out and change the world for the better."
- "This class spoke about some extremely important topics that I believe most college age students are extremely apathetic towards. This class presented real time, real life issues that are affecting billions of people and non-human animals and I believe this course should be REQUIRED for all students, especially as we move into the future."
- "The fact that my 'norm' was challenged and I got to see a different side of my everyday choices."

CONCLUSION

This chapter has relied heavily on relevant research examining the development of moral attitudes and social change, and suggests applying these findings to higher educational settings for both educators and learners to benefit from framing animal protection issues as a social justice concern, intersected with other social justice concerns. There is a need for thorough, empirical work that essentially teaches human *processes* in thinking, feeling, and behaving *along* with specific content around a variety of animal protection issues within a humane pedagogy framework across disciplines in higher education. The author is currently analyzing detailed data taken before and after relevant courses related to behavior and attitude shifts toward animal protection issues and the intersection of human rights and environmental preservation among students. The intention is to add knowledge and provide valuable tools for higher educators, as well as to clarify best practices in humane pedagogy when including animals in higher education social justice discourse. The hope is to remove ethical blind spots around animal protection issues in higher education, and society as a whole, to drive social progress toward a more humane, equitable, peaceful and safer world for all sentient beings.

References

Adams, C. J. (2015). *Sexual politics of meat*. Bloomsbury Publishing.

Allport, G. W. (1954). The nature of prejudice. Oxford, England: Addison-Wesley

Animal Legal Defense Fund. (n.d.). Laws that protect animals. Retrieved from https://aldf.org/article/laws-that-protect-animals

Ascione, F. R. (2001). *Animal Abuse and Youth Violence. Juvenile Justice Bulletin*. Juvenile Justice Clearinghouse.

Bartlett, M. (2005). Hanging on to our roots. *SecEd*, *2005*(12). doi: 10.12968/sece.2005.12.537

Bastian, B., Costello, K., Loughnan, S., & Hodson, G. (2011). When closing the human-animal divide expands moral concern. *Social Psychological and Personality Science*, *3*(4), 421-429. doi: 10.1177/1948550611425106

Beckoff, M. (2019). After 2,500 Studies, It's Time to Declare Animal Sentience Proven. Livescience.com. https://www.livescience.com/39481-time-to-declare-animal-sentience.html

Beston, H. (1928). *The outermost house*. New York, NY: Ballantine.

Brandenberger, J. W., & Bowman, N. A. (2015). Prosocial growth during college: Results of a national study. *Journal of Moral Education*, *44*(3), 328–345. doi: 10.1080/03057240.2015.1048792

Cameron, Daryl. Empathy & Moral Psychology Lab. (n.d.). Retrieved from https://emplab.la.psu.edu/people/cdc49

Carey, S. (1985). *Conceptual change in childhood*. Cambridge,MA: MIT Press.

Caviola, L., Everett, J., & Faber, N. (2019). The moral standing of animals: Towards a psychology of speciesism. *Journal Of Personality And Social Psychology*, *116*(6), 1011-1029. doi: 10.1037/pspp0000182

Chatterton, T., & Wilson, C. (2010, February 1). The 'Four Dimensions of Behaviour' framework: a tool for characterising behaviours to help design better interventions. Retrieved from https://www.tandfonline.com/doi/full/10.1080/03081060.2013.850257.

Crenshaw, K. (2006). Intersectionality, identity politics and violence against women of color. *Kvinder, Køn & Forskning*, (2-3). doi: 10.7146/kkf.v0i2-3.28090

Ehrlich, T. (2000). *Civic responsibility and higher education*. Westport (Conn.): Oryx Press.

Evans, L. (2001). Delving deeper into morale, job satisfaction and motivation among education professionals. *Educational Management & Administration*, *29*(3), 291–306. doi: 10.1177/0263211x010293004

Freire, P. (1970). *Pedagogy of the ppressed*. New York: Herder and Herder.

Frankl, V. E., Boyne, J., & Winslade, W. J. (2017). *Mans search for meaning*. Boston: Beacon Press.

Gaertner, S., Dovidio, J., Anastasio, P., Bachman, B., & Rust, M. (1993). The common ingroup identity model: Recategorization and the reduction of intergroup bias. *European Review of Social Psychology, 4*(1), 1-26. doi: 10.1080/14792779343000004

The Good Food Institute. (2017, December 31). Retrieved from https://www.gfi. org

Hatfield, D.B., & Wallace, (D.C.). Successive approximation (shaping). In W.E. Craighead & C.B. Nemeroff (Eds.), *The concise corsini encyclopedia of psychology and behavioral science.* (Hoboken, NJ: John Wiley and Sons.

Hazel, S., Signal, T., & Taylor, N. (2011). Can teaching veterinary and animal-science students about animal welfare affect their attitude toward animals and human-related empathy?. *Journal Of Veterinary Medical Education, 38*(1), 74-83. doi: 10.3138/jvme.38.1.74

Harper, A. B. (2010). *Sistah Vegan: Black female vegans speak on food, identity, health, and society.* New York: Lantern Books.

Heleski, C. R., Mertig, A. G., & Zanella, A. J. (2006). Stakeholder attitudes toward farm animal welfare. *Anthrozoös, 19*(4), 290-307.

Hidjo, F.S. (2013, April 29). Meat subsidies strip other food industries to the bone. Retrieved from http://usmfreepress.org/2013/04/29/meat-subsidies-strip-other-food-industries-to-the-bone

Itle-Clark, S. & Comaskey, E. (in press). A proposal for a humane pedagogy. *International Journal of Humane Education, 1*(1).

Johnston, V. S. (1999). *Why we feel: The science of human emotions.* Cambridge, Mass: Perseus.

Joy, M. (2019). *Powerarchy: Understanding the psychology of oppression for social Transformation.* Oakland, CA: Berrett-Koehler Publishers.

Joy, M. (2011). *Why we love dogs, eat pigs, and wear cows.* San Francisco: Conari Press.

Kasperbauer, T. (2018). *Subhuman.* 1st ed. Oxford: Oxford University Press.

Kim, C.J. (2011) Moral extensionism or racist exploitation? The use of holocaust and slavery analogies in the animal liberation movement, *New Political Science*, 33:3, 311-333, DOI: 10.1080/07393148.2011.592021

Ko, A., & Ko, S. (2019). *Aphro-ism: Essays on pop culture, feminism, and black veganism from two sisters.* Vancouver, B.C.: Langara College.

Ko, A. (2019). *Racism as zoological witchcraft: A guide for getting out.* Brooklyn, NY: Lantern Books

Kornfield, J. (2008). *The wise heart: Buddhist psychology for the west.* London: Rider.

Kornfield, Jack. Author, Buddhist Practitioner. (2020, May 21). Retrieved from https://jackkornfield.com

Krznaric, R. (2015). *Empathy: Why it matters, and how to get it.* London: Rider Books.

Lang, A. (2019, May 14). Our choices impact animals: The dynamics of choice. Retrieved from https://blogs.psychcentral.com/veganism/2019/05/our-choices-impact-animals-the-dynamics-of-choice

Lang, A. Animal Persuasion: A guide for ethical vegans and animal ... (n.d.). Retrieved from https://www.amazon.com/Animal-Persuasion-advocates-emotional-challenges/dp/1540617408

Larson, G., & Fuller, D. Q. (2014). The evolution of animal domestication. *Annual Review of Ecology, Evolution, and Systematics, 45*(1), 115–136. doi: 10.1146/annurev-ecolsys-110512-135813

Lawford-Smith, H. (2012). Non-ideal accessibility. *Ethical Theory and Moral Practice, 16*(3), 653–669. doi: 10.1007/s10677-012-9384-1

Levine, B. (2013, December 28). Empathy does not discriminate. Retrieved from https://freefromharm.org/animal-rights/empathy-does-not-discriminate

Malahy, S., & Monin, B. (2014). Checking ethical blind spots: Being aware of potential harm. *PsycEXTRA Dataset.* doi: 10.1037/e512142015-232

Manjoo, F. (2019, August 28). Stop Mocking Vegans. Retrieved from https://www.nytimes.com/2019/08/28/opinion/vegan-food.html

Mann, C., & Wollen, P. (2018). *Vystopia: The anguish of being vegan in a non-vegan world.* Sydney, NSW: Communicate31 Pty Ltd.

Mattaini, M., & Holtschneider, C. (2017). Collective leadership and circles: Not invented here. *Journal of Organizational Behavior Management, 37*(2), 126-141. doi: 10.1080/01608061.2017.1309334

Neff, K. (2013). *Self compassion.* London: Hodder & Stoughton.

Nussbaum, M. *Hiding from humanity: Disgust, shame, and the law.* Princeton University Press, 2004. *JSTOR*, www.jstor.org/stable/j.ctt7sf7k.

Nussbaum, M. (2013). *Creating capabilities.* Cambridge, Mass.: The Belknap Press of Harvard University Press.

Park, Y., & Valentino, B. (2019). Animals are people too: Explaining variation in respect for animal rights. *Human Rights Quarterly, 41*(1), 39-65. doi: 10.1353/hrq.2019.0002

Rozin, P., & Fallon, A. E. (1987). A perspective on disgust. *Psychological Review, 94*(1), 23–41. doi: 10.1037//0033-295x.94.1.23

Ryder, R. (2004). Speciesism revisited. *Think, 2*(6), 83-92. doi: 10.1017/s1477175600002840

Scully, M. (2011). *Dominion: The power of man, the suffering of animals, and the call to mercy.* London: Souvenir.

Siegel, D. J. (2012). *Mindsight: Change your brain and your life.* Brunswick, Vic.: Scribe Publications.

Singer, P. (1975). *Animal liberation.* Harper Collins.

Smith, J. A., Marsh, J., & Mendoza-Denton, R. (2010). *Are we born racist?: New insights from neuroscience and positive psychology.* Boston, MA: Beacon Press.

Spiegel, M. (1997). *The dreaded comparison: Human and animal slavery.* New York: Mirror Books.

Staub, E. (2015). *The roots of goodness and resistance to evil.* Oxford: Oxford University Press.

Tedeschi, P., Jenkins, M. A., & Perry, B. D. (2019). *Transforming trauma: Resilience and healing through our connections with animals.* West Lafayette, IN: Purdue University Press.

Tuttle, W. M. (2014). *Circles of compassion: Essays connecting issues of justice.* Danvers, MA: Vegan Publishers.

Urban, W. J., Wagoner, J. L., & Gaither, M. (2019). *American education: A history.* New York: Routledge, Taylor & Francis Group.

Wang, Y., Tran, D., & Liao, Z. (2011). Learning hierarchical poselets for human parsing. *Cvpr 2011.* doi: 10.1109/cvpr.2011.5995519

World Animal Protection. (2020, June 9). Retrieved from https://www.worldanimalprotection.us

Zajda, J., Majhanovich, S., & Rust, V. (2006). *Education and social justice.* Dordrecht: Springer.

Zaki, J., & Cikara, M. (2015). Addressing Empathic Failures. *Current Directions in Psychological Science, 24*(6), 471–476. doi: 10.1177/0963721415599978

CHAPTER FIVE

SOCIAL WORK EDUCATION AND HUMANE EDUCATION: OPPORTUNITIES FOR INCORPORATION

Cini Bretzlaff-Holstein, Trinity Christian College

The role of social work education is essentially the socialization of students into the social work profession. Housed within higher education institutions, social work education is rooted in the liberal arts (the humanities, the arts, and the natural and social sciences), and its curriculum is informed by various disciplines such as psychology, sociology, history, political science, economics, ecology, biology, philosophy, statistics, communications, and so on. The mission of the social work profession is to seek mutually beneficial relationships between people and society. And yet, this is no longer enough. Certainly, social work cannot be the answer to all the intersecting issues humans, the environment, and other living species experience. Nevertheless, social workers and social work educators have a responsibility to shift away from a human-centric perspective toward a more inclusive frame of reference for the well-being of humans, animals, and the natural world.

With its holistic emphasis on the intersectionality of people, the environment, and animals, humane education can help social work education raise the ecological consciousness of social work students. The opportunity for interdisciplinary collaboration between social work education and humane education is evident in that humane education has the potential to complement or integrate with social work education, particularly considering the social work profession's continued understanding and expansion of environmental ethics, environmental justice (eco-centrism), and human-animal relationships. Moreover, interprofessional and interdisciplinary collaboration is a norm and a prominent part of the social work intervention approaches to practice.

Before examining the opportunities for humane education and social work education to work together, this chapter will first provide a broad introduction to what social work is, while briefly highlighting its historical roots and contextualizing the profession in the 21st century. Following this introduction, an articulation of the similarities and differences between social work and humane education will be offered. Next, an overview of social work education will be provided to afford an understanding of what social work education broadly entails. This overview will include drawing attention to social work education programs in the United States that specifically incorporate some humane education principles and/or components in their program offerings and curriculum. And lastly, suggestions for incorporating humane education principles into social work curriculum and partnering with humane education will be offered.

Social Work 101 – What is Social Work?

Social work is a helping profession whose mission focuses on social justice and the advancement of human rights. As a global profession, social work is an advocacy-based, empowerment-driven, and systems-changing discipline at its core. More specifically, the global definition of social work is as follows:

> Social work is a practice-based profession and an academic discipline that promotes social change and development, social cohesion, and the empowerment and liberation of people. Principles of social justice, human rights, collective responsibility and respect for diversities are central to social work. Underpinned by theories of social work, social sciences, humanities and indigenous knowledge, social work engages people and structures to address life challenges and enhance wellbeing. The

above definition may be amplified at national and/or regional levels (International Federation of Social Workers, 2014).

In the United States, the National Association of Social Workers (NASW) is the member organization of professional social workers and articulates the mission of the social work profession via the NASW Code of Ethics "to enhance human well-being and help meet the basic human needs of all people, with particular attention to the needs and empowerment of people who are vulnerable, oppressed, and living in poverty" (National Association of Social Workers, 2017, p. 2). Accrediting body for social work education programs in the United States, the Council on Social Work Education (CSWE) (2015), articulates the following definition:

> The purpose of the social work profession is to promote human and community well-being. Guided by a person-in-environment framework, a global perspective, respect for human diversity, and knowledge based on scientific inquiry, the purpose of social work is actualized through its quest for social and economic justice, the prevention of conditions that limit human rights, the elimination of poverty, and the enhancement of the quality of life for all persons, locally and globally.

While the history of social work is much more extensive than will be articulated here, the profession's historical development is often cited as commencing in the United Kingdom and the United States particularly in response to the Industrial Revolution of the late 19th and early 20th centuries. Because of the Industrial Revolution, immigration and urban migration to city centers for employment in factories resulted in numerous challenges in urban centers such as poverty, illiteracy, hunger, disease, and mental health issues (McNutt, 2013). Two primary movements influenced the social work profession's development in response to these issues and its current foundational structure. They were the Settlement House Movement and the Charity Organization Society (COS) both of which addressed these challenges in unique ways and had two different philosophical focuses of social reform and individual reform (DuBois, 2011).

The Settlement House Movement originated in England at Toynbe

Hall in July 1884 by Canon Barnett and first reached the United States shores in New York City (DuBois, 2011; Scheuer, 1985). This first settlement house was established by Stanton Coit in 1886 and was known as the Neighborhood Guild, leading to the expansion of the Settlement House Movement in the United States to cities such as Chicago by social work pioneers Jane Addams and Ellen Gates Starr at Hull House (DuBois, 2011; Scheuer, 1985). These settlement houses essentially served as community centers in which settlement house workers (social reformers) lived in the house, worked with the residents and leaders of the community to address the challenges they identified, and served as "an outpost of culture and learning" (Scheuer, 1985). They provided education for adults and for children of immigrants; trade and vocational training; art, music and theater classes; and after-school recreational programming, as well as public health and juvenile delinquency initiatives (Trainin Blank, 1998). The settlement houses emphasized systemic and policy change, as well as social responsibility, and were rooted in social science research for understanding and addressing urban problems (McNutt, 2013). In fact, regarding a humane society, social reformers' valued animal welfare and anti-cruelty to animals influenced the formation of legislation to counter cruelty, abuse, and neglect of children, as there were no child protective laws at the time (Ryan, 2014).

The Charity Organization Society (COS) emphasized individual reform through a scientific approach to administering social services via the coordination of neighborhood/private charities by volunteers known as "friendly visitors," who used social casework to collect information and register and supervise residents applying for charitable assistance due to the many problems facing the urban poor that the settlement workers were also seeking to address: poverty, unemployment, disease, hunger, and so on (Hansan, 2013; McNutt, 2013). The primary goal was to enhance self-sufficiency and individual responsibility. Mary Richmond, a pioneer of the social work profession, who is described as the founding mother of social casework, wrote the book titled *Social Diagnosis* in 1917, which outlined social research strategies for establishing contact with residents applying for charitable assistance, gathering information, and methodologies for conducting interviews (Steyaert, 2013).

Out of these two movements–and other key historical moments in the profession's history–evolved the values, knowledge and skills of the social work profession that serve as a common base for all social work education programs. They are as follows:

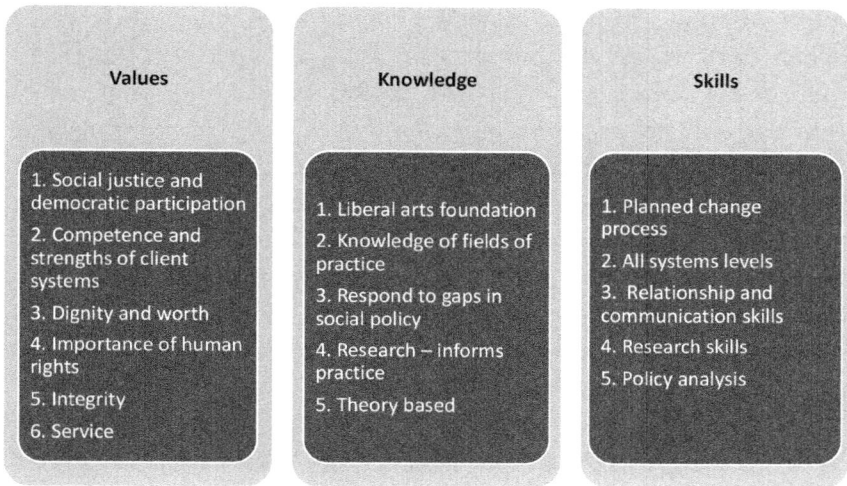

Values	Knowledge	Skills
1. Social justice and democratic participation	1. Liberal arts foundation	1. Planned change process
2. Competence and strengths of client systems	2. Knowledge of fields of practice	2. All systems levels
3. Dignity and worth	3. Respond to gaps in social policy	3. Relationship and communication skills
4. Importance of human rights	4. Research – informs practice	4. Research skills
5. Integrity	5. Theory based	5. Policy analysis
6. Service		

Foundations of Social Work Practice (DuBois & Miley, 2011)

SOCIAL WORK: THEORY AND PRACTICE

Social work is not just a profession, it is a lens and identity influenced by specific theoretical frameworks that inform social work practice. Most notably, the ecological perspective and person-in-environment lens are two important frameworks in social work for informing practice, both of which posit a reciprocal relationship between the person and the social environment (Gitterman & Germain, 2008; Hutchinson, 2014; Payne, 2014). The environment is a result of human behaviors and the people who make up the environment. The environment is comprised of the habitat, such as the physical and social contexts that are culturally specific, as well as the various human niches within the broader communal structure (Gitterman & Germain, 2008). The person and the environment influence each other, they occur within the various life-course functions of historical, individual, and social time, and transactions are ever-changing and dynamic (Gitterman & Germain, 2008; Hutchinson, 2014; Payne, 2014). In other words, social work's interventions for fostering change is where people interact with their environment and the various social systems that they comprise. Social supports, assets, resources, strengths within the person and the environment help create change in both the person and the environment.

Within social work practice there are three systemic levels of intervention in which social workers implement what is known as the helping process. Those three systemic levels are micro (working with individuals), mezzo (working with groups and families) and macro (working with communities, organizations, policy) (Hutchinson, 2014; Payne, 2014). The helping process is a change process in social work practice including engagement, assessment, contracting intervention, evaluation, and termination (Cummins & Sevil, 2017), and is a process of planned change based on a strengths-based perspective and empowerment theory. In essence, social work operates from the stance that all clients (individuals, groups, families, communities, etc.) have assets and strengths with the capacity for change.

SOCIAL WORK FIELDS OF PRACTICE

This helping process occurs in numerous contexts, as social work is a profession that is quite versatile. To be a professional social worker is to have received a social work degree, as well as a certification or licensure (although some jobs do not require licensure or certification) (Cox, Tice, & Long, 2016). While not exhaustive, the list below demonstrates various fields and contexts for social work practice:

- Child and Family Services
- Adoption and Foster Care
- Health and Rehabilitation
- Mental Health
- Occupational Social Work
- Juvenile and Adult Corrections
- Gerontological Services
- School Social Work
- Housing
- Income Maintenance
- Community Development
- Government agencies
- Public service-elected official

- Community organizing
- Non-profit or non-government organizations
- Community-based mental health agencies
- Faith-based organizations
- Military/ veterans programs
- Private practice (therapy)
- Veterinary social work/animal-assisted
- Environmental

These are but a few examples of where social workers may be found. Indeed, for some of these contexts there is a greater familiarity and recognition of social workers practicing in these fields. Nonetheless, because of the versatility of the profession, social work can readily connect and partner with humane educators.

SOCIAL WORK AND HUMANE EDUCATION: SIMILARITIES AND DIFFERENCES

While social work and humane education are each their own distinct disciplines, in many ways they are more alike than they are different. Both disciplines are social justice focused, with a broad understanding of systems that exist with various forms of injustices. Social work and humane education both most noticeably work toward the promotion of human rights and social justice. They are both on "the same train working for positive change," and both have a goal of improving the world and empowering "other people to bring equity, to bring justice" (Bretzlaff-Holstein, 2017, p. 69). Both disciplines are broad and interdisciplinary, rooted in solution-focused, strengths- and asset-based frameworks for addressing real-world problems through systemic transformation (Weil, 2016). Humane education and social work are interdisciplinary in their pursuits of justice. Additionally, they are both research- and evidence-based in their efforts to address real-world issues.

Where the two disciplines tend to diverge from each other is regarding environmental justice and animal welfare and rights. These two areas have tended to be specializations within the social work profession and social work education. Regarding animals, social work has tended to focus on animals when assessing the role of companion animals in a family system (Risley-Curtiss, 2010). This, however, is not an automatic inclusion for all social workers, as viewing animals as part of a family system is not part of the foundational education of social workers. Social work does recognize the link between animal cruelty and various forms of violence against humans (i.e. child abuse, domestic violence) (Risley-Curtiss, 2010; Tedeschi, Fitchett, Molidor, 2005). And social work does integrate and partner with animals as part of an intervention strategy with clients through animal-assisted therapy (Risley-Curtiss, Rogge, & Kawam, 2013; Tedeschi, Fitchett, Molidor, 2005). These tend to be the broader areas in which animals are recognized in social work practice.

Pertaining to environmental justice and environmental preservation, this has become a greater focus within the social work profession as it sees the negative impacts of climate change, environmental racism, pollution, water accessibility, and so on amongst people and communities around the world (Miller & Hayward, 2014). As of 2015 the Council on Social Work Education (CSWE), a social work education program accrediting body, has required a greater emphasis on environmental justice in accredited social work programs. While more attention is being paid to the natural environment within social work, it is not all-inclusive amongst social work education programs and the profession as a whole. As such, humane education can be a helpful resource for social work and social work education for widening its person-in-environment and ecological perspective frameworks.

Social Work Education Overview

Social work education plays a vital role in the broader profession in its educating and socializing of social workers. Within social work education there are three degree levels–baccalaureate, master's, and doctoral (PhD in Social Work or Doctor of Social Work practice degree). The International Federation of Social Workers (IFSW) & the International Association of Schools of Social Work's (IASSW) (2012) *Global Standards for Social Work Education and Practice* provides universal guidelines and core curricula for educating and training social workers around the world, which includes content emphasis such as the person-in-environment, human behavior in the social environment, cultural competence and humility, practice skills, the helping process/planned change process, research, social welfare and policy practice, values and ethics, and field education (International Federation of Social Workers, 2012).

For social work education in the United States, the Council on Social Work Education (CSWE) is the accrediting body for all Bachelor of Social Work (BSW) and Master of Social Work (MSW) programs at public and private colleges and universities. BSW and MSW programs undergo reaffirmation of accreditation every 8 years after initial accreditation. CSWE has the sole responsibility for accrediting social work programs in the United States per the Council for Higher Education Accreditation (CHEA) (Watkins & Holmes, 2012). Accreditation is based on a social work program's ability to demonstrate compliance with the Educational Policy and Accreditation Standards (EPAS) developed and updated every 7 years by CSWE's Commission on Accreditation (COA) and informed by CSWE's Commission on Educational Policy (COEP) policies. These standards are rooted in a performance approach to curriculum design through competency-based education and are designed "to demonstrate the integration and application of the competencies in practice with individuals, families, groups, organizations, and communities" (CSWE Commission on Accreditation, 2017). There are 9 competencies under the current 2015 EPAS. Those are as follows:

1. Student demonstrates ethical and professional behavior.
2. Student engages diversity and difference in practice.
3. Student advances human rights and social, economic, and environmental justice.
4. Student engages in practice-informed research and research-informed practice.
5. Student engages in policy practice.
6. Student engages with individuals, families, groups, organizations, and communities.
7. Student assesses individuals, families, groups, organizations, and communities.
8. Student intervenes with individuals, families, groups, organizations, and communities.
9. Student evaluates practice with individuals, families, groups, organizations, and communities.

(Council on Social Work Education, 2015)

As of CSWE's February 2020 Commission on Accreditation (COA) meeting, there are 532 accredited baccalaureate social work programs, 282 accredited master›s social work programs, 17 baccalaureate social work programs in candidacy, and 27 master's social work programs in candidacy (CSWE, n.d.). Although CSWE is currently in the process of mapping out an accreditation of practice doctoral programs (DSW), the Group for the Advancement of Doctoral Education in Social Work (GADE) (2014) has historically been "an organization made up of over 80 social work doctoral program directors worldwide who represent their member Universities" and seeks to provide guidelines for the development, review, and improvement of social work doctoral programs. For the purposes of this examination of social work education, however, an emphasis on the bachelor and master's levels will be the focus.

BSW CURRICULUM AND MSW CURRICULUM

To understand where social work education and humane education might interact within higher education, it would be beneficial to take a brief glance at what the BSW and MSW curriculum entails. As stated previously, grounded in the liberal arts and the person-in-environment construct, social work promotes human and social well-being. This is reflected throughout both the explicit curriculum (formal educational structure, social work & cognate courses and curriculum design) and the implicit curriculum ("the program's commitment to diversity; admissions policies and procedures; advisement, retention, and termination policies; student participation in governance; faculty; administrative structure; and resources") in social work education programs at both the BSW and MSW levels (CSWE Commission on Accreditation, 2017). Social work generalist practice uses a range of prevention and intervention methods with individuals (micro), families & groups (mezzo), organizations & communities (macro). It encompasses professional knowledge, values, and skills that can be adapted in various contexts and with diverse client systems.

The curriculum at the BSW level includes courses covering human behavior in the social environment (life span development), knowledge about and appreciation for diverse populations and populations at risk of oppression and discrimination, research to inform social work practice, historical and contemporary social policy, social work practice courses at the micro, mezzo, and macro levels, and field education as the signature pedagogy. Typically, students complete a 400-hour field placement for their field education.

At the master's level, there are two options for earning an MSW degree, which also includes a field education experience of 900 hours. The first is through what is called a one-year advanced standing program for students who have already obtained their BSW degree from a CSWE accredited program. For master-level students whose undergraduate degree is not social work, the degree requirement is two years, with the first year serving as the foundation year covering the generalist practice content covered at the BSW level, and the second year is the concentration or specialization year. Examples of concentrations in MSW programs include focus areas such as advanced clinical practice, health care, mental health, school social work, children, youth and family services, community development or community practice, and social administration, to name a few. Additionally, a number of MSW programs offer dual degrees in which students may earn an MSW and a second master's degree at the same time, such as a Master of Business Administration (MBA), a Master of Public Health (MPH), a Master of Divinity (MDiv), Master of Science in Education (MSEd), Master of Science in Social Policy (MSSP), etc.

INCLUSION OF ANIMALS AND/OR THE ENVIRONMENT IN SOCIAL WORK EDUCATION PROGRAMS

Today, there are a few well-established master-level social work programs whose curriculum have a distinct focus area(s) on social work and the various types of human-animal relationships in social work practice and/or the environment. One university whose MSW program offerings include both is the University of Denver (DU) Graduate School of Social Work (GSSW). DU's GSSW (n.d.) has an MSW concentration in Sustainable Development & Global Practice. Additionally, it has an Institute for Human-Animal Connection (IHAC) (n.d.) that emphasizes the interrelationship and health of people, animals and the environment and offers graduate certificates in Animals & Human Health (AHH) Certificate, Equine-Assisted Mental Health Practitioner Certificate, an Animal Assisted Social Work (AASW) Certificate, and a

Humane Education Practitioner Certificate.

Other social work programs also offer certificates inclusive of animals in social work practice. For instance, Arizona State University School of Social Work (n.d.) offers a Graduate Certificate in Treating Animal Abuse in partnership with the Animals and Society Institute. The University of Tennessee Knoxville College of Social Work (n.d.), in partnership with the College of Veterinary Medicine, offers an MSSW Veterinary Social Work Certificate, a Postgraduate Veterinary Social Work Certificate Program, an Animal Assisted Interactions Certificate, and an Animal Related Grief and Bereavement Certificate. A final example of social work education integrating human-animal relationships in the curriculum is Michigan State University School of Social Work (n.d.) and the College of Veterinary Medicine's Veterinary Social Work Services (VSWS), which provides a learning environment for veterinary students, field placement opportunities for social work graduate students, grief and loss support for clients making difficult decisions about their companion animals, and community outreach.

INCORPORATING HUMANE EDUCATION INTO SOCIAL WORK CURRICULUM: PRELIMINARY SUGGESTIONS

While the above noted social work programs demonstrate more ecocentric versus humancentric approachs to their programming, they are outliers in social work education. The curriculum integration suggestions here are preliminary. Social work education programs at both the BSW and MSW levels have ample opportunities to partner with humane education in the expansion of their curriculum to be more explicitly inclusive of animals and the environment with their recognition of the interrelationship between the well-being of humans, animals and the environment. Indeed, a curriculum map linking social work courses with the CSWE competencies and behaviors, program assignments, and so on that demonstrates the interconnections of humans, animals, and the environment within the curriculum would be an extensive project for any social work program to undertake. To do so, assistance and collaboration with humane educators would be most beneficial and helpful. Though a big endeavor, this could be a collaborative project that a social work program could undertake as a formal partnership between social work education and humane education.

Together, the two disciplines could then present the outcome of this project at a professional social work education conference–most notably the Council on Social Work Education's Annual Program Meeting (APM).

At the BSW level and MSW foundations level, the generalist practice courses provide many prospects for humane education principles and expertise to be incorporated into the curriculum through the guidance and direction of humane educators. Most notable would be the human behavior in the social environment (HBSE) course, which introduces students to the person-in-environment and ecological perspective frameworks that inform all social work practice. Inclusion of the natural environment and animals in social work curriculum within this course is an obvious location, and humane education could assist with the course design to be more inclusive and/or a humane educator could be a guest lecturer.

Certainly, the other courses in the social work curriculum could include projects, simulations, service learning, and so on that incorporate humane education principles and pedagogy. One such course could be the social welfare course that introduces students to the history of social welfare in the United States and demonstrates how policy impacts social work practice and how social work practice impacts policy. Learning about food insecurity and food assistance programs such as the Supplemental Nutrition Assistance Program (SNAP) (formally known as food stamps) is one topic area within this course that could have an overt humane education integration. Students could look at the broader food system in order to gain a better understanding of the various social, economic, political and environmental impacts food production and accessibility has on humans, the environment, and animals, coupled with a service learning component at a community garden that is holistic in its approach to sustainable food growth (Bretzlaff-Holstein, 2018).

Regarding field education at both the BSW and MSW levels, field education is particularly apropos to formal collaboration with humane education. Humane education could work with social work field directors in examining the social work program's field site partners and looking for opportunities for the social work student interns to include humane education programming as part of their learning contract. For example, field placement sites in which humane educators and social work students/social work education programs could interact and work together most obviously could be school settings. A student intern could partner with a humane educator to do classroom lessons on anti-bullying or work together on a community garden project within the school. Residential homes for youth are also a more traditional social work field placement site whose programming may or may not include animal-assisted therapy or nature-based therapy. If it does not, humane education could provide guidance to the social work program and the organization for beginning to think about the incorporation of some of these therapies for their programming. This could be an important project for a student intern.

Humane education could also work with field directors in social work programs to identify and build partnerships with less traditional social work field sites, such as animal shelters. For instance, a social work intern could be helpful with animal surrenders, as surrenders are often not straightforward cases and other circumstances such as lack of resources, etc. may be impacting such a decision.

While it would be a challenge for a BSW student to double major in social work and humane education with the numerous requirements between the two degree requirements and the amount of time and thus economic layers that come into play, offering a humane education minor could be another opportunity for BSW students to formally connect with humane education principles and ethics. Co-teaching a cross-listed social work and humane education course at the master's level could be an important starting point for a formal collaboration between the two disciplines within a higher education institution (Bretzlaff-Holstein, 2017). Also, humane education programs could partner with social work programs in offering a humane education certificate as part of the MSW degree or as a continuing education option for MSW professionals, such as at the Institute for Human-Animal Connection at the University of Denver Graduate School of Social Work noted previously. Expanding upon this, a dual degree could be a great option in an MSW program in which a student could earn their MSW degree and M.A. in Humane Education at the same time.

CONCLUSION

While humane education as a discipline is yet to be formally included as an academic field at the university level, this does not negate social work education, and therefore, the social work profession's need for humane education's principles, ethics, and expertise for creating sustainable systemic change. As a discipline informed by other disciplines, which regularly engages in interdisciplinary and interprofessional collaborations, social work must continue to evolve and adapt. Together, social work education and humane education can operate from a mutually beneficial partnership in which social work brings its knowledge and expertise in working with people and their communities to the table, and humane education can bring its knowledge and expertise of the interconnectedness of the well-being of humans, animals, and the environment to the table.

References

Arizona State University School of Social Work. (n.d.). *Graduate certificate in treating animal abuse.* Retrieved from https://socialwork.asu.edu/content/graduate-certificate-treating-animal-abuse

Bretzlaff-Holstein, C. (2018). The case for humane education in social work education. *Social Work Education*, doi: 10.1080/02615479.2018.1468428

Bretzlaff-Holstein, C. (2017). *The case for humane education in social work education* (Doctoral dissertation). Retrieved from http://sophia.stkate.edu/dsw/3

Council on Social Work Education. (2015). *Educational policy and accreditation standards.* Retrieved from https://cswe.org/getattachment/Accreditation/Standards-and-Policies/2015-EPAS/2015EPASandGlossary.pdf.aspx

Council on Social Work Education. (n.d.). *About CSWE accreditation.* Retrieved from https://www.cswe.org/Accreditation/Information/About-CSWE-Accreditation

CSWE Commission on Accreditation. (2017). *EPAS handbook.* Retrieved from https://www.cswe.org/Accreditation/Standards-and-Policies/EPAS-Handbook

Cox, L.E., Tice, C.J., & Long, D.D. (2016). *Introduction to social work: An advocacy-based profession.* Thousand Oaks, CA: Sage Publications.

Cummins, L.K., & Sevel, J.A. (2017). *Social work skills for beginning direct practice* (4th ed.). Boston, MA: Pearson Education, Inc.

DuBois, B. & Miley, K.K. (2011). *Social work: An empowering profession* (7th ed.). Needham Heights, MA: Allyn & Bacon.

Group for the Advancement of Doctoral Education in Social Work. (n.d.). *Home.* Retrieved from https://www.gadephd.org

Gitterman, A. & Germain, C. B. (2008). *The life model of social work practice: Advances in theory and practice* (3rd ed.). New York, NY: Columbia University Press.

Hansan, J.E. (2013). Charity organization societies (1877–1893). *Social Welfare History Project.* Retrieved from http://socialwelfare.library.vcu.edu/eras/civil-war-reconstruction/charity-organization-societies-1877-1893

Hutchinson, E. D. (2014). *Dimensions of human behavior: Person and environment.* (5th Ed.). Thousand Oaks, CA: Sage.

International Federation of Social Workers. (2014, July). *Global definition of social work.*

Retrieved from http://ifsw.org/get-involved/global-definition-of-social-work

McNutt, J. G. (2013, September). *Social work practice: History and evolution.* Encyclopedia of Social Work. National Association of Social Workers and Oxford University Press. doi: 10.1093/acrefore/9780199975839.013.620

Michigan State University School of Social Work. (n.d.). *Veterinary social work services.* Retrieved from http://socialwork.msu.edu/Programs/Community-Outreach/Veterinary-Social-Work-Services

National Association of Social Workers. (2017). *Code of ethics.* Washington, DC: NASW Press.

Payne, M. (2014). *Modern social work theory.* (4th Ed.). Chicago, IL: Lyceum Books, Inc.

Risley-Curtiss, C. (2010). Social work practitioners and the human-companion animal bond: A national study. *Social Work, 55*(1), 38–46. doi: 10.1093/sw/55.1.38

Risley-Curtiss, C., Rogge, M.E., & Kawam, E. (2013). Factors affecting social workers' inclusion of animals in practice. *Social Work, 58*(2), 153–162. doi: 10.1093/sw/swt009

Ryan, T. (2014). Chapter 6: The moral priority of vulnerability and dependency: Why social work should respect both humans and animals. In Ryan, T. (Ed.) *Animals and social work: Why and how they matter* (pp. 80–101). New York, NY: Palgrave McMillan.

Scheuer, J. (1985). *Legacy of light: University Settlement's first century.* New York, NY: University Settlement Society of New York. Retrieved from http://social-welfare.library.vcu.edu/settlement-houses/origins-of-the-settlement-house-movement

Steyaert, J. (2013, April). *1917 Mary ellen richmond: The founding mother of social casework.* History of Social Work. Retrieved from https://www.historyofso-cialwork.org/eng/details.php?cps=7

Tedeschi, P., Fitchett, J., & Molidor, C. E. (2005). The incorporation of animal-assisted interventions in social work education. *Journal of Family Social Work, 9*(4), 59–77. doi: 10.1300/J039v09n04_05

The University of Tennessee Knoxville. (n.d.). *Veterinary social work.* Retrieved from http://vetsocialwork.utk.edu

Trainin Blank, B. (1998, Summer). Settlement houses: Old idea in new form builds communities.

The New Social Work, 5(3). Retrieved from https://www.socialworker.com/feature-articles/practice/Settlement_Houses%3A_Old_Idea_in_New_Form_Builds_Communities

University of Denver Graduate School of Social Work. (n.d.) *Concentration in sustainable development & global practice.* Retrieved from https://socialwork.du.edu/academics/msw/denver/sustainable-development-global-practice

University of Denver Graduate School of Social Work Institute for Human-Animal Connection. (n.d.). *Education and certificates.* Retrieved from https://social-work.du.edu/humananimalconnection/education-about-human-animal-interactions

Watkins, J. & Holmes, J. (2012). Educating for social work. In Dulmus, C. N. & Sowers, K. M. (Eds.), *The profession of social work: Guided by history, led by evidence* (pp. 35-50). Hoboken, NJ: John Wiley & Sons.

Weil, Z. (2016). *The world becomes what we teach: Educating a generation of solu-tionaries.* New York, NY: Lantern Books.

CHAPTER SIX

HUMANE ETHICS IN THE HUMANITIES, SCIENCES, AND BEYOND: HUMANE EDUCATION AND ANTHROZOOLOGY

Brian W. Ogle, Beacon College

WHAT IS ANTHROZOOLOGY?

Often defined as the scientific examination of the interactions between humans and non-human animals, the field of anthrozoology attempts to empirically examine the complex relationship we share with our animal counterparts. The field is inter- and multi-disciplinary in nature, represented by a diversity of academic disciplines focused on investigating all aspects of this intricate connection between humans and non-human animals.

There are noticeable variations in the terminology to name this field to study. Traditionally, anthrozoology has been well represented by an abundance of sciences. Additionally, the term anthrozoology is often associated with empirical evidence collected through proven methodologies. Those individuals approaching their examination through a lens pulling from the humanities and the arts have leaned into a term called human-animal studies or even animal studies. However, these terms have recently become more of a marketing mechanism and representation of an organization's brand to carve out a niche in this growing field of study.

The field of study is relatively new, with the first dedicated academic journal being founded in 1989 and the first organization dedicated to supporting researchers in this discipline being founded in 1991 (Bradshaw, 1991). Since then, the field has continued to grow on a continued basis. This growth in the field of study is reflective in the emergence of academic programs being offered across the globe focused on exploring the complex relationship between humans and non-human animals. At the time of this publication, there were six undergraduate majors, sixteen undergraduate minors, and eleven graduate programs, all focused on anthrozoology or animal studies. There are numerous academic institutions offering certificates, related degree programs, and classes in the area of anthrozoology (Animals & Society Institute, n.d.). These numbers are projected to continue to grow each year as higher education continues to focus on the offering of specialized degree programs.

Studies within the field of anthrozoology/human-animal studies/animal studies are represented by each of the major fields of science, including biomedical (human and veterinary), psychology, ethology, zoology, and biology. Additionally, you will find an equal representation of other fields of study regularly publishing on the topic of human-animal interactions. These include education, historians, geographers, political science, sociology, and the fine arts.

The diversity in disciplines represented in the field is reflective of the diversity of interactions shared between humans and animals. The most prevalent themes of anthrozoology often focus on the species most humans interact with regularly, which include our companion animals like cats, dogs, and horses. Pet-keeping, animal-assisted interventions, pet loss, and the human-animal bond are well-represented topics within the literature.

Yet, the interactions between humans and animals do not only occur with these few representatives. Other critical topics for study include our interactions with farm animals, animals used for sport, wildlife, and captive wildlife. This examination can extend to particular examples of human-animal interactions, including zoos, aquariums, rodeos, conservation, and human-wildlife conflict. Many current sub-themes found within major disciplines can be classified as anthrozoology. This overlap of disciplinary research often creates synergy for multiple applications to solve problems facing both humans and animals. Human-wildlife conflict is a great example of this synergy between traditional natural science fields and the interdisciplinary field of anthrozoology.

APPLICATIONS OF ANTHROZOOLOGY

There are a few topics and areas of interest that have been historically favored by researchers in the field of anthrozoology. Animal-assisted interventions (therapy) is one of those dominating themes in the research landscape of classic anthrozoology that has been present from the founding of the field of study, in part due to the direct and relevant application of findings. This topic continues to be relevant to the research community due to the increasing utilization of emotional support animals and the shifting public perception of this practice (Binfet, 2017; Becker, Rogers, & Burrows, 2017; Nimer & Lundahl, 2007; Marino, 2012; Souter & Miller, 2007). A far less focused field of anthrozoology also includes the examination of animals as symbols, representation in mythology, and their significance within many cultures around the world. Furthermore, we are beginning to see a re-emergence of research focused on the integration of live animals into the educational environment to promote learning gains and holistic growth within students (Herbert & Lynch, 2017; Kalof, Zammit-Lucia, Bell, & Granter, 2016; Molnár, Iváncsik, DiBlasio, & Nagy, 2020).

Due to the overarching themes represented in the field of anthrozoology, the application to real-world scenarios is as bountiful as the non-human animals we encounter in our life. Organizations that have a central task of connecting humans to animals and the environment should be familiar with the emerging research in the field. Likewise, researchers should strive to inform practitioners of the real-world implications of their research.

Animal sheltering has the potential to benefit the most from this collaboration between researchers and practitioners, as the central core of their operation focuses on addressing the challenges facing humans and animals within the community. Much of the work by Dr. Emily Weiss can be classified as anthrozoological in nature. Throughout her body of work, the theme of the human-animal bond and the characteristics influencing the connection to animals are apparent. In one particular study, her team identified the factors influencing the likelihood of an animal being considered adoptable. These findings have salient outcomes that should be used when designing messaging for potential adopters as well as shelter-specific educational programming (Weiss, Miller, Mohan-Gibbons, & Vela, 2012). Likewise, similar work by key players in the development of the field of study has been done to examine the anthropogenic reasons for surrendering an animal to a local shelter (Segurson, Serpell, & Hart, 2005). The same approaches can, and should, be taken to examine other related topics, such as community cats.

The examination can also be extended to that of zoos and aquariums, which also strive to connect humans to wildlife. While many continue to debate the ethics of zoological institutions, it is important to recognize the power and influence accredited facilities have on the landscape. Many studies have set out to examine the influences that motivate individuals to visit the zoo and preliminary evaluation of their behavior inside the park. There is limited research available demonstrating the effectiveness of educational programming. However, the literature demonstrates the potential for zoos and aquariums to leverage their unique place in the community to foster respect and reverence for wildlife (Clayton, Fraser, & Saunders, 2009; Roe & McConney, 2015; Bruni, Fraser, & Schultz, 2008; Lindemann-Matthies, & Kamer, 2006; Davey, 2006; Moss & Esson, 2010; Luebke & Matiasek, 2013). These facilities also offer an opportunity for researchers to examine the relationship between a variety of humans and varying non-human animals. Little work has been done to elucidate and place empirical measurements on the relationship between people with invertebrates, fish, and reptiles.

Many animals across the globe face particular pressures due to the conflict that exists with humans. Using an anthrozoological lens, we can begin to create new approaches to conservation guided by the understanding of the human element. Additionally, the combination of anthrozoology and humane education demonstrates the potential to create a robust conservation program designed to mitigate conflict. One prime example of this potential can be seen with the rattlesnake round-ups that occur throughout the United States. To reduce the frequency and impacts of these events on the landscape, it is critical to understand the motivations behind the events as well as the perceptions of the event and animals held by the local community members. Effective and targeted messaging can then be crafted to help decrease the prevalence of, and participation in, these events.

Both formal and informal education programming have been

popular for research by anthrozoologists, as well. This area of examination also has the potential for long-lasting impacts when placed into practice. The inclusion of classroom animals by teachers is an area for frequent examination by researchers. As with the education research in zoos, the findings are conflicting; however, the research is promising. There is evidence to support the use of classroom animals in the development of the child's character, including enhancing and fine-tuning empathy (Daly & Suggs, 2010). The term "educational anthrozoology" has been developed as a method for the specific programming designed not only to increase a student's awareness of animals, but to enhance and foster the bond between human and animal. These programs also strive to maximize the demonstrated benefits to the students involved in the program (Mariti, Papi, Mengoli, Moretti, Martelli, & Gazzano, 2011).

THE INTERCONNECTION BETWEEN ANTHROZOOLOGY & HUMANE EDUCATION

Anthrozoology has often been associated with the studies of queer theory and feminism, in part due to their shared examination of the "other," who is often underrepresented or ill-appreciated by the status quo. This area of study can also extend to the examination of the sense of "self" that is perceived by humans, creating an "us and them" framework of understanding non-human animals. Allowing ourselves to open up and move beyond the Cartesian dualistic modes of thought (Taylor, 2007) will allow the anthrozoologist to adopt a more humane mindset when approaching their thoughts, values, and interactions with all non-humans.

I would be remiss if I did not discuss one of the most important topics of study connecting the field of anthrozoology to humane education: The Link. Abuse to animals and humans, as well as the aggression displayed by humans toward other living things, is a core component of humane pedagogy. Furthermore, this has been an area of interest for anthrozoologists since the 1980s (Lockwood & Hodge, 1986) and continues to be a frequent topic of interest in the literature. Findings from this research can help to provide synergy between the two fields as they each attempt to find their academic niche within the educational system.

There is a natural collaboration and supportive effort that exists between the field of anthrozoology and the practice of humane education. It is my personal belief that one cannot exist without the other, and the two fields are explicitly bonded to one another. Humane education is a major pillar to the field of anthrozoology, not only in study but also in application. Through the application of the research, humane educators are better able to provide targeted programming to enhance the human-animal bond. Likewise, anthrozoologists should learn the principles of educating about animals as well as the foundation of empathy development to enhance their understanding of the interactions between humans and non-human animals.

COMBINING ANTHROZOOLOGY AND HUMANE EDUCATION IN THE COLLEGE CLASSROOM

The development of interest-driven education should not only exist in the K-12 system, but also should be incorporated into the context of university teaching. Animals provide a natural point of interest for any learner, both science majors and non-majors, due to their applicability and universal tie to the human experience. Constructing courses, individual lessons, and unique learning experiences within the college environment provides college faculty the perfect opportunity to integrate the foundations of anthrozoology as well as humane education.

Interest-driven education helps develop the identity of the individual learner (Edelson & Joseph, 2004). This is one of the most fundamental aspects of the college experience and one of the primary reasons why most employers require a college education. Learners who have had the ability to examine their own identity, as well as the cultural identities of other individuals, are more likely to experience career successes. Self-efficacy in post-graduation tasks, such as career tasks, is often directly linked to the development of identity during the college experience (Stringer & Kerpelman, 2010; Mancini, Caricati, Panari, & Tonarelli, 2015).

Experiences focused on capitalizing on the natural appeal of animals should be carefully constructed in a manner that reflects modern andragogy but is also inclusive of the practices of humane education and using the academic prowess of anthrozoology. These experiences can be designed for courses in the humanities, fine arts, and any of the sciences. Consideration should also be given to providing these experiences to teacher preparation programs in order to support the development of educational anthrozoology in the K-12 classroom.

Since animals are a universal concept, and directly link to every field of study, the establishment of relevancy for the learning experience should not be a difficult task for the instructor. Instead, this effort should be placed on maintaining the initial interest while connecting the interest to specific skill development, both academic and professional in nature.

A potential benefit to the academic department or program can be the increase in students from outside of the department in the courses. The universal appeal of animals can be a mechanism for increasing student enrollment in elective courses and may encourage students to 'sample' the main field of study through a less-intense lens or experience.

For those discipline areas often avoided by students, this also provides them with the ability to engage in the discipline in a more comfortable format. At Beacon College, this is used to decrease student anxiety in the science lab course required as part of the general education core. In addition to the following practices for creating experiences for non-majors, the use of animals is the driving mechanism to engage students in science learning. Combined with a real-world focus, the course allows students to examine the local ecosystem and engage in impact experiences involving the observation of live animals. The incorporation of humane education is a central component of this course, as well. Since all students require this course, this means only approximately 15% of students are life science majors. As a result, an emphasis has been placed on developing environmental awareness, active citizenship, and fostering the appreciation for wildlife through the implementation of humane education themes. This not only increases science-based knowledge but also offers a measurable increase in the respect and appreciation for wild animals. The course also serves as a mechanism for science majors to connect to the real-world application of their particular major and observe the benefits of employing humane education.

Humane education is also a natural fit in several courses throughout the major, including the year-long biology sequence. The college has adopted a platform and practice of not utilizing dissection as a teaching activity. As such, this opens the door for many conversations about the use of animals in dissection as well as laboratory animal procedures during this course sequence. Students engage in biology learning but are receiving humane education training as well. This helps to reaffirm their attachment to animals and allows them to reconcile their passion for majoring in a field of study focused on animals with the demand for learning anatomy and physiology.

Other potential opportunities for including those learning experiences combining anthrozoology and humane education do not have to be as complex. These opportunities can be as simple as a singular exercise in one class. One activity that naturally lends itself to either a history, humanities, or art class is the analysis of visual primary sources demonstrating an interaction between humans and non-human animals. This allows students to practice analytical skills while learning about the research supporting their analysis. Through this analysis, there is an opportunity to include information on humane education and how this practice could be used to enhance the human-animal bond or remedy a given situation within the source.

One popular activity in the behavioral sciences focuses on the examination of the daily life of one single animal. In this activity, students are asked to view the world from the animal's perspective for a given length of time. Through this analysis, the student develops an understanding of the concept of umwelt. This theory postulates that each individual living thing has its own unique reality, and many experiences shape this reality. This includes the physical interpretation of the world. For students, the opportunity to see a room from the level of a cat presents a new understanding of the cat's interpretation of a given situation. This form of thinking is also present in the work of Dr. Temple Grandin, in which she takes on the perspective of the animal to understand how the animal is reacting to given environmental structures. The application of umwelt is a prevalent theme in anthrozoology. It provides the humane educator a unique opportunity to enhance the understanding of, or empathy toward, non-human animals. This activity also provides students with an opportunity to practice many unique academic and real-world skills.

The incorporation of learning experiences designed to examine the themes of anthrozoology is a natural fit for most academic departments and programs. In many of the sciences, this is already being done to a certain extent. Most veterinary medicine programs include some training on the human-animal bond as well as the exploration of the supporting literature on the topic. Natural resource and environmental studies programs include an exploration of human-wildlife conflict and conservation psychology. However, it can be argued that not enough of this integration is done in other fields of study, particularly the humanities and fine arts. As mentioned previously, our connection to non-human animals is a universal trait, and animals serve as a central figure in many cultures. Understanding the cultural aspect of our relationship with animals, and how this differs based on culture, presents a prime opportunity to reinforce many of the foundational skills or theories in these particular areas of study.

Additionally, the conversation needs to be had on how to integrate humane education with these anthrozoological themes naturally. Due to the primary function of educating about animals, it is critically important for many of these fields of study to instill the knowledge of how to increase respect and reverence for non-human animals. Veterinary students of all levels should not only have a firm understanding of how the human-animal bond shapes the interactions between clients and their animals, but also the strategies needed to enhance this bond through practices shaped by humane education principles. As recognized leaders in the community when it comes to addressing community issues with companion animals, veterinarians should have a fundamental understanding of how to effectively deliver messaging designed to not only be factual but also focused on ethics, values, and creating a fair world for all living beings.

The same can be extended to that individual who desires a career in conservation. While many individuals often hold onto an image of saving animals in the wild through the application of scientific research, the reality is these efforts are not successful without the pairing of educational initiatives within the local community. The act of conservation centers on the principle of mitigating human activities that have caused damage to local ecosystems. Without the understanding of the human element, a sustainable solution to protect the animals or habitat cannot be effectively created. A true conservationist not only needs to understand the relevant sciences, but also needs to have an understanding of relevant anthrozoological findings and foundations of conservation psychology while being equipped with the ability to create effective educational messaging to create culture change.

Humane education also provides anthrozoologists with the training and ability to recognize bias within their approach to communicating with groups about animals. The language selected by anthrozoologists can shape and inform a community's perception of their interactions with animals. This skill is needed to not only recognize bias held regarding specific types of animals or the particular role humans play in the life of an animal (speciesism), but also to acknowledge those biases of specific populations of humans. The ability to effectively deliver messaging to any age group, any socio-economic status, and any education level is incredibly important. This is often a difficult task for the academic researcher, who often views communicating with the general public as a waste of time. This bias not only limits the distribution and application of their findings, but also has the potential to create a damaging bias in the community against those in higher education.

Higher education will continue to evolve and transform as each academic institution finds a way to carve out a marketable niche within the field. However, those institutions recognized within the industry are those who focus on developing the leaders of the future. Bringing this vision of a world where sustainability has been achieved and harm to the "other" has been eliminated begins with the faculty in the classroom. Exposure to, and the inclusion of, humane education in the college classroom is vital to develop future leaders into those who not only focus on their understanding of their discipline of study, but also use critical thinking to examine ways to act in a manner that reduces the impact on the planet, wildlife, and their fellow humans.

References

Animals & Society Institute. (n.d.). *Degree Programs*. https://www.animalsand-society.org/human-animal-studies/degree-programs

Becker, J. L., Rogers, E. C., & Burrows, B. (2017). Animal-assisted social skills training for children with autism spectrum disorders. *Anthrozoös, 30*(2), 307-326.

Binfet, J. T. (2017). The effects of group-administered canine therapy on university students' wellbeing: A randomized controlled trial. *Anthrozoös, 30*(3), 397-414.

Bradshaw, J.W.S. (1991). ISAZ International Society for Anthrozoology Newsletter, 1, 1.

Bruni, C. M., Fraser, J., & Schultz, P. W. (2008). The value of zoo experiences for connecting people with nature. *Visitor Studies, 11*(2), 139-150.

Clayton, S., Fraser, J., & Saunders, C. D. (2009). Zoo experiences: Conversations, connections, and concern for animals. *Zoo Biology, 28*(5), 377-397.

Daly, B., & Suggs, S. (2010). Teachers' experiences with humane education and animals in the elementary classroom: Implications for empathy development. *Journal of Moral Education, 39*(1), 101-112.

Davey, G. (2006). Visitor behavior in zoos: A review. *Anthrozoös, 19*(2), 143-157.

Edelson, D. C., & Joseph, D. M. (2004). The interest-driven learning design framework: Motivating learning through usefulness. In *Proceedings of the 6th international conference on Learning sciences* (pp. 166-173). International Society of the Learning Sciences.

Friedmann, E. (1991). Welcome from the President. ISAZ International Society for Anthrozoology Newsletter, 1, 1.

Herbert, S., & Lynch, J. (2017). Classroom animals provide more than just science education. *Science & Education, 26*(1-2), 107-123.

Kalof, L., Zammit-Lucia, J., Bell, J., & Granter, G. (2016). Fostering kinship with animals: Animal portraiture in humane education. *Environmental Education Research, 22*(2), 203-228.

Lindemann-Matthies, P., & Kamer, T. (2006). The influence of an interactive educational approach on visitors' learning in a Swiss zoo. *Science Education, 90*(2), 296-315.

Lockwood, R., & Hodge, G. R. (1986). The tangled web of animal abuse: The links between cruelty to animals and human violence. *Humane Society News, Summer*, 10-15.

Luebke, J. F., & Matiasek, J. (2013). An exploratory study of zoo visitors' exhibit experiences and reactions. *Zoo Biology, 32*(4), 407-416.

Mancini, T., Caricati, L., Panari, C., & Tonarelli, A. (2015). Personal and social aspects of professional identity.: An extension of Marcia's identity status model applied to a sample of university students. *Journal of Vocational Behavior, 89*, 140-150.

Marino, L. (2012). Construct validity of animal-assisted therapy and activities: How important is the animal in AAT?. *Anthrozoös, 25*(1), 139-151.

Mariti, C., Papi, F., Mengoli, M., Moretti, G., Martelli, F., & Gazzano, A. (2011). Improvement in children's humaneness toward non-human animals through a project of educational anthrozoology. *Journal of Veterinary Behavior, 6*(1), 12-20.

Molnár, M., Iváncsik, R., DiBlasio, B., & Nagy, I. (2020). Examining the effects of rabbit-assisted interventions in the classroom environment. *Animals, 10*(1), 26.

Moss, A., & Esson, M. (2010). Visitor interest in zoo animals and the implications for collection planning and zoo education programmes. *Zoo Biology, 29*(6), 715-731.

Nimer, J., & Lundahl, B. (2007). Animal-assisted therapy: A meta-analysis. *Anthrozoös, 20*(3), 225-238.

Roe, K., & McConney, A. (2015). Do zoo visitors come to learn? An internationally comparative, mixed-methods study. *Environmental Education Research, 21*(6), 865-884.

Segurson, S. A., Serpell, J. A., & Hart, B. L. (2005). Evaluation of a behavioral assessment questionnaire for use in the characterization of behavioral problems of dogs relinquished to animal shelters. *Journal of the American Veterinary Medical Association, 227*(11), 1755-1761.

Souter, M. A., & Miller, M. D. (2007). Do animal-assisted activities effectively treat depression? A meta-analysis. *Anthrozoös, 20*(2), 167-180.

Stringer, K. J., & Kerpelman, J. L. (2010). Career identity development in college students: Decision making, parental support, and work experience. *Identity: An International Journal of Theory and Research, 10*(3), 181-200.

Taylor, N. (2007). 'Never an it': Intersubjectivity and the creation of animal personhood in animal shelters. *Qualitative Sociology Review, 3*(1).

Weiss, E., Miller, K., Mohan-Gibbons, H., & Vela, C. (2012). Why did you choose this pet?: Adopters and pet selection preferences in five animal shelters in the United States. *Animals, 2*(2), 144-159.

PART THREE

BUILDING THE
HUMANE INSTITUTION

CHAPTER SEVEN

OPPORTUNITIES AND PRIORITIES IN A PUBLIC INSTITUTION: EDUCATION AND/OR QUALITY CARE

Mary Lee A. Jensvold

WHY CHIMPANZEES?

Chimpanzees share biological, behavioral, and social traits with humans. In blood chemistry, for example, chimpanzees are not only the closest species to humans, but chimpanzees are closer to humans than chimpanzees are to gorillas or to orangutans (Ruvolo, 1994; Stanyon, Chiarelli, Gottlieb, & Patton, 1986), and 98% of human and chimpanzee DNA shares the same structure (The Chimpanzee Sequencing and Analysis Consortium, 2005; Sibley & Ahlquist, 1984). Chimpanzees share with humans timing of developmental milestones such as first smile, eruption of milk teeth, and puberty. Both human and chimpanzee infants have a long period of dependency on maternal care (Goodall, 1986).

Wild chimpanzees live in communities of individuals with fluid subgroups. They have complex social relationships, networks, and politics. Chimpanzees use tools for a variety of purposes, including obtaining insects and honey, nutcracking, for bodily protection, and as weapons. The total tool set and functions of tools in one community varies from other communities. Thus, each community has a unique repertoire of tool use. Chimpanzees gesture as part of communication and the repertoire of gestures within a community differs from other communities (see Boesch, 2012 for review). The gestures are used referentially and intentionally and appear in sequences (McCarthy, Jensvold, & Fouts, 2013; Roberts, Roberts, & Vicks, 2014; Roberts, Vicks, & Buchanan-Smith, 2013). With these similarities, humans have much to learn from chimpanzees about our place in nature. Understanding the continuity between humans and other species helps us develop empathy for other species. This in turn increases our compassion. Thus, chimpanzees can be seen as a means to provide humane education.

CROSS-FOSTERED CHIMPANZEES

Cross-fostering is an ethological procedure in which the young of one species are reared by the adults of another species (Stamps, 2003). Cross-fostering for chimpanzees Washoe, Moja, Tatu, and Dar occurred at the University of Nevada-Reno from 1966 to 1980 under the supervision of Allen and Beatrix Gardner. The chimpanzees' psychological environment was identical to that of human children. They wore clothes, sat in high chairs, used spoons and bowls, played games, and helped with chores (Gardner & Gardner, 1989). The human foster families used only American Sign Language (ASL) during everyday activities with the chimpanzees. They encouraged the cross-fosterlings to sign by expanding on fragmentary utterances and asking questions. Under these conditions, the cross-fosterlings acquired the signs of ASL in patterns similar to those of human children (Gardner & Gardner, 1994; Gardner, Gardner, & Van Cantfort, 1989).

PROJECT LOULIS 1978-1982

Cross-fostering ended for Washoe in 1975 when she relocated with caregivers Roger and Deborah Fouts to Institute of Primate Studies (IPS) in Norman, OK. There, as a young adult, Washoe adopted 10-month-old Loulis. To determine whether Loulis would acquire signs without human intervention, all human signing, except for seven signs (WHO, WHAT, WHERE, WHICH, WANT, SIGN, and NAME), was prohibited in his presence. Loulis spent all of his time with Washoe and other signing chimpanzees. He began to sign in seven days and combined signs into phrases in five months. In the five-year period of signing restriction, Loulis learned 51 signs (Fouts, Fouts, & Van Cantfort, 1989; Fouts, Hirsch, & Fouts, 1982). Like the cross-fostered chimpanzees and human children, Loulis acquired his signs in a conversational setting, and later he used his signs in conversations with human caregivers and with the other chimpanzees (Fouts, 1994; Jensvold, Wilding, & Schultze, 2014; Leitten, Jensvold, Fouts, & Wallin, 2012).

CENTRAL WASHINGTON UNIVERSITY

Cross-fostering ended for Moja in 1979 when she joined Washoe and Loulis at the IPS. Then in 1980, Washoe, Loulis and Moja moved to the campus of Central Washington University (CWU) in Ellensburg, WA, with the Foutses. Cross-fostering ended for Tatu and Dar in 1981 when they arrived at CWU directly from UNR. All five chimpanzees lived on the third floor of the Psychology Building in 300 square feet of indoor space. CWU did not fiscally support the chimpanzees' care. In response, the Foutses founded Friends of Washoe (FOW), a private non-profit 501c3 with a central mission to raise funds to support care for the chimpanzees. Then in 1993, the chimpanzees moved to a large, state-of-the-art, 7,000-square=foot facility with indoor and outdoor space also on the CWU campus. The name of this new facility and the organization in it was the Chimpanzee & Human Communication Institute (CHCI). CWU owned and maintained the building while FOW continued to provide support for chimpanzee care. Moja died in 2002, Washoe in 2007, and Dar in 2012.

Studies at CWU explored the ways that the chimpanzees used their signs. They initiated conversations in ways appropriate to the conversational partner (Bodamer & Gardner, 2002). They repaired misunderstandings and adjusted appropriately to the conversational partner (Jensvold & Gardner, 2000; Leitten et al, 2012). The chimpanzees' utterances functioned to answer questions, request objects and actions, describe objects and events, make statements about internal states, accomplish tasks such as initiating games, protest interlocutor behavior, and as conversational devices (Leeds & Jensvold, 2013). The chimpanzees even signed to each other under controlled conditions when no humans were present (Fouts, 1994). They signed privately to themselves (Bodamer, Fouts, Fouts, & Jensvold, 1994) and in imaginary play (Jensvold & Fouts, 1993).

TRAINING IN HUMANE AND COMPASSIONATE CARE

There were many educational programs over these years, and the new facility allowed for the expansion of those programs, which created humane education programs. Educational programs at the institute were for the public, K-12 students, and university-level students. Students of CWU uniquely had the opportunity to learn all aspects of chimpanzee research and care through a student intern program. They gained experience caring for the group of signing chimpanzees and learned all levels of care from cleaning enclosures, preparing meals, and enrichment preparation to more advanced levels such as unlocking enclosures, shifting the chimpanzees between enclosures, and supervising and training other student interns. They received university credits or volunteered. This program served up to 30 students per year from 1980 to its end in 2013. Some students participated for one quarter while many others continued for years.

The approach to caring for chimpanzees at CHCI was based upon cooperation, respect, and friendship rather than obedience, fear, and domination. Caregivers operated on principles of reliability, predictability, and respect. Operant techniques were never used until the very end of the project, and in a very limited capacity, to train for injection.

Staff and advanced students considered different personalities and interpersonal attitudes when choosing new intern caregivers. The caregiving staff had to be accepted by the chimpanzees; individuals who elicited aggressive behaviors from the chimpanzees were not allowed to work in proximity to them. Most relationships take time to develop, so the three-month training period was one where experienced staff guided and fostered positive relationships between the trainee and the chimpanzees.

Before training began, all potential caregiving interns demonstrated an understanding of chimpanzee behaviors and their meanings. A behavioral taxonomy that listed over 200 different chimpanzee behaviors and the contexts in which they occurred was used (McCarthy et al., 2012). Next, caregiving interns were trained in safe procedures for interactions, and they incorporated chimpanzee behaviors in all their interactions. For example, upon greeting the chimpanzees, a caregiver presented head nods, breathy pants, and a pronated wrist. These behaviors are typical greeting behaviors between chimpanzees. The chimpanzees at CHCI were unique in that they signed, so caregivers also communicated with ASL in all interactions. If caregivers used their voice to talk to the chimpanzees or fellow humans, they avoided loud voices. Loud voices often elicit vocalizations and other signs of arousal from chimpanzees. Thus, they are disturbing and should be avoided.

All new caregiving interns were explicitly trained with a humble attitude to ensure that human arrogance was avoided. Caregivers spent a major part of their time on daily chores and caring for the individual needs of the chimpanzees. They cleaned their rooms, cooked three meals, prepared their snacks, and ensured they had interesting activities. They acted as maid, cook, and trusted family butler. They also played the role of understanding and reassuring friends when a group member became upset with another. Using chimpanzee behaviors facilitated these relationships, integrating caregivers into the chimpanzee's social group.

Chimpanzee groups contain a social hierarchy, and CHCI caregivers respected and integrated into this hierarchy. Caregivers treated the alpha chimpanzee with deference. They served and greeted her first, which made it unnecessary for her to assert her dominance. If a caregiver did not respect her dominance, she began to hoard food and display aggressive behaviors toward that individual. The caregiver's interpersonal attitude was made obvious by the chimpanzee's reaction. Similarly, in early days at the Fauna Foundation in Quebec, when caregivers began to treat the oldest member of the group with deference her aggressive behaviors decreased. Caregivers showed submissive postures and gestures such as crouching and avoiding eye contact during any chimpanzee aggressive displays. This made caregivers appear less threatening.

Analysis of the hierarchy at CHCI showed humans held the lowest place (Hayashida et al., 2002). Malone, Fuentes, and Vaughan (2000) examined post-conflict interactions at CHCI. When the chimpanzees directed aggression at another individual following a conflict, 63% were directed at humans rather than other chimpanzees. This is in contrast to a biomedical facility where 78% of aggression was intragroup (Maki, Alford, & Bramblett, 1987). Since humans were the lowest-ranking individuals at CHCI, they were safe outlets for aggression, yet the humans could not be injured since they were always separated by a fence. Additionally, the wounding rate at CHCI was lower than at other facilities that did not have this same philosophy of care (Jensvold, Field, Cranford, Fouts, & Fouts, 2005). This approach to managing aggression increased chimpanzee well-being and taught the students humility.

The chimpanzees began each day in their nighttime enclosure with a greeting from a friend, and they returned the blankets and other nighttime enrichment to the caregiver. Next the caregiver served breakfast, which was vitamins, monkey chow, a fruit smoothie, and whole fruit. The chimpanzees then entered the indoor and outdoor playrooms where there were toys, clothes, magazines, and other objects to enrich the environment. At noon, the caregiver offered a lunch of monkey chow, a cooked bean and vegetable soup, and fresh vegetables in the night enclosures. Those who wished to eat entered the night enclosure. After lunch they were allowed back into the playrooms. At the end of the day, the caregiver offered dinner in the nighttime enclosures. Dinner was usually monkey chow and cooked cereal, potatoes, or some other carbohydrate-based entrée. Once again those who wished to eat entered the night enclosure. After dinner, caregivers distributed blankets and nighttime enrichment such as toys, magazines, hairbrushes, and toothbrushes in the night enclosures. The chimpanzees stayed there until the following morning. If a chimpanzee chose not to eat dinner, he or she slept in one of the playrooms.

The regular movement of the chimpanzees ensured that each enclosure was vacant during a 24-hour period, usually at a regular time, and then the caregivers could enter the vacant enclosure to clean it. From the chimpanzees' perspective, they had a predictable sequence of events, and they could choose to participate or not participate in an event. This provided the chimpanzees with a sense of control and choices in their daily activities, and they were not punished for lack of participation. Sometimes the chimpanzees' participation was essential for the routine to continue; then the choice for the chimpanzees was to have the routine continue or not. For example, in the morning, caregivers asked the chimpanzees to return their blankets before breakfast began, and breakfast did not begin until the blankets were returned. This is much like starting the car in the morning; the key must be inserted and turned before the car starts. It is a feedforward system in which an action creates the subsequent action. When the chimpanzees' interests are a priority, relationships between chimpanzees and caregivers are much more harmonious. In contrast, when the human's needs are a priority, there is increased conflict between chimpanzees and caregivers. Our system circumvented that situation and let interns experientially learn about putting another individuals' needs first; it was a unique service experience.

For this method to work, it was important for staff to be consistent and follow the same set of rules. Failure to do this introduced unpredictability and robbed the chimpanzees of their ability to choose. If a staff person did not follow the routine and made up his or her own routine, then the chimpanzees were unable to predict events and consequences and make choices. This also taught interns the importance of working as a team with other caregivers.

HUMANE STUDIES

Amid all this caregiving, noninvasive behavioral studies also occurred. Still, the chimpanzees' needs always came first. All decisions on acceptable research designs were based on what was in the chimpanzees' best interest. Human arrogance of any kind was not allowed; in fact, there was a sign that said, "Leave your ego at the door." The chimpanzees were never forced to participate in any studies. Any testing was subject-paced, the chimpanzees were never bribed or coerced into participation, and they were always free to leave the testing situation. Typical experiments involved conversational probes or conditions of enrichment.

The role of researcher and caregiver blended seamlessly. The most interesting observations were often made during routine care activities. Methods of data collection were similar to the way trusted family servants make discoveries about the family that they serve. Caregivers unobtrusively and sometimes covertly observed the family members interacting with each other. Other times, the caregiver introduced systematic probes into conversations as part of the sign language research (Bodamer & Gardner, 2002; Jensvold & Gardner, 2000; Leitten et al., 2012). How could we expect the chimpanzees to converse with us and participate in trials if we did not have a good relationship? Allen and Beatrix Gardner reasoned that the chimpanzees needed interesting things to talk about and interesting people to talk to (Gardner & Gardner, 1994). This provided the foundation of an enriching environment and an ethological approach to study the roots of human language and chimpanzee behavior.

Students were involved in all aspects of these behavioral studies. They contributed to ongoing data collection by systematically recording signs, interactions, behaviors, diet, and enrichment. They systematically video recorded and participated in analysis. Some designed their own studies, and graduate students completed a thesis. These activities resulted in many co-authored publications and presentations (e.g., Campion, Jensvold, & Larsen, 2011; Jensvold, Buckner, & Stadtner, 2010; Jensvold et al., 2005; Jensvold et al., 2001; Leeds & Jensvold, 2013; Leitten et al., 2012; McCarthy et al., 2012). Our research approach was a humane one. This was a very different approach than the tradition in captive chimpanzee research.

LESSONS OF CAPTIVITY AND COMPASSION: A HUMAN EDUCATION

The lesson at CHCI of putting the chimpanzees' needs first was an unusual lesson in our culture of "selfies." Most individuals found it refreshing to put their own needs aside for a time, yet for others it didn't mesh with their values.

Many conversations occurred in the halls of CHCI between mentors and students. We talked about taking the chimpanzees on their own terms. We talked about what is wrong with captivity. We talked about exploitation of chimpanzees and other vulnerable beings. The interns also talked with the chimpanzees. The chimpanzees were ambassadors—telling interns what it is like to be a member of another species. The interns became friends with the chimpanzees, which benefitted the quality of caregiving and changed perspectives.

With these face-to-face daily interactions, at some point the interns had to grapple with the dilemma of keeping chimpanzees in captivity. Self-reflection would lead to questions: "How can I do this to my friends? How can I keep those who I love inside a cage, incarcerated, for the duration of their lives?" There is no better way to teach this lesson than to be a part of it. The interns learned this lesson in an environment that was congruent with their feelings. One said that we should treat captive chimpanzees with dignity and respect and do the best that we can for them. There was no sugar coating, no euphemizing the locks and cages, and no reasonable justification for why we rightly should keep chimpanzees in captivity. Captive chimpanzees are captive for no other reason than being born in the wrong place. There is no justification with educational or research gain for this. Quite simply, chimpanzees do not belong there, it is wrong to have them there, but they have no other option, particularly those born in North America. But rather than linger on what is wrong and muster daily sympathy in interactions with the chimpanzees, there was a daily objective of providing excellent care with a positive attitude, knowledge of chimpanzees, and humility. These interns grew to widen their circle of compassion and seek ways to improve the lives of the CHCI chimpanzees and all other chimpanzees. They came to see chimpanzees, and all other nonhumans, in a different light. They realized chimpanzees are not so different from humans. And if they aren't that different from humans then what about humans' relations to gorillas, monkeys, cats, rats, sea urchins and so on? This was probably the most valuable lesson that came out of CHCI.

Graduates from the programs received B.S. and M.S. degrees in Primate Behavior or Experimental Psychology. Many went on to work in other sanctuaries; some went to zoos; some pursued advanced degrees; some went into the field to study wild apes; some went into animal law; and some went into animal welfare, protections, and advocacy. One worked in a maximum security psychiatric ward. He said his experience at CHCI prepared him for his work there. Some started their own chimpanzee sanctuaries. They all went into the world with a changed heart. We can define human education as an approach that considers all beings, human and non-human. In this approach, students at CHCI received a humane education.

OUTREACH PROGRAMS

Programs at CHCI also served individuals not enrolled at CWU. Over 11 years, approximately 400 Earthwatch volunteers participated in a Caring for Chimpanzees project. These volunteers assisted in both data collection and husbandry. For nearly 20 years, the CHCI Summer Apprentice Program hosted an average of 12 individuals per year. These university-level individuals participated in data collection and husbandry. Finally, for nearly 20 years, 3,000 to 6,000 individuals per year attended Chimposiums. These members of the general public or K-12 students learned about chimpanzees and sign language studies in a one-hour program. These programs affected visitors' attitudes on humane issues such as the use of chimpanzees in entertainment and biomedical research and the value of conservation (McCarthy et al., 2009). The outreach and student programs were immensely powerful and far-reaching and would contribute to the objectives of a humane educational program.

CHCI CLOSES

Chimpanzees in the U.S. have no more legal standing than a car, so they are owned by individuals or organizations. Tatu and Loulis were under the care of FOW. FOW had a legal agreement with CWU regarding the housing and care of the chimpanzees. FOW's obligation was to provide care for the chimpanzees and raise the funds for their care. CWU owned the building that housed the chimpanzees and was obliged to maintain it.

Chimpanzees as social individuals must live in social groups. Breeding falls outside the mission of ethical sanctuaries since it only brings more individuals into a life deprived of freedom. Additionally, there are many chimpanzees in the US who are in need of placement at quality sanctuaries, and space and funding is very limited. With inevitable attrition in the CHCI family of chimpanzees, CHCI had in its strategic plan introduction of more chimpanzees to the facility. This would require renovations to the facility to allow introduction areas. Over the course of years, CWU took steps in this direction. It hired consultants to make recommendations on renovation, requested $1.7 million from state capital funding, and began the initial work of the renovation. At that time, there were three remaining chimpanzees: Dar, Tatu and Loulis. Then Dar died suddenly on November 24, 2012, of heart failure. With only two remaining chimpanzees, FOW requested that the university take stop-gap measures to complete phases of the renovation that would allow immediate introduction of chimpanzees. Then CWU administration began to waiver in its commitment to fund renovations. At the same time, it was imperative that Tatu and Loulis be in a social situation as soon as possible. They were depressed, and FOW was concerned about another death, potentially leaving a chimpanzee alone. This would make future introductions more difficult.

After five months of CWU's failure to make a commitment, FOW decided to move the chimpanzees to Fauna Foundation near Montreal, Quebec. At the time, Fauna provided a home to 11 chimpanzees retired from biomedical research and zoos. Fauna presented a high potential for integration with other chimpanzees and immediately available space. The move occurred in late August 2013, three months after the decision was made.

FOW handled all costs associated with the move and did it in the best way possible. The chimpanzees traveled in a private jet with an old friend and expert chimpanzee vet. While this sounds nice, it is not like typical air travel. Chimpanzees are confined to transport cages. The process involves multiple events of anesthesia for physicals and then moving into transport cages. Tatu and Loulis were trained for injection to minimize stress. Yet after the first physical, Tatu signed HURT each day for a week.

The initial week at Fauna was difficult. Tatu asked to go out the first few days. She was depressed and Loulis was fearful. Fauna and FOW ensured that Tatu and Loulis always had a signing caregiver present. These caregivers were from CHCI, so Tatu and Loulis had old friends as well. It was a difficult time, but they were integrated with other chimpanzees immediately after the quarantine ended.

At CHCI, the student intern program–and all the outreach programs including the weekly Chimposiums and summer Apprentice Program–ended. The move created upset students and parents. Many students, instead of a lesson in humility and compassion, learned a lesson of failing in commitments.

NON-HUMAN ANIMALS ON UNIVERSITY CAMPUS?

This leads to a larger question. Should we be housing chimpanzees on public campuses where they are vulnerable to administrative climate change? Tatu and Loulis' story is not unique. The bonobos at Georgia State University moved to Iowa Trust, and today their future is uncertain (Gardyasz, 2013). Ohio State University moved the chimpanzees on its campus without the cooperation of the project director. The move occurred in a way that resulted in two moves and two chimpanzee deaths (Gerns, 2007). University of Georgia recently closed its monkey lab (Davis, 2013). While all the students in these programs had experience working with nonhuman primates, what is the cost in to the non-human primates?

Instead, university programs can partner with privately owned sanctuaries. Students can attend classes and participate at internships at sanctuaries. Currently students of CWU participate in credit-bearing internships at Chimpanzee Sanctuary Northwest in Cle Elum, WA. There they gain experience in chimpanzee husbandry. Fauna has provided international internships for CWU students. They have participated in both husbandry and behavioral studies. This type of collaboration allows the sanctuary to continue its commitment to the residents, while the university maintains its own mission.

It is through regular face-to-face interactions that students learn about the depth of the person in chimpanzees and other apes. This experience coupled with their academic learning allows for this insight into our fellow beings. This humane education is valuable for the students and society, but it must occur in a way that is consistent with the values transmitted in a human education. One where there is no hardship or cost to the non-human teachers.

References

Bodamer, M. D., Fouts, R. S., Fouts, D. H., & Jensvold, M. L. A. (1994). Functional analysis of chimpanzee (*Pan troglodytes*) private signing. *Human Evolution, 9*(4), 281-296.

Boesch, C. (2012). *Wild cultures: A Comparison between chimpanzee and human cultures.* Cambridge, United Kingdom: Cambridge University.

Campion, T. L., Jensvold, M. L., & Larsen, G. (2011). Use of gesture sequences in free-living chimpanzees (*Pan troglodytes schweinfurthii*) in Gombe National Park, Tanzania. *American Journal of Primatology, 73(Suppl. 1)*, 97.

The Chimpanzee Sequencing and Analysis Consortium (2005). Initial sequence of the chimpanzee genome and comparison with the human genome. *Science, 437*(7055), 69-87. doi:10.1038/nature04072

Davis, J. (2013, November 13). UGA to retire monkeys used in research. *The Atlanta Journal-Constitution.* Retrieved from www.ajc.com/news/news/uga-to-retire-monkeys-used-in-research/nbrZz

Fouts, D. (1994). The use of remote video recordings to study the use of American Sign Language by chimpanzees when no humans are present. In R. A. Gardner, B. T. Gardner, B. Chiarelli, & F. X. Plooij (Eds.), *The ethological roots of culture* (pp. 271-284). Dordrecht, Netherlands: Kluwer.

Fouts, R. S., Fouts, D. H., & Van Cantfort, T. E. (1989). The infant Loulis learns signs from cross-fostered chimpanzees. In R. A. Gardner, B. T. Gardner, & T. E. Van Cantfort (Eds.), *Teaching sign language to chimpanzees* (pp. 280-292). Albany: State University of New York.

Fouts, R. S., Hirsch, A. D., & Fouts, D. H. (1982). Cultural transmission of a human language in a chimpanzee mother-infant relationship. In H. E. Fitzgerald, J. A. Mullins, & P. Page (Eds.), *Psychobiological perspectives: Child nurturance* (Vol. 3, pp. 159-196). New York, NY: Plenum Press.

Gardner, B. T., & Gardner, R. A. (1994). Development of phrases in the utterances of children and cross-fostered chimpanzees. In R. A. Gardner, B. T. Gardner, B. Chiarelli, & F. X. Plooij (Eds.), *The ethological roots of culture* (pp. 223-256). Dordrecht, Netherlands: Kluwer.

Gardner, R. A., & Gardner. B. T. (1989). A cross-fostering laboratory. In R. A. Gardner, B. T. Gardner, & T. E. Van Cantfort (Eds.), *Teaching sign language to chimpanzees* (pp. 1-28). Albany: State University of New York.

Gardner, R. A., Gardner, B. T. & Van Cantfort, T. E. (Eds.). (1986). *Teaching sign language to chimpanzees.* Albany: State University of New York.

Gardyasz, J. (2013, November 1). Saving the sanctuary. *Business Record.* Retrieved from businessrecord.com/Content/Culture/Culture/Article/Saving-the-Sanctuary/170/832/60728

Gerns, K. (2007, March 12). Judge to rule on chimp lawsuit. *The Scientist.* Retrieved from www.the-scientist.com/?articles.view/articleNo/24836/title/ Judge-to-rule-on-chimp-lawsuit

Goodall, J. (1986). *The chimpanzees of Gombe.* Cambridge, MA: Harvard University Press.

Hayashida, C., Jensvold, M. L., Grandia, A., Blake, S., Eburn, A., Jung, C., ... Fouts, R. (2002, Winter). Social hierarchy of five captive chimpanzees. *Friends of Washoe, 23*(2), 7-13.

Jensvold, M. L. (2007). Promoting positive interactions between chimpanzees (*Pan troglodytes*) and caregivers. *Laboratory Primate Newsletter, 46*(1), 1-4.

Jensvold, M. L. (2008). Chimpanzee (*Pan troglodytes*) responses to caregiver use of chimpanzee behaviors. *Zoo Biology, 27*(5), 345-359.

Jensvold, M. L., Buckner, J., & Stadtner, G. (2010). Caregiver-chimpanzee interactions with species-specific behaviors. *Interaction Studies, 11*(3), 396-409.

Jensvold, M. L., Field, A., Cranford, J., Fouts, R. S., & Fouts, D. H. (2005). Incidence of wounding within a group of five signing chimpanzees (*Pan troglodytes*). *Laboratory Primate Newsletter, 44*, 5-7.

Jensvold, M. L. A., & Fouts, R. S. (1993). Imaginary play in chimpanzees (*Pan troglodytes*). *Human Evolution, 8*(3), 217-227.

Jensvold M. L. A., & Gardner R. A. (2000). Interactive use of sign language by cross-fostered chimpanzees. *Journal of Comparative Psychology, 114*(4), 335-346.

Jensvold, M. L. A., Sanz, C. M., Fouts, R. S., & Fouts, D. H. (2001). The effect of enclosure size and complexity on the behaviors of captive chimpanzees (*Pan troglodytes*). *Journal of Applied Animal Welfare Science, 4*(1), 53-69.

Jensvold, M. L., Wilding, L., & Schulze, S. M. (2014). Signs of communication in chimpanzees. In G. Witzany (Ed.), *Biocommunication of animals* (pp. 7-19). Dordrecht, Netherlands: Springer.

Leeds, C. A., & Jensvold, M. L (2013). The communicative functions of five signing chimpanzees (*Pan troglodytes*). *Pragmatics & Cognition, 21*(1), 224-247.

Leitten, L., Jensvold, M. L., Fouts, R., & Wallin, J. (2012). Contingency in requests of signing chimpanzees (*Pan troglodytes*). *Interaction Studies, 13*(2), 147-164.

McCarthy, M., Brown, H., Gray, A., Lee, K., Steele, R., Jensvold, M. L., & Fouts, D. (2009, May). The effects of the Chimposium educational program on visitor knowledge and attitudes. Paper presented at the Symposium on University Research and Creative Expression, Ellensburg, WA.

McCarthy, M., Jensvold, M. L., & Fouts, D. H. (2012). Use of gesture sequences in captive chimpanzee (*Pan troglodytes*) play. *Animal Cognition, 16*(3), 471-481. doi: 10.1007/s10071-012-0587-6

Roberts, A. I., Roberts, S. G. B., & Vick, S. J. (2014). The repertoire and intentionality of gestural communication in wild chimpanzees. *Animal Cognition, 17*(2), 317-336.

Roberts, A. I., Vick, S. J., & Buchanan-Smith, H. M. (2013). Communicative intentions in wild chimpanzees: Persistence and elaboration in gestural signaling. *Animal Cognition, 16*(2), 187-196.

Ruvolo, M. (1994). Molecular evolutionary processes and conflicting gene trees: The hominoid case. *American Journal of Physical Anthropology, 94*(1), 89-113. doi:10.1002/ajpa.1330940108

Sibley, C. G., & Ahlquist, T. E. (1984). The phylogeny of the hominoid primates indicated by DNA-DNA hybridization. *Journal of Molecular Evolution, 20*(1), 2-15. doi:10.1007/BF02101980

Stamps, J. (2003). Behavioral processes affecting development: Tinbergen's fourth question comes of age. *Animal Behavior, 66*(1), 1-13. doi:10.1006/anbe.2003.2180

Stanyon, R., Chiarelli, B., Gottlieb, D., & Patton, W. H. (1986). The phylogenetic and taxonomic status of *Pan paniscus*: A chromosomal perspective. *American Journal of Physical Anthropology, 69*(4), 489-498.

CHAPTER EIGHT

THE HUMANE UNIVERSITY: INCORPORATING ANIMAL ISSUES AND HUMANE EDUCATION IN ACADEMIC INSTITUTIONS

Jonathan Balcombe

A FROG RESCUE

I was always drawn to animals. By age five, I was exploring the backyard of my suburban home in Auckland, New Zealand, looking for insects. My mother placed a plump monarch butterfly caterpillar in a glass jar, and we plied it with leaves from its New Zealand host, the swan plant (*Asclepias fruticosa*). A few mornings later, we found the vibrant black-orange-white grub miraculously transformed into a lime-green chrysalis, a delicate row of tiny golden dots across its upper mantle. Months passed, and the chrysalis turned almost black. Then another miracle occurred: a fully-fledged monarch butterfly, which we released outside.

In 1967, when I was eight, we immigrated to Canada. Upon our arrival by the sea in Vancouver, my mother gave me a coloring book of common North American birds. It also had stickers, and I spent much of the three-day train journey to Toronto carefully licking and placing the stickers into their prescribed rectangles and coloring the accompanying drawings. The day after we settled into temporary lodgings in downtown Toronto, I wandered out into the back garden and recognized one of the birds from my coloring book. It was a white-breasted nuthatch, and I have been hooked on birds since.

A year later, at a beloved childhood summer camp north of Toronto, I discovered what would become one of my favorite nature spots—the ditches bordering the railroad tracks that carried freight around the Great Lakes region of southern Ontario. These ditches filled with rainwater and gradually became serviceable wetland habitats for the local wildlife. I would go there when time permitted to watch frogs, dragonflies, and whirligig beetles. I saw my first pileated woodpecker there, and I would occasionally find a garter snake.

It was also at this location that my deep empathy for animals found expression one day, when a thin, scruffy, bearded man came ambling along the tracks. In one hand, he held a dip-net and a heavy, dripping cloth sack. In the other, he held a leopard frog. He approached me and asked me to hold the frog for a minute. I was a compliant nine-year-old and took the frog in my hand while he waded into the ditch. It didn't take much imagination to figure out what was in the sack. I looked at the frog in my hand and felt sorry for it. I didn't want it to end up crammed with the other hapless frogs in that sack. An overwhelming urge rose up inside me to let the frog go. So, I did.

The man came back. He was angry at what I'd done, and I learned some useful new swear-words that day. I felt humiliated, but I didn't like what that man was doing, and I felt I had done the right thing by setting the frog free. I don't know what the fate of the other frogs was, but I suspect they were most likely to become fishing bait—to be impaled dead or alive with a hook through the mouth, as if they were pieces of rubber. Or perhaps they were destined for a biology lab, where their gray, lifeless forms would be pinned out on dissection trays by impressionable youngsters to experience the slipperiness of a gastrocnemius muscle and see that an amphibian heart has three chambers instead of four.

There is another, implicit lesson that the traditional animal dissection exercise may reinforce in the minds of many young students: animals were put here for us, and we can do with them as we please. Dissection sends students the message that in Western science even relatively trivial human interests take priority over animal interests (Shapiro, 1991). The frog's most precious possession—his life—has been sacrificed for a biology lesson that can be taught effectively using non-lethal methods (Balcombe, 2000; Oakley, 2013).

A simple ethical analysis might conclude that we don't dissect frogs because we should, but rather because we can. This is the same might-makes-right doctrine that has infused some of humankind's worst social injustices, including colonialism, slavery, ethnic cleansings, the suppression of women, and the denial of civil rights. We have done much to relegate those social ills to the history books, but when it comes to our relations with other animals, we continue to carry the banner of might-makes-right.

During my ensuing education as a biology student, I participated in dissections of several frogs and a parade of other species including cats, fetal pigs, sparrows, starlings, dogfish sharks, salamanders, locusts, clams, and crayfish. I didn't like it, but the powers of authority and peer pressure kept me from rocking the boat until I was a university-level student. As an undergraduate biology student at Toronto's York University, I met with my entomology professor to discuss what I considered inhumane treatment of locusts. As a doctoral student at the University of Tennessee, I campaigned successfully for students to be given a choice to use humane alternatives in lieu of purchasing a fetal pig at the campus bookstore. That my students comprised a small proportion of the entire course enrollment, yet accounted for about 98% of the conscientious objectors to the pig dissection, speaks to the importance of a welcoming environment before students will assert a preference. Understandably, students are reluctant to publicly reject a teaching method that an instructor tacitly deems superior because she or he has chosen it for instruction.

TOWARD CULTURAL CHANGE

Curiously, there seems to have been little progress in humane education (see Bernard Unti's paper in this book). To be sure, there are organizations doing important work to advance the cause, such as the Academy of Prosocial Learning, the Institute for Humane Education, the Humane Education Committee of the United Federation of Teachers, and Humane Education Advocates Reaching Teachers (HEART). But, as yet, there has been no formal establishment of humane education principles in the classrooms of America. The animal dissection issue is symptomatic of this general stagnation. While the number of laws giving students the option to opt out of consumptive classroom uses of animals has been growing steadily in the United States (there were none before 1985; today there are 16), animal dissection remains a default method for most U.S. life science teachers (Oakley, 2012).

None of this need surprise anyone. Across all domains, the human-animal relationship remains fundamentally anthropocentric. Animals continue to be legally defined as the property of humans, and the right to consume animals for food, clothing, fashion, and entertainment remains entrenched as a cultural and societal norm. As the human populace continues to expand, animals continue to lose ground as suitable living spaces for most species inevitably dwindle. Globally, our species confines, kills, and eats more animals today than at any point in history—some 60 billion land animals (Food and Agriculture Organization of the United Nations [FAO], 2006)—and we terminate the lives of between 200 billion and 2.7 trillion fishes each year (Cooke & Cowx, 2004; Mood, 2010).

That sounds quite depressing if you care about animals. But there are reasons for optimism. The rise of the Internet means that large media corporations—which often have their own corporate-driven agendas—no longer control information dissemination. Today, web presence and social networks allow citizens to share information and foster advocacy. There is now wide and growing awareness of the ecological unsustainability of meat-centered diets for the masses (FAO, 2006), as well as its links to diseases and mortality and to climate change (Akhtar et al., 2009). It was awareness of these undeniable links that compelled the United Nations in 2010 to call for a significant worldwide diet change, away from animal products (UNEP, 2010).

Cultural change happens much faster than geological change. A boulder takes eons to disintegrate, but a social injustice can be breached and banished in the span of decades—witness the campaigns for suffrage and civil rights. Today, laws to protect animals are being enacted in the United States at unprecedented rates, about 100 yearly. With ratification of the Lisbon Treaty in 2009, the European Union includes animal sentience as a factor with legislative weight.

Several phase-outs and bans of factory farming practices have occurred on both sides of the Atlantic since Switzerland voted in 1981 to ban the use of battery cages to house egg-laying hens. Meatless Mondays are embraced on over 130 American university campuses, more than a dozen international universities, and in several cities around the world. And for the first time in our history, Americans are eating substantially fewer chickens, turkeys, pigs, and cattle. U.S. consumption of meat has dropped 10% over the last decade (CME Group, 2011). As to why, the options and futures exchange CME Group (2011) says it's for many reasons, mainly health, but notes the efforts of a "large number of non-governmental agencies that oppose meat consumption for reasons ranging from the environment to animal rights to social justice and one could conclude that it was amazing that consumption held up as long as it did."

ANIMALS RISING

There is another trend that should hearten anyone with a concern for animals. Following a period of quiescence during the first two-thirds of the 20th century, today scientific interest in animals' capacity to think and feel is unprecedented. And, due in part to an equally unprecedented availability of information through electronic social media, public access to information on the complexity and sophistication of animals' lives is like never before. Almost as soon as scientists discover that crocodiles use tools, orangutans announce their next days' plans, dolphins nip at puffer-fishes for a toxic drug high, or two different species of fish team up on a reef to make hunting more successful through cooperation, the story appears on a news feed and in a YouTube video. A 2012 video of a crow using a jar lid to ski repeatedly down a snowy rooftop in Russia quickly went viral, as did a 2013 video of macaque monkeys leaping playfully into the ocean shallows from a 30-foot boulder on the coast of Thailand. If someone doubts that black swans go surfing, that an African fish catches swallows in mid-air, or that chimpanzees have better spatial memory than humans do, the argument can be settled at the click of a (computer) mouse.

These information conduits are as useful to scientists as they are to laypersons. I like to consult the scientific source, but my initial awareness of a new scientific finding—and there are legions of them these days—comes to me through an online news feed or social network. As a biologist and an advocate, I seek to raise the status of animals by synthesizing and popularizing emerging scientific information about their behavior, their cognition, and their emotions. My main conduits are books, lectures, and electronic media: Facebook posts, Twitter tweets, email blasts, my website, and blogs. Because feelings rival facts in their power to drive behavioral change, I include some stories and personal accounts to make the material more emotive.

Work for animals is not just for animals. The animal movement is also a movement for human advancement. Cruelty is indivisible, and violence fosters more violence. When we cause others to suffer, we demean ourselves and tear the social fabric. As 19th century social reformer George Angell famously responded when criticized for devoting time to animal welfare when there was so much human suffering in the world: "I am working at the roots."

Enter the University

What is the role of the university in generating social and cultural change? Are centers of higher learning just about learning, or are they also about improving the human condition? I looked up (online, of course) the mission and vision statements of my alma maters. Each spoke to a broader purpose beyond the classroom. York University's mission seeks to test the boundaries and structures of knowledge and cultivate the critical intellect. In a nod to nascent cultural change, the school's motto is *Tentanda Via*: The way must be tried. And Carleton University (Ottawa, Canada) seeks "to create greater accessibility and a more inclusive world" (CU, n.d.).

Universities are well positioned to play an important role in the genesis and advancement of social change. A campus is a community, a microcosm of the global human society, a mixture of nationalities, ethnicities, cultures, religions, and socioeconomic backgrounds. People live there, they eat and sleep there (though preferably not during lectures), and they even shop there. Universities have their own policies and, to a degree, their own culture. Because it is smaller, the university can be more nimble than the city or the nation. Universities have the creative resources to be test cases for cultural change, and that includes how animals are perceived and treated.

Because universities can function as largely autonomous social entities, my vision for humane universities of the future is an integrated one. Humane universities will have institution-wide policies that embrace an ethic of respect for all. I refer to the inclusive "all," which embraces all sentient animals—beings whose lives matter because they can feel pain and pleasure and can experience suffering and joy. And by "respect," I mean considering the animals' own interests, which essentially translates to not willfully inflicting serious harm. Such policies would apply to all facets of the institution: teaching, research, food services, "pest" control, pets, etc., and they serve the dual functions of reducing suffering and fostering a culture of compassion.

What sorts of policies might we expect for the humane university of the future? Here are a few examples of what I envision.

CHANGES IN RESEARCH

If it conducts animal research at all, the university will do so with the utmost consideration for the well-being of the animals involved. Institutional Animal Care and Use Committees (IACUCs)—which paradoxically exist to protect animals used in institutional research while simultaneously approving procedures that cause their suffering and death—will mirror the mission and the spirit of their human equivalent, the Institutional Review Board (IRB), which exists to protect human subjects in research.

Classroom teaching practices will similarly do away with consumptive uses of animals, and animal-friendly learning tools will be integrated into the curriculum. Just as responsibly procured human cadavers are used in nursing and medical schools, so too can the animal equivalent be arranged for biology classrooms. Any dissections carried out will be performed on animals that died of unrelated or natural causes. This is a challenge of logistics, not numbers. Veterinary clinics and animal shelters alone collectively euthanize millions of animals yearly. Innovative, animal-friendly instructional and field techniques will be adopted that show respect and compassion for animals (see the following section for an example).

INTEGRATED CURRICULUM

There are also many opportunities for a less anthropocentric ethic to be expressed beyond science education by incorporating animal dimensions into disciplines typically taught with only humans in mind (Caine, 2008). For example, as it is traditionally perceived and taught, the subject of geography is intrinsically human-centered when, in fact, land is equally fundamental to the functioning and survival of other animals as to humans. This is similarly true for history, and an integrated curriculum ought to include reflection and discussion on how human beliefs, policies, and practices have affected animals through time; how these paradigms are changing in the present era; and the implications for the evolving human condition.

I envision a day when education makes room for teaching values and life skills. The traditional focus on factual curricula leaves little room for teaching students how to live compassionately, how to deal with the inevitable emotional challenges that life presents, peaceful conflict resolution, and spiritual self-awareness. By the time students reach university age, they ought to have grounding in these concepts and skills. The humane university of tomorrow will offer a mandatory freshman course in principles of compassion.

CAMPUS ENVIRONMENT

The physical environment of the campus will be both eco- and animal-friendly. Because humans are embedded within nature (Callicott, 1985), our consideration of all sentient members of the living community is not only valid but required. Furthermore, as Aldo Leopold (1949) emphasized in his influential land ethic, all biotic and abiotic components of the landscape warrant consideration because they are integral to ecological completeness and to the wellbeing of all who live there. To the extent possible, green spaces will be planted with native species and corridors will allow the movement of terrestrial wildlife between plots. Bird nesting boxes and bat houses will be erected, with interpretive signs.

Understandably, some urban campuses will have little opportunity to add or modify green space. Other campuses offer many opportunities to bring nature into the students' daily surroundings. I have made many visits to Cornell University as a guest lecturer and a parent, and it must rank as one of the top campuses in the nation when it comes to natural habitats. Fall Creek flows through campus, filling 300-acre Beebe Lake and spilling down spectacular gorges. Despite a history of damming and dredging, the lake is surrounded by woods and a one-mile trail. Aquatic and woodland birds, deer, and other mammals, including students, are drawn to this green jewel at the campus center. The Cornell Plantations program features a native plant education program and a wildflower garden of over 200 species. On a visit to Florida Gulf Coast University (FGCU), I watched fishes guarding their underwater nests in a pond just meters from one of the campus buildings. These fishes are safe from persecution because FGCU policy restricts fishing to catch-and-release on 80-acre North Lake. The sort of campus I'm advocating would not tolerate fishing at all, and an intermediate step would be to require that only barbless hooks be used, which would bring practice slightly more in line with the current policy's clause that caught fishes be returned to the water without causing them significant injury (FGCU, 2009).

CAMPUS DINING

Campus menus will be free of factory-farmed products; any meat and dairy products available will come from suppliers whose practices follow the highest standards of that oft-misused term "free-range." Animals will have had free and easy access to the outdoors, dairy cows will have nursed and reared their calves (which in modern dairy production are separated from cows at birth), and slaughter—which doesn't really belong in the same breath as "humane"—will at least not involve prods, loading ramps, transport trucks, stockyards, or abattoirs. Campus markets will stock a wide selection of meat alternatives, and all dining menus will have daily vegetarian and vegan options. Inevitably, students will become more familiar with plant-based meal options. I am certain that following the lead of the University of North Texas which in 2011 opened *Mean Greens*, a vegan dining hall, a vegetarian or vegan campus meal plan at all institutions is only a matter of time (Holland, 2014). It's already happening at elementary schools. An elementary school in Flushing, New York, switched to a completely vegetarian meal plan in 2012 (Spector, 2013), and a private school in Los Angeles intends to expand its all-vegan menu from one-day per week to all five days by 2015 (Chait, 2014).

PRODUCTS AND MERCHANDISE ON CAMPUS

Merchandise linked to animal suffering, such as hunting and fishing equipment, animal-tested products, fur, and cruel pest-control devices, will not be sold on campus and will be discouraged from use. In sum, the integrated humane university will not serve veal, sell fur-trimmed jackets, or allow glue traps. That's a broad and ambitious scenario, but moral principles are compelling. I believe it is only a matter of time before a campus with such principles comes to life.

ONE MAN'S CONTRIBUTION

Let me finish with a specific example of how one person's awakening resulted in substantial and measurable progress in the realms of humane education and social advancement at the university level.

Mike Howell is an ichthyologist and emeritus professor of biology at Samford University in Birmingham, Alabama. As a graduate student in 1964, Howell had the first of two experiences that ultimately moved him to alter the course of his professional life. On a class field trip with several other graduate students led by his professor, a prominent ichthyologist and curator of the university's fish collection, the group happened upon a large male bowfin (*Amia calva*) swimming in a shallow swamp, guarding about 50 of his 3-inch-long young swimming in a tight school alongside him.

Within minutes, the team had caught the parent fish, and they had a net full of wriggling baby bowfins. The professor loudly instructed the students: "You boys take all those fish and put them into our five-gallon jugs." In keeping with the traditional methods by which fish collectors collect fish, the jugs were half-filled with formaldehyde solution. Meanwhile, the huge male was put in a separate jug, where he thrashed about violently, flinging formaldehyde droplets everywhere. Howell reports that "after about ten minutes of an excruciating death, he finally succumbed to the noxious solution, and his quivering motion finally ceased."

As other students were busy dumping handfuls of the fledgling bowfins into the formalin pickling solution, Howell turned to the professor: "Do we have to kill all of these small bowfins?"

"Yes," the professor said, "take 'em all. We need them for records and maybe some scientist will need to do a statistical analysis of their features."

It took five minutes before the chemicals overwhelmed the young fish and their bodies became still. Howell recalls his feelings: "For the first time, and for some unknown reason, I felt nauseous about my participation in this immense, senseless killing. Even when I, again, asked my professor, 'Why do we have to kill all of those fishes?' the reply was, 'Well, that's just what professional field biologists do.'"

In the 1970s, while leading his own vertebrate field zoology class on its first fish collecting trip, Howell was asked the same question he had asked of his professor years earlier. In response, he parroted the words of his mentor: "Because that is the way it has always been done in field biology courses. Besides, we need to collect numerous specimens for statistical analyses." The student then abruptly stated, "Your course is genocide and I'm going to drop it!" And he did.

That student made an everlasting impression on Howell. He lost sleep thinking about the experience and the ensuing confrontation. He wondered if there might be a way to deliver quality teaching without killing the organism. He asked himself: "Couldn't we capture a fish in our net, place it into some kind of holding tank, pass it around to each student, point out its identifying characteristics and adaptations, photograph it, and return it back into its native stream unharmed?"

After experimenting with many prototypes, Howell came up with a narrow, V-shaped design that he called the "Teaching-Photographic (T-P) Tank." Several of his field biology friends tried out the T-P Tank during the late 1970s and 1980s. They liked it, and soon a small but growing band of converts were placing field-caught fishes in T-P tanks and passing them around while they gave a mini-lecture on the fish's anatomy and adaptations to its habitat. Students were required to then take a digital image of the fish in its natural colors (soon lost in formaldehyde). Today, these images are downloaded to a website repository, which can be used for identification and record keeping. Informal student surveys indicate that students prefer the T-P Tank to lethal methods.

Howell patented the device in 1991, and it is sold through a major biological supply company. Royalties go into a special fund to support undergraduate student research. Howell credits the T-P Tank—as well as the jarring field experiences that led to it—with sparing the lives of millions of individual fishes, and perhaps igniting the embers of empathy in more than a few students.

CONCLUSION

Howell's story reminds us that one person can make a big difference, and that it is never too late to get started on creating meaningful change. For me, it invokes the words of one of history's most tragic optimists, Anne Frank (1952): "How wonderful that nobody need wait a single moment before starting to change the world."

As organized communities, universities are incubators of innovation and first-string players in cultural change. Universities don't need to wait for society to change; they help drive societal change. The first humanely integrated universities are not far off, and I believe they will serve as epicenters of expanding change in broader society.

References

Akhtar A. Z., Greger M., Ferdowsian H., & Frank E. (2009). Health professionals' roles in animal agriculture, climate change, and human health. *American Journal of Preventive Medicine, 36*(2), 182-187.

Balcombe, J. P. (2000). *The use of animals in higher education: Problems, alternatives, and recommendations.* Washington, DC: Humane Society Press.

Caine, R. S. E. (2008). *Towards a framework of humane non-anthropocentric environmental education* (Unpublished doctoral dissertation). University of Toronto, Toronto, ON.

Callicott, J. B. (1985). Intrinsic value, quantum theory, and environmental ethics. *Environmental Ethics, 7*(3), 257-275.

Chait, J. (2014). MUSE School in Los Angeles will be the first entirely vegan school in the U.S. Retrieved from http://www.inhabitots.com/muse-school-in-los-angeles-will-be-the-first-entirely-vegan-school-in-the-u-s/

CME Group. (2011, December 20). Daily livestock report. *CME Group, 9*(243), 1-2.

Cooke, S. J., & Cowx, I. G. (2004). The role of recreational fisheries in global fish crises. *BioScience, 54*(9), 857–859.

Carleton University. (n.d.) Mission statement and goals. Carleton University. Retrieved from https://carleton.ca/read/about-read/mission-statement

Food and Agriculture Organization of the United Nations. (2006). *Livestock's long shadow: Environmental issues and options.* Available from http://www.fao.org/docrep/010/a0701e/a0701e00.htm

Florida Gulf Coast University. (2009). Policy 3.018: Fishing on campus. Retrieved from http://www.fgcu.edu/Housing/current/the-community-guide.html

Frank, A. (1952). *Diary of a young girl.* New York, NY: Pocket Books.

Holland, C. (2014). Texas university opens vegan-friendly dining hall. *VegNews.* Retrieved from http://vegnews.com/articles/page.do?pageId=6544&catId=1

Leopold, A. (1949). *A sand county almanac.* New York, NY: Oxford University Press.

Mood, A. (2010). Worst things happen at sea: The welfare of wild-caught fish. Retrieved from http://www.fishcount.org.uk

Oakley, J. (2012). Science teachers and the dissection debate: Perspectives on animal dissection and alternatives. *International Journal of Environmental and Science Education, 7*(2), 253-267.

Oakley, J. (2013). Animal dissection in schools: Life lessons, alternatives, and humane education. Ann Arbor, MI: Animals and Society Institute.

Shapiro, K. J. (1991, November). The psychology of animal dissection. *The Science Teacher, 59*(7), 43.

Spector, K. (2013). N.Y. school goes vegetarian, student test scores improve. Retrieved from http://ecowatch.com/2013/10/21/school-lunch-goes-vegetarian-students-reap-better-test-scores

United Nations Environment Program. (2010). Report: Assessing the environmental impacts of consumption and production. Retrieved from http://business-publicpolicy.com/?p=2188

CHAPTER NINE

TECHNOLOGICAL ADVANCES AND NEW APPROACHES TO WILDLIFE RESEARCH IN THE 21ST CENTURY

Kerrie Anne T. Loyd, Arizona State University
Colleges at Lake Havasu

WILDLIFE RESEARCH THEN

Ecologists, conservation and wildlife biologists, zoologists, and ethologists often conduct field studies requiring the use of live, free-roaming wild animals. Researchers interested in animal habitat use and ranging behavior must outfit individual animals with collars and transmitters for tracking. If research goals include population estimation, a common methodology is capture-mark-recapture which involves (live) capturing animals, tagging individuals for identification using a species-appropriate marker, and counting recaptured animals at a later date. Tags may be metal or plastic ear tags (mammals), leg bands (birds), branding (marine mammals), unique toe clipping (amphibians), or Passive Integrative Transponders (PIT), which are inserted subcutaneously or intramuscularly for many taxa. Additionally, tags are used for research on animal movement and life history parameters (growth rates, survivorship), and PIT tags are increasing in popularity due to reduced tag loss from their internal nature (Smythe & Nebel, 2013). Individual identification allows tracking of response to a management option and researching of differences in animal condition as a result of a treatment (Pollard, Blumstein & Griffin, 2010). Animals are also captured for physiological studies, disease research, phenotypic manipulation (bird plumage), and hormonal supplementation (behavioral research) (Cuthill, 1991). Capture methods are dependent on species, size, and population density and include dip nets, pitfall traps, live box traps, snares, cannon net guns, and more (Shemnitz, Batcheller, Lovallo, White, & Fall, 2012). Larger animals often require chemical immobilization to assist in the physical restraint necessary to mark or collect samples. Unfortunately, anesthetizing animals often results in higher mortality than nonchemical handling and restraint (Shemnitz et al., 2012).

In the 20th century, invasive techniques for wildlife research such as those listed above were widely adopted in ecological and behavioral research. There is now an increasing base of evidence suggesting that animal capture and handling results in negative effects on research animals (Jewell, 2013). Capture may lead to injury, physiological distur-bances, or non-natural behavior due to interference. The stress of cap-ture and handling is thought to be related to reduced immune function. Behavioral effects may include disruption to an animal's social group or hierarchy, changes in mating or breeding behavior, or behaviors result-ing in increased susceptibility to predation (Jewell, 2013). Reduced feeding and reproductive behaviors have been noted in mammals post-capture and handling (Reeder & Kramer, 2005). The capture of animals for capture-mark-recapture population estimation sometimes results in individuals remaining in traps too long, repeated captures, injuries from the trap, and exposure to extreme weather (Monamy & Gott, 2001). Death of captured wildlife has been reported from several minutes to weeks after the experience; this includes diverse groups: ungulates, marsupials, primates, birds, and pinnipeds (Jewell, 2013). Repeated captures are likely to raise this risk of Shock Disease (capture myopathy). A long-term study recently reported that banding of King Penguins (via flipper tags) significantly impaired population growth rate through reduced survival and reproduction (Saraux et al., 2011). The 39% fewer chicks produced by banded individuals and the higher mortality of adult penguins is likely associated with reduced foraging efficiency exhibited by banded birds.

The insertion or attachment of VHF transmitters on small animals for tracking often increases the stress and energy needs of animals when the weights approach the recommended limit (Cuthill, 1991). Parris et al. (2010) evaluated individual animal welfare resulting from alternative sampling methods and concluded that marking adult frogs via toe clipping is the least appropriate method for species (reduced survival rate post sampling) and individual welfare. Toe clipping is widely used and remains an Animal Welfare Act acceptable method of marking, yet some amphibians die just from the stress of handling. Increased infection and decreased mobility are also a concern (Parris et al., 2010). Tissue damage, pain, and stress are obvious effects of hot branding pinnipeds, but Walker, Mellish, and Weary (2010) additionally documented behavioral changes, and Scordina (2006) reported reduced juvenile survival as a result.

For many invasive field procedures and research, the monitoring of animals post sampling is rare, and information on the effects of post-capture, handling, or marking is understudied (Cuthill, 1991). A common goal of field researchers should be to reduce any harm or suffering of wildlife to improve the validity of the research itself. Field data is more reliable if the animals studied are not impaired in any way as a result of researcher interference (Dubais & Hershaw, 2013). The behavior and ecology of study animals are unlikely to mirror those of unstudied, undisturbed wildlife. Jewell (2013) also noted the need to reconsider the validity of data collected in the field using invasive methods in light of negative effects on researched individuals. She suggests poor ethics in research can be related to judgments of poor science.

DOES WILDLIFE FIELD RESEARCH HAVE AN ANIMAL WELFARE ETHIC?

The past 10 years have witnessed a call for ecological ethics, driven by institutional and societal concerns for the welfare of research animals (Minteer & Collins, 2005). Traditionally, field researchers played a minor role in animal welfare reforms as compared to biomedical professionals (Cuthill, 1991). Today, the work of ethologists and ecologists may be more highly scrutinized by the public because our use of animals does not benefit human society the way biomedical research does. Cuthill (1991) suggests some uses of animals may be more acceptable in biomedical fields because of the potential for reducing human illness and suffering. Often conservation research or animal behavior studies contribute to academic and management progress rather than directly benefiting human health and disease.

Some disagreement exists between conservation biologists concerned with the recovery and protection of a species, and animal welfare supporters concerned with the suffering of individual animals used in research. Conservation biologists view some degree of loss or pain acceptable in work that prevents the extinction of threatened species. Species recovery sometimes includes actions such as selective culling of diseased organisms (which pose a threat to healthy individuals) or predator control (lethal control of predators to benefit threatened prey species). Biologists often agree that the science information gained by disrupting or even culling wild animals is fundamental to future conservation planning and management (McMahon, Harcourt, Bateson & Hindell, 2012). Invasive species management is one example, whereby the removal of an invasive species directly benefits the recovery of endangered species; however, this is often unacceptable to animal welfare and rights groups who only support economically unfeasible control measures such as relocation or sterilization (Perry & Perry, 2008). In many cases, programs require culling to prevent more widespread animal suffering (within and sometimes across multiple species) due to overpopulation; elephants in southern Africa are one example (McMahon et al., 2012). Animal welfare and conservation both share the common goal of reducing negative impact on native wildlife in our age of exploding human population growth (Dubas & Harshaw, 2013). Wildlife reintroductions are one case where biologists and welfare activists overlap due to the requirement to provide care for each individual reintroduced, with the goal of successful population restoration (Harrington et al., 2013). Harrington et al. (2013) provide decision trees to assist with the improved success of reintroductions through animal welfare considerations at each stage of the process.

The issues faced by biodiversity researchers and managers are unique enough to warrant a new field of ethics (ecological ethics) to address welfare concerns. Minteer & Collins (2005) call for professional organizations in conservation and ecology to incorporate workshops and interdisciplinary panels to discuss the moral responsibilities of field researchers. These should consider public perceptions and demand for improved welfare of animals in science. The number of stakeholders affected by ecological research is much greater than sciences using laboratory animals and includes interests of biologists; federal, state and local agencies; private landowners; and the general public (Farmer, 2013). Diverse social and ethical concerns exist, and values of animals and wildlife may not always be aligned. This makes agreement upon an ideal set of guidelines difficult to achieve (Farmer, 2013). Common beliefs of the public should inform current standards of research with animals. Animal research activities are deemed acceptable when suffering of individuals remains low and the potential benefit and research importance is high (McMahan et al., 2012).

A recent survey of public opinions about wildlife management decisions found overwhelming majorities of respondents were not willing to trade the suffering of individual animals to protect populations or to accept the culling of one species to protect an endangered species (Dubas & Harshaw, 2013). This reflects an animal rights perspective. Rollins (2011) discusses how the animal rights movement (with regards to agricultural reform) has become so mainstream in America, and human dimensions research suggests the movement is becoming more influential in wildlife management. The U.S. has undergone a recent shift in the second half of the 20th century, from a public reflecting more utilitarian attitudes toward wildlife (valuing wildlife for human use and manipulation) to protectionist values. Human attitudes toward wildlife are influenced by values. Values are enduring beliefs, the foundation for an individual's thought and action (Bright, Manfredo, & Fulton, 2000). Value orientations describe patterns of direction and intensity among a set of beliefs about wildlife across several dimensions (Fulton, Manfredo, & Lipscomb, 1996). Wildlife value orientations are changing as part of a broader shift in values from materialist to post-materialist, influenced by modernization and a rise in environmentalism and mutualism orientations (i.e., the belief that wildlife have rights) (Inglehart, 1997; Teel & Manfredo, 2010; Teel, Manfredo, & Stinchfield, 2007). Materialist values were prevalent when existence needs required the use of wildlife as a food source. Since this need has been alleviated in recent decades, human contact with wildlife changed, and people now focus more frequently on caring and emotional bonding with wildlife (Teel et al., 2007). One post-materialist goal involves progression toward a more humane society (Manfredo, Teel, & Bright, 2003). Trends supporting this shift include the decrease in recreational hunting, growth of organizations addressing animal welfare issues, and emerging social conflict over issues involving wildlife (Teel et al., 2007). This value shift is connected to the increased affluence and education related to urbanization (Manfredo et al., 2003). The possibilities of shifting wildlife values orientations due to post-modernism theory (Manfredo et al., 2003) could translate to public support for protection and wildlife rights. U.S. residents with the highest mutualism orientations (animal welfare and animal rights) tend to be female, college educated, residents of large cities, or recent participants in wildlife viewing (Teel & Manfredo, 2010). People with a stronger feeling that rights of wildlife exist are more likely to engage in animal welfare enhancing behaviors (Teel et al., 2007). Williams, Ericsson, & Heberlein (2002) predicted that education and urbanization will lead to an increase in positive attitudes over time. Additionally, Champ (2002) discussed the relationship of wildlife media (television programs and documentaries) and modern attitudes and wildlife value orientations.

People tend to value animals more when they become rare (Schwartz, Landres, & Parsons, 2003), and this is likely reflected in today's beliefs and perceptions. Kauphof (2001) suggests that online animal webcams may be driving some of this shifting perspective. Members of the general public are now regularly logging on to webcams (for example, of newborn animals at zoos and on falcon, eagle, and owl nests) to check in on their favorite "wild pets." Viewers are developing an attachment to wildlife animals and a desire to improve situations for animals; the videos may activate personal responsibilities to care for animals. "The magnificence of seeing animals go about their daily lives is crucial for the seeds of compassion it sows" (Armitage, 2003 p.4).

The *Guide for the Care and Use of Laboratory Animals* is the principle reference for use of animals in research in the U.S.; however, this primarily relates to biomedical research with little relevance to wild animals (Sikes, Paul, & Beupre, 2012; Wallace & Curzer, 2013). Institutional Animal Care and Use Committee (IACUC) members are often uninformed or ill trained in ecological research involving wild animals and the ethical issues that may arise (Wallace & Curzer, 2013). There are now taxon-specific guides for appropriate conduct in field research, developed by the professional societies for each taxon, such as the *Guidelines of the American Society of Mammalogists for the Use of Wild Animals in Research* (Sikes et al., 2011) and the *Guidelines for Use of Live Amphibians and Reptiles in Field and Laboratory Research* (American

Society of Ichtyologists and Herpetologists, 2004). These guides should be formally recognized as the appropriate standards for research involving wildlife. They should continue to evolve and be incorporated by IACUCs because they are more relevant than references developed and geared toward biomedical uses of laboratory animals in research (Sikes et al., 2012). The *Australian Code for Care and Use of Animals in Scientific Efforts* was recently overhauled to include further guidelines related to wildlife field research (Monamy & Gott, 2001). Researchers are encouraged to discuss ethical and social issues surrounding their uses of animals and are required to undertake training to develop appropriate plans of action for multiple unexpected situations. Research proposals are peer-reviewed, and stated justification for research includes thoroughly considering all of the following: whether the number of wild animals used can be reduced or replaced with invertebrates; whether all prior research has been completely reviewed to be certain the study is needed; statistical verification that researchers are not oversampling; consideration of all impact on individual animals involved in the research; and exploration of alternative, non-invasive methods (Monamy & Gott, 2001). Curzer, Wallace, Perry, Muhlberger, & Perry (2013) outline moral ethics for ecological and wildlife research expanding on the replacement, reduction, and refinement themes required of laboratory research under the guide for care and use of lab animals. Reinforced is the notion that research plans and designs should minimize the harm to individual animals per piece of knowledge gained (Curzer et al., 2013). However, it is difficult to estimate and compare harms to animals because the fields of ecology and animal behavior are still young (Curzer et al., 2013). Cattet (2013) suggests improved communication between field biologists and veterinarians is needed, and that it would allow reduction of harm to wild animals used in research. Veterinarians remain concerned about the capturing and marking techniques that are standard in field research, and reject the common assumption that handled and marked individuals will continue to behave normally upon release (Cattet, 2013). Veterinarians may assist in plans to alleviate some of the impacts of research on individual animals or encourage the use of alternative methods.

WILDLIFE RESEARCH NOW

Field research is undergoing an evolution at present, with a vast expansion of non-invasive techniques for studying wild animals (Altmann & Altmann, 2002). Non-invasive approaches for vertebrate sampling include techniques that are either "unperceived by an animal subject or are perceived by an animal but do not elicit a chronic stress response or reduction in fitness" (Pauli, Whiteman, Riley, & Middleton, 2009, p. 2). Tools range from use of tracking and sign indices to auditory (vocalization) markers to remote cameras to genetic sampling of hair or feces for current capture-mark-recapture population estimates. In addition to benefitting study animals through avoidance of invasive procedures, most non-invasive approaches result in increased safety to researchers, increased accuracy of data collected and, in many cases, decreased investments in time and cost (Pauli et al., 2009). Non-invasive methods now allow researchers to gather information on wild animals living in wilderness areas while preserving the character of such protected land (Schwartz et al., 2011).

Capture-mark-recapture, life history parameter estimates, and population response to management requires identification of individual animals. Many animals have unique acoustic signatures that can be used to answer questions about population size and activity, including African wild dogs, primates, ground squirrels, and multiple avian species (e.g., kingfishers, flycatchers, and owls) (Pollard, Blumstein, & Griffin, 2010). These authors specifically studied the vocalization of marmots and ground squirrels and tested the use of this metric, concluding that it is possible to determine the number of individuals in the population as well as to discriminate between them (Pollard et al., 2010). The use of acoustic techniques (detection of species-specific ultrasonic echolocation vocalizations) to study bat species' habitat use and distribution has become routine over the last decade (e.g., Farrell & Gannon, 1999; Russo & Jones, 2003; Vaughan, Jones, & Harris, 1997).

Photography of individuals with unique phenotypic variation (terrestrial carnivore pelage, marine mammal spots, scars, or whiskers) is becoming useful to avoid artificial markings and the behavioral and physiological disruptions accompanying them. Photographic capture-mark-recapture techniques are growing in popularity. McCullum (2012) documents the large increase in the use of remote cameras ("camera traps") in wildlife research in the past two decades. Remote cameras are digital cameras triggered by an infrared sensor. When something warmer than the ambient temperature passes in front of the lens, the camera captures a photo. With improvements in sensitivity, image resolution, and battery life, remote cameras are now a reliable and cost-effective tool for wildlife researchers. Cameras are being used to gather objective data on a wide variety of mammals including elusive, nocturnal species living at very low densities (McCallum, 2012). Remote camera use in field ecology has occurred on almost every continent, in several habitat types, to study behavior, occupancy, population size, species richness, and management impacts on mammals (McCallum, 2012). The most common orders studied included artiodactyla (even-toed ungulates) and rare carnivores (including tigers and leopards), but lagomorphs (rabbits), primates, and rodents have also been studied using camera traps. Recently, remote cameras have documented the return and roaming habits of an endangered jaguar to the southwestern U.S. (Cheng, 2013), the discovery of a rare Asian saola (ungulate) in Vietnam (Lendon, 2013), and a new species of tapir in the Brazilian Amazon (Cozzuol et al., 2013). Published applications of remote camera research include estimating the density and sex ratio of two species of rare Asian bears using chest-mark patterns (thickness, tapering, smooth/jagged edge, size of tips, etc.) photographed at baited camera trap stations (Ngoprasert, Reed, Steinmetz, & Gale, 2012). Photographic capture-mark-recapture is also proving successful at monitoring an abundance of mammals without obvious individual differences. Goswami, Lauretta, Madhusudan, & Karanth (2012) used presence of fixed traits (e.g., tusk arrangement, angle, thickness, length, ear fold, and lobe shape or tear) of Asian elephants to establish identities.

Other innovative uses of camera tools have contributed to a move toward more humane sampling. Decades ago, we learned about domestic cat diet and impact on wildlife via stomach content analysis, which requires subjects to be euthanized (e.g., Catling, 1988; Comen & Brunner, 1972; McMurray & Sperry, 1941; Paltridge, Gibson, & Edwards 1997; Read & Bowen, 2001; van Aarde, 1980). Recently, suburban domestic cat-wildlife interactions were studied via "KittyCams," small, lightweight, animal-borne video cameras that captured all activity of roaming pet cats, allowing researchers to quantify wildlife captures and consumption (Loyd, Hernandez, Carroll, Marshall, & Abernathy, 2013).

This method provided an improvement in the estimates of cat impact on wildlife because domestic cats do not consume or bring home all prey; the authors found a significant amount of wildlife prey was left at the site of capture by hunting cats. This sampling method attempted to bridge the polarized debate about domestic cats in our ecosystems by providing objective video evidence of cat activities. The same images and videos from this research are now being used as educational tools to encourage pet owners to keep their cats indoors for the safety and well-being of both the cats and wildlife. Olea and Mateo-Tomas (2013) used Google Street View mapping functions to remotely survey areas for endangered cliff nesting vultures. Google Street View allowed easy identification of cliffs occupied by vultures, outperforming digital elevation models (Olea & Mate-Tomas, 2013). Similar techniques can be useful for mapping or assessing potential habitat in developed areas, saving time and money when compared to traditional ground searches and sampling.

Non-invasive genetic sampling is being used with increasing frequency to identify individuals of diverse species (including whales, bears, turtles, canids, and felids) via hair, feathers, feces, or other tissues collected in a way that avoids capture and handling of the animals (Luckacs & Burnham, 2008). Each animal has a unique "molecular fingerprint" allowing researchers to identify individuals and even associate them with family members (Shemnitz et al., 2012). DNA-based capture-mark-recapture procedures are considered superior to traditional tactics due to the increase in robustness resulting from the avoidance of tag-loss (Luckacs & Burnham, 2008) and reduced efficacy of traditional techniques for elusive or rare species. Population estimates for diverse species, from whales to eagles to wallabies, have been determined using DNA techniques, and molecular samples have also helped to determine survival rates for foxes and grizzly bears (Shemnitz et al., 2012). Recent papers have confirmed the efficacy of collecting and sampling DNA from the hair of canids (Ausband et al., 2011) and large felids (Sawaya, Ruth, Creel, Rotella, & Stetz, 2010), which often have large home ranges and live at low densities. Traditional methods of studying large felids like mountain lions involved capture, marking, and outfitting animals with a VHF radio collar for tracking. Sawaya et al. (2010) found that snow-tracking mountain lions in cold climates yielded abundant samples, allowing them to identify and sex individuals in a reliable and cost-effective manner. Coyotes were detected in a much shorter period of time using lure and rub stations to collect hair for genetic analysis than other non-invasive methods like remote cameras or track-plates (Ausband et al., 2011). DNA analysis can be used to estimate population abundance, growth rates, and distribution, and to examine patterns of genetic structure and diversity in wild populations; and non-invasive hair sample methods rival the genetic data collected from blood and tissue (Sawaya et al., 2010). Recently, environmental DNA (secreted by organisms via skin, gametes, mucous, and waste) protocols have been established to monitor aquatic species, including fish and amphibians, through detection of mitochondrial DNA in water samples (Pilliod, Goldberg, Laramie, & Waits, 2013).

Hair and feathers can also be used in stable isotope analysis, whereby ratios of carbon and nitrogen in hair and feathers provide information on animal diets and distribution over time. Recent applications include feeding ecology in great apes (Oelze et al., 2011), origin of African migrant birds (Hobson et al., 2012), and seasonal movements in bats (Britzke, Loebs, Romanek, Hobson, & Vonhof, 2012). Emerging methods also include the use of urine and feces to provide noninvasive insight into animal endocrine physiology (Altmann & Altmann, 2002). Fecal samples are easy to collect, and Palme, Rettenbacher, Touma, El-Bahr, & Mostl (2005) determined that fecal samples are superior for use in measuring stress hormones (glucocorticoids and catecholamines) in some species because the concentrations of glucocorticoid metabolites in the feces reflected secretory patterns better than blood (where concentrations can change very quickly and often). The use of dogs to locate scat of wild animals increases sample size and data quality (Schwartz et al., 2011). Alternatively, some sampling methods labeled noninvasive or nonintrusive may disturb animals by flushing wildlife from a nest or cover (often eliciting a stress response from subjects) to collect needed samples (Pauli et al., 2009).

Yet another emerging trend contributing to the movement toward less-invasive research at the university level and beyond is the notion of citizen science. Citizen science shares natural history observations from communities with scientific researchers who can use this information to expand ecological databases with species observations, date, and locations contributed by backyard birdwatchers (as one example). Citizen science is becoming a fantastic tool for ecological research, public engagement, and environmental education (Dickenson et al., 2012). Programs range from documenting the presence, number, and demographics of organisms across broad spatial scales (e.g., eBird and Monarch Larva Monitoring Project) to long-term monitoring of natural features and phenomena (e.g., Save our Streams water quality monitoring and Nature's Notebook phenology monitoring). Citizen science observations are currently supplementing research on invasive species, climate change, and wildlife disease (Dickensen et al., 2012). The general public has contributed to marine monitoring in addition to terrestrial projects. Scuba divers documented trends in shark and ray abundance on reefs (Ward-Paige & Lotze, 2011; Ward-Paige, Pattengiull-Semmens, Meyers, & Lotze, 2010), and tourist photographs have been valuable in identifying whale sharks for photographic capture-mark-recapture modeling (Davies, Stevens, Meekan, Struve, & Rowcliffe, 2012).

CONCLUSION

Historically, the quality of data collected in years past improved with increasing intrusiveness of sampling techniques; however, with advances today, data quality can be greater with less invasive methods (Schwartz et al., 2011). The above methods describe some recent trends in noninvasive sampling, where the probability of animal injury and suffering from sampling should be nonexistent. The wildlife techniques manual (Shemnitz et al., 2012) assists wildlife researchers in choosing appropriate equipment for animal capture, guided by the Animal Welfare Act and required by institutional IACUCs. Powell and Proulx (2003) evaluate the performance of alternative invasive trapping and marking techniques for terrestrial mammals. The guidelines prepared by the professional societies for each vertebrate taxon and recent literature on sampling focal taxa should be considered for further suggestions of non-invasive sampling designs. With the continued call from academics for a wildlife research ethic, appropriate and comprehensive guidelines may soon be available allowing standardization of field research proposal reviews.

ACKNOWLEDGEMENTS

Thank you to Dr. Sharon Harvey, environmental ethicist, Arizona State University, for reviewing this manuscript and providing feedback.

References

Altmann, S. A., & Altmann, J. (2003). Anniversary essay: The transformation of behavior field studies. *Animal Behavior, 65*, 413-423.

Armitage, P. (2003). *The show must go on!* Johannesburg, South Africa: Ripple Effect.

Ausband, D. E., Young, J., Fannin, B., Mitchell, M. S., Stenglein, J. L., Waits, L. P., & Shivik, J. A. (2011). Hair of the dog: Obtaining samples from coyotes and wolves noninvasively. *Wildlife Society Bulletin, 35*(2), 105-111.

Bright, A. D., Manfredo, M. J., & Fulton, D. C. (2000). Segmenting the public: an application of value orientations to wildlife planning in Colorado. *Wildlife Society Bulletin, 28*(1), 218-226.

Britzke, E. R., Loebs, S. C., Romanek, C. S., Hobson, K. A., & Vonhof, M. J. (2012). Variation in catchment areas of Indiana bat (*Myotis sodalist*) hibernacula inferred from stable hydrogen (δ2H) isotope analysis. *Canadian Journal of Zoology, 90*(10), 1243-1250.

Catling, P. C. (1988). Similarities and contrasts in the diets of foxes and cats relative to fluctuating prey populations and drought. *Australian Wildlife Research, 15*(3), 307-317.

Cattet, M. R. L. (2013). Falling through the cracks: Shortcomings in the collaboration between biologists and veterinarians and their consequences for wildlife. *ILAR Journal, 54*(1), 33-40.

Cheng, J. (2013). Rare jaguar sighting in Arizona's Santa Rita Mountains. *Time Magazine Newsfeed*. Retrieved from http://newsfeed.time.com/2013/06/28/rare-jaguar-sighting-in-arizonas-santa-rita-mountains

Coman, B. J. & Brunner, H. (1972). Food habits of the feral house cat in Victoria. *Journal of Wildlife Management, 36*(3), 848-853.

Cozzuol, M. A., Clozato, C. L., Holanda, E. C., Rodrigues, F. H. G., Nienow, S., de Thiosy, B., ... Santos, F. R. (2013). A new species of tapir from the Amazon. *Journal of Mammalogy, 94*(6), 1331-1345.

Curzer, H. J., Wallace, M. C., Perry, G., Muhlberger, P. J., & Perry, D. (2013). The ethics of wildlife research: A nine R theory. *ILAR Journal, 54*(1), 52-57.

Champ, J. G. (2002). A culturalist-qualitative investigation of wildlife media and value orientations. *Human Dimensions of Wildlife, 7*(4), 273-286.

Cuthill, I. (1991). Field experiments in animal behaviour: Methods and ethics. *Animal Behavior, 42*(6), 1007-1014.

Davies, T. K., Stevens, G., Meekan, M.G., Struve, J., & Rowcliffe, J. M. (2012). Can citizen science monitor whale-shark aggregations? Investigating bias in mark-recapture modeling using identification photographs sourced from the public. *Wildlife Research, 39*(8), 696.

Dickinson, J. L., Shirk, J., Bonter, D., Bonney, R., Crain, R. L., Martin, J., & Purcell, K. (2012). The current state of citizen science as a tool for ecological research and public engagement. *Frontiers in Ecology and the Environment, 10*(6), 291-297.

Dubois, S., & Harshaw, H. W. (2013). Exploring "humane" dimensions of wildlife. *Human Dimensions of Wildlife, 18*(1), 1-19.

Farmer, M. C. (2013). Setting up an ethics of ecosystem research structure based on the precautionary principle. *ILAR Journal, 54*(1), 58-62.

Fulton, D. C., Manfredo, M. J., & Lipscomb, J. (1996). Wildlife value orientations: A conceptual and measurement approach. *Human Dimensions of Wildlife, 1*(2), 24- 47.

Gannon, W. L., Sikes, R. S., & The Animal Care and Use Committee of the American Society of Mammalogists. (2011). Guidelines of the American society of mammalogists for the use of wild mammals in research. *Journal of Mammalogy, 92*(1), 235-253.

Goswami, V. R., Lauretta, M. V., Madhusudan, M. D., & Karanth, K. U. (2011). Optimizing individual identification and survey effort for photographic capture-recapture sampling of species with temporally variable morphological traits. *Animal Conservation, 15*(2), 1-10.

Harrington, L. A., Moehrenschlager, A., Gelling, M., Atkinson, R. P., Hughes, J., & Macdonald, D. W. (2013). Conflicting and complementary ethics of animal welfare considerations in reintroductions. *Conservation Biology, 27*(3), 486-500.

Herpetological Animal Care and Use Committee of the American Society of Ichthyologists. (2004). Guidelines for the use of live amphibians and reptiles in field and laboratory research. *Copeia,* 1-43.

Hobson, K. A., van Wilgenburg, S. L., Wassenaar, L. I., Powell, R. L., Still, C. J., & Craine, J. M. (2012). A multi-isotope (δ13C, δ15N, δ2H) feather isoscape to assign Afrotropical migrant birds to origins. *Ecosphere, 3*(5), 1-20.

Inglehart, R. (1997). *Modernization and post modernization: Culture, economic, and political change in 43 societies.* Princeton, NJ: Princeton University Press.

Jewell, Z. (2013). Effect of monitoring technique on quality of conservation science. *Conservation Biology, 27*(3), 501-508.

Kamphof, I. (2011). Webcams to save nature: Online space as affective and ethical space. *Foundations of Science, 16*(2), 259-274.

Lendon, B. (2013). Rare "Asian unicorn" caught on camera. *CNN Online News.* Retrieved from http://www.cnn.com/2013/11/13/world/asia/vietnam-rare-mammal

Loyd, K. T., Hernandez, S. M., Carroll, J. P., Marshall, G. J, & Abernathy, K. J. (2013). Quantifying free-roaming domestic cat predation using animal-borne cameras. *Biological Conservation, 160*, 183-189.

Lukacs, P. M., & Burnham, K. P. (2005). Review of capture-recapture methods applicable to noninvasive genetic sampling. *Molecular Ecology, 14*(13), 3909-3919.

Manfredo, M. J., Teel, T. L., & Bright, A. D. (2003). Why are public values toward wildlife changing? *Human Dimensions of Wildlife, 8*(4), 287-306.

McCallum, J. (2012). Changing use of camera traps in mammalian field research: Habitats, taxa and study types. *Mammal Review, 43*, 196-205.

McMahon, C. R., Harcourt, R., Bateson, P., & Hindell, M. A. (2012). Animal welfare and decision making in wildlife research. *Biological Conservation, 153*(3), 254-256.

McMurry, F. B., & Sperry, C. C. (1941). Food of feral house cats in Oklahoma: A progress report. *Journal of Mammalogy, 22*(2), 185-190.

Minteer, B. A., & Collins, J. P. (2005). Why we need an "ecological ethics." *Frontiers in Ecology and the Environment, 3*(6), 332-337.

Monamy, V., & Gott, M. (2001). Practical and ethical considerations for students conducting ecological research involving wildlife. *Austral Ecology, 26*(3), 293-300.

Ngoprasert, D., Reed, D. H., Steinmetz, R., & Gale, G. A. (2012). Density estimation of Asian bears using photographic capture-recapture sampling based on chest marks. *Ursus, 23*(2), 117-133.

O'Farrell, M. J. & Gannon, W. L. (1999). A comparison of acoustic versus capture techniques for the inventory of bats. *Journal of Mammalogy, 80*(1), 24-30.

Oelze, V. M., Fuller, B. T., Richards, M. P., Fruth, B., Surbeck, M., Hublin, J. J. & Hohmann, G. (2011). Exploring the contribution and significance of animal protein in diet of bonobos by stable isotope ratio analysis of hair. *Proceedings of the National Academy of Science, 108*(24), 9792-9797.

Olea, P. P., & Mateo-Tomas, P. (2013). Assessing species habitat using Google Street View: A case study of cliff-nesting vultures. *PLoS One, 8*(1), 1-7.

Palme, R., Rettenbacher, S., Touma, C., El-Bahr, S. M., & Mostl, E. (2005). Stress hormones in mammals and birds: Comparative aspects regarding metabolism, excretion, and noninvasive measurement in fecal samples. *New York Academy of Sciences, 1040*(1), 162-171.

Paltridge, R., Gibson, D. & Edwards, G. (1997). Diet of the feral cat in central Australia. *Wildlife Research, 24*(1), 67-76.

Parris, K. M., McCall, S. C., McCarthy, M. A., Minteer, B. A., Steele, K., Bekessy, S., & Medvecky, F. (2010). Assessing ethical trade-offs in ecological field studies. *Journal of Applied Ecology, 47*(1), 227-234.

Pauli, J. N., Whiteman, J. P., Riley, M. D., & Middleton, A. D. (2009). Defining noninvasive approaches for sampling of vertebrates. *Conservation Biology, 24*(1), 349-352.

Perry, D., & Perry, G. (2007). Improving interactions between animal rights groups and conservation biologists. *Conservation Biology, 22*(1), 27-35.

Pilliod, D. S., Goldberg, C. S., Laramie, M. B., & Waits, L. P. (2013). *Application of environmental DNA for inventory and monitoring of aquatic species* (Publication No. FS 2012-3146). Retrieved from https://pubs.usgs.gov/fs/2012/3146/pdf/fs2012-3146.pdf

Pollard, K. A., Blumstein, D. T., & Griffin, S. C. (2010). Pre-screening acoustic and other natural signatures for use in noninvasive individual identification. *Journal of Applied Ecology, 47*(5), 1103-1109.

Powell, R. A., & Proulx, G. (2003). Trapping and marking terrestrial mammals for research: Integrating ethics, performance criteria, techniques, and common sense. *ILAR Journal, 44*(4), 259-272.

Read, J., & Bowen, Z. (2001). Population dynamics, diet, and aspects of the biology of feral cats and foxes in arid South Australia. *Wildlife Research, 28*(2), 195-203.

Reeder, D. M. & Kramer, K. M. (2003). Stress in free-ranging mammals: Integrating physiology, ecology, and natural history. *Journal of Mammalogy, 86*(2), 225-235.

Reiter, D. K., Brunson, M. W., & Schmidt, R. H. (1999). Public attitudes toward wildlife damage management and policy. *Wildlife Society Bulletin, 27*(3), 746-758.

Rollins, B.E. (2011). Animal rights as a mainstream phenomenon. *Animals, 1*(1), 102-115.

Russo, D. & James, G. (2003). Use of foraging habitats by bats in a Mediterranean area determined by acoustic surveys: Conservation implications. *Ecography, 26*(2), 197-209.

Saraux, C., Le Bohec, C., Durant, J. M., Viblanc, N. A., Gauthier-Clerck, M., Beune, P., ... Maho, Y. L. (2011). Reliability of flipper-banded penguins as indicators of climate change. *Nature, 469*(7329), 203-206.

Sawaya, M. A., Ruth, T. K., Creel, S., Rotella, J. J., & Stetz, J. B. (2011). Evaluation of noninvasive genetic sampling methods for cougars in Yellowstone National Park. *The Journal of Wildlife Management, 75*(3), 612-622.

Schemnitz, S. D., Batcheller, G. R., Lovallo, M. J., White, H. B., & Fall, M. W. (2012). Capturing and handling wild animals. In N. J. Silvy (Ed.), *The Wildlife Techniques Manual.* (pp. 64-117). Baltimore, MD: Johns Hopkins University Press.

Schwartz, M. K., Landres, P. B., & Parsons, D. J. (2011). Wildlife scientists and wilderness managers finding common ground with noninvasive and nonintrusive sampling of wildlife. *International Journal of Wilderness, 17*(1), 4-7.

Scordino, J. (2006). *Steller sea lions (Eumetopias jubatus) of Oregon and Northern California: seasonal haulout abundance patterns, movements of marked juveniles, and effects of hot-iron branding on apparent survival of pups at Rogue Reef* (Master's Thesis). Corvallis, Oregon State University.

Sikes, R. S., Paul, E., & Beaupre, S. J. (2012). Standards for wildlife research: Taxon-specific guidelines versus US public health service policy. *Bioscience, 62*(9), 830-834.

Smyth, B., & Nebel, S. (2013) Passive integrated transponder (PIT) tags in the study of animal movement. *Nature Education Knowledge, 4*(3), 3.

Teel, T. L., & Manfredo, M. J. (2010). Understanding the diversity of public interests in wildlife conservation. *Conservation Biology, 24*(1), 128-139.

Teel, T. L, Manfredo, M. J., & Stinchfield, H.M. (2007). The need and theoretical basis for exploring wildlife value orientations cross-culturally. *Human Dimensions of Wildlife, 12*(5), 297-305.

Vaughan, N., Jones, G. & Harris, S. (1997). Habitat use by bats (Chiroptera) assessed by means of a broad-band acoustic method. *Journal of Applied Ecology, 34*(3), 716-730.

van Aarde, R. J. (1980). The diet and feeding behavior of feral cats at Marion Island. *South African Journal of Wildlife Research, 10*(3-4), 122-128.

Wallace, M. C., & Curzer, H. J. (2013). Moral problems and perspectives for ecological field research. *ILAR Journal, 54*(1), 3-4.

Walker, K. A., Mellish, J. E., & Weary, D. M. (2010). Behavioural responses of juvenile Steller sea lions to hot-iron branding. *Applied Animal Behaviour Science, 122*(1), 58-62.

Ward-Paige, C. A., & Lotze, H. K. (2011). Assessing the value of recreational divers for censusing elasmobranchs. *PloS One, 6*(10), 1-10.

Ward-Paige, C. A., Pattengill-Semmens, C., Myers, R. A., & Lotze, H. K. (2011). Spatial and temporal trends in yellow stingray abundance: Evidence from diver surveys. *Environmental Biology of Fishes, 90*(3), 263-276.

Williams, C. K., Ericsson, G., & Heberlein, T. A. (2002). A quantitative summary of attitudes toward wolves and their reintroduction (1972-2000). *Wildlife Society Bulletin, 30*(20), 575-584.

CHAPTER TEN

HAPPY ANIMALS PROMOTE GOOD SCIENCE: ALTERNATIVES TO THE TRADITIONAL LABORATORY APPROACH

Evan MacLean and Brian Hare, Duke University

Historically, research on animal behavior and animal cognition has been conducted in two very different traditions. The first approach has roots in ethology and emphasizes the study of animals in their natural habitat. The second approach is to maintain a captive population of animals for which the environment and experimental conditions can be precisely controlled. Research with wild animals benefits from the naturalistic conditions under which animals are observed, and there tend to be few welfare concerns in these contexts (but see Goldberg et al., 2007; Shutt et al., 2014; Westin, 2017). However, due to the natural ecological setting, researchers have limited control over important variables, rendering many experimental studies impossible (but see Pritchard, Hurly, Tello-Ramos, & Healy, 2016). Consequently, most experimental research with animals is conducted in captivity where researchers have much more control over the animals they study, including their rearing history, diet, and life experiences. Under these conditions, scientists can make highly controlled experimental manipulations and collect many types of data that are difficult to obtain in the field. However, animals in traditional laboratory environments often live in austere conditions with potentially negative consequences both for animal welfare and the validity of research findings (Calisi & Bentley, 2009; Garner & Mason, 2002; Rowan, 1990).

One approach for improving animal welfare in captive research settings is to "enrich" standard biomedical facilities to accommodate species-typical needs and preferences (Baumans et al., 2007; MacLean et al., 2009; Olsson et al., 2003). For example, seemingly small changes, such as providing mink with access to a water pool, can greatly reduce the stress of captivity (Mason et al., 2001). A less common approach, however, is for researchers to forgo laboratory housing altogether in favor of nontraditional research settings. In this chapter, we highlight how nontraditional research settings can borrow strengths from both field and laboratory environments, while simultaneously leading to major improvements in animal welfare. Drawing on our own research, we present two examples of alternative models for research with great apes and domestic dogs and illustrate their scientific, animal welfare, and financial benefits in comparison to a traditional laboratory-based approach.

GREAT APE RESEARCH AT AFRICAN SANCTUARIES

Background and Purpose

As humans' closest living relatives, bonobos (*Pan paniscus*) and chimpanzees (*Pan troglodytes*) play a special role in understanding our species' evolution and the similarities and differences between humans and our nearest primate cousins. However, research with captive great apes also poses major ethical considerations and welfare challenges (Gagneux et al., 2005; Goodall et al., 2010). As large-bodied, highly social primates who are adapted to life in tropical rain forests, great apes require spacious facilities that accommodate their arboreal lifestyles and fission-fusion social dynamics (Goodall, 1986; Kano, 1992; Nishida et al., 1999). Although some research centers have succeeded in creating high-quality living conditions for captive apes (Idani & Hirata, 2007; Matsuzawa et al., 2006; Morimura et al., 2011), the majority of U.S. research facilities do not adequately accommodate the needs of these species (Fritz et al., 1992; Woods & Hare, 2010).

In their habitat countries, wild populations of great apes are threatened by habitat loss, and the illegal hunting of apes for food, known as the "bushmeat trade" (Farmer, 2002; Peterson, 2003; Rose, 1998). Sadly, in addition to killing ape mothers, poachers frequently capture the orphaned infants, who are kept as pets in local villages or illegally sold into the exotic pet trade. African sanctuaries work with local authorities to confiscate these orphans of the bushmeat trade and to provide refuge and rehabilitation in protected forested enclosures (Andre et al., 2008; Farmer, 2002; Woods & Hare, 2010). Often infants arrive at sanctuaries malnourished and/or wounded and initially require intensive medical care. However, as these infants are nursed back to health, they are integrated into peer groups and begin to live independently from humans once again. With time, younger individuals can be transitioned into mixed-age, species-typical social groups that spend the majority of their days in large forested enclosures where they can forage and interact with the natural world similarly to wild populations (Figure 1). Ultimately, these populations can potentially be reintroduced to the wild to promote the conservation and the genetic viability of remaining wild great ape populations (Andre et al., 2008; Beck et al., 2007; Goossens et al., 2005). For additional information on African sanctuaries and their role in great ape protection, see PASA primates (pasa.org), Stokes et al. (2018), Pasaprimates and see Trayford & Farmer (2013).

Research at African Sanctuaries

In addition to providing care and refuge for orphaned apes, African sanctuaries collaborate with scientists on projects ranging from observational studies of free-ranging social groups to experimental tests of ape cognition and health, genetic, and morphological research. These diverse types of projects are facilitated through the unique infrastructure at sanctuaries, which consist of large, outdoor, forested enclosures; sheltered sleeping dormitories; and veterinary care facilities. Although sanctuary apes spend the majority of their days in large outdoor enclosures, even hundreds of acres of primary tropical forest cannot provide enough food for these populations. Thus, animals return to sheltered sleeping dormitories each evening, where they receive additional food and can be monitored by sanctuary staff.

These facilities provide an amazing opportunity for scientists to conduct noninvasive behavioral research with apes. Similar to zoos and research labs, most sanctuary dormitories contain multiple rooms, where researchers can work with individual subjects temporarily separated from their group mates for voluntary participation in problem-solving tasks. Because apes participate for food rewards, most individuals are eager to interact with humans and enjoy the novelty of problem-solving tasks, which are designed as games for animal participants (e.g., MacLean & Hare, 2012; MacLean & Hare, 2013; Rosati & Hare, 2011; Tan & Hare, 2013; Wobber, Herrmann, et al., 2013). In addition to problem-solving games, researchers can easily collect urine, feces, and saliva while apes are in these dormitories. Thus, research at sanctuaries is conducive not only to behavioral work but also to hormonal and genetic studies (e.g., Fischer et al., 2011; Prüfer et al., 2012; Wobber, Hare, et al., 2013; Wobber et al., 2010). Lastly, to monitor the health of sanctuary populations, veterinary staff conduct routine health checks during which other types of data (e.g., physiology, blood draws, morphological measures) can be collected (e.g., Mcintyre et al., 2009). In addition to facilitating basic research, these health checks provide an opportunity to obtain information relevant to conservation efforts for wild apes (Gamble et al., 2011; Jones et al., 2011), as well as the origins and spread of emerging infectious diseases (Krief et al., 2010; Nunn & Hare, 2012). Thus, sanctuaries can easily accommodate the vast majority of behavioral and medical research currently conducted in laboratories. However, sanctuaries also provide researchers with a wide range of opportunities that far surpass those available in traditional research settings.

First, due to the large and demographically diverse populations at sanctuaries, researchers have the potential to collect data with hundreds of individuals in the course of a study. These sample sizes have allowed scientists to probe questions about individual and species differences with a scope that is not feasible in traditional laboratories. For example, sanctuary research permitted the first large-scale comparison of cognition in human children and nonhuman apes in order to powerfully test the leading hypothesis for what makes human cognition unique (Herrmann et al., 2007; Herrmann, Hernandez-Lloreda, et al., 2010). Similarly, because sanctuary populations are demographically diverse, researchers were able to directly compare the cognitive development of human children and nonhuman apes (Wobber, Herrmann, et al., 2013).

Second, because sanctuary apes live in highly complex social and ecological environments, measures of cognition and behavior from these individuals are more likely to be representative of species-typical traits than those from captive populations deprived of these opportunities (Ongman et al., 2013). In addition, the naturalistic enclosures at sanctuaries allow researchers to pose experimental questions in ecologically relevant contexts. For example, studies of spatial memory can be carried out in naturalistic foraging areas, mirroring the contexts in which apes would use these skills in nature (Rosati & Hare, 2012). Studies of tool use benefit from the natural opportunities that animals have to learn about and use tools in their forested enclosures (Gruber et al., 2010; Herrmann et al., 2008). Additionally, access to large populations of bonobos has also allowed for the first studies of this species' vocal repertoire (Clay et al., 2011); unusual sharing behavior (Tan & Hare, 2013); and quantitative comparisons with chimpanzee cognition (Hare et al., 2007; Herrmann, Hare, et al., 2010) and endocrinology (Wobber, Hare, et al., 2013; Wobber et al., 2010; Wobber & Herrmann, 2014).

Third, research at sanctuaries can be conducted at a fraction of the cost of similar work in traditional research labs. In the U.S., the care and maintenance of a laboratory chimpanzee costs a minimum of $40 per day, whereas these costs are closer to $5 per day in Africa (Hare, 2011). However, even in light of this huge financial difference, animals housed at sanctuaries experience far superior conditions relative to apes in more traditional lab settings. Thus, not only are sanctuaries a low-cost alternative to research labs, they provide "more for the money" by accommodating species-typical social groups in vast expanses of tropical forest rather than small social groups housed in barren enclosures. Although we believe that sanctuaries should be the preferred research environments based on welfare considerations alone, the financial advantages of this model are also sure to appeal to funding agencies that support research with captive apes.

Are Sanctuary Apes Psychologically Healthy?

The inhabitants of African sanctuaries are predominantly orphans of the bushmeat trade, and many of these individuals have endured traumatic life experiences involving premature separation from their mothers (e.g., Lopresti-Goodman et al., 2012). Are these populations psychologically and behaviorally healthy? How do they compare to mother-reared apes? Wobber and Hare (2011) investigated these questions by comparing aberrant and species-typical behavior, cortisol levels, and performance in a cognitive test battery between chimpanzee and bonobo orphans and age-matched mother-reared subjects. With respect to behavior, sanctuary orphans exhibited lower levels of rocking and coprophagy (aberrant behaviors) than subjects in a state-of-the-art zoological facility. Orphans and mother-reared individuals did not differ in their cortisol levels, and both groups performed similarly across the vast majority of cognitive tests (Wobber & Hare, 2011). Thus, current data suggest that although many sanctuary apes have undergone trauma during infancy, rehabilitation programs at these sanctuaries are effective, and these apes are psychologically healthy in comparison to mother-reared individuals (Rosati et al., 2013).

Research at Sanctuaries Promotes
Humane Education and Conservation

A central benefit of research collaborations between sanctuaries and scientists is that research fees directly contribute to educational and conservation initiatives in ape habitat countries. As noted above, wild ape populations are threatened both by habitat loss and hunting. One of the best strategies to protect these species is to work with local populations to encourage sustainable economic development and to educate individuals about the dangers of the bushmeat trade and the value of conserving ape populations (Andre et al., 2008). For example, Lola ya Bonobo–the world's only bonobo sanctuary–leads education programs designed for Congolese children to learn about bonobos and how and why they should protect this unique species. The sanctuary has helped to establish "Kindness Clubs" at nearly forty Kinshasa schools and sponsors field trips for children to visit the sanctuary. During these visits, children learn about bonobo behavior and biology, bonobos' special relationship with humans, and why Congolese children play such an important role in determining the fate of this species (Andre et al., 2008). Thus, sanctuaries play a critical role in humane education through programs designed to foster compassion for great apes and instill a sense of responsibility for the welfare of these species, both in captivity and in the wild. Research collaborations with sanctuaries help to promote these educational programs through financial support from research fees and through scientific partnerships to evaluate the impact of conservation education programs.

The End to the Era of Laboratory Ape Research?

Due to the financial and ethical challenges of working with apes in labs, the National Institutes of Health (NIH) announced plans to retire the vast majority of its research chimpanzees (Office of the Federal Register, 2013). This decision stemmed from an internal study by the National Academy of Sciences' Institute of Medicine (IOM) designed to assess the need for, and current uses of, chimpanzees in health research. In December 2011, this committee reported that chimpanzees were not needed in the vast majority of biomedical applications and that the "moral costs" of chimpanzee research require heightened justification for the continued use of chimpanzees in biomedical research (Altevogt et al., 2011). Following this report, NIH Director Francis Colllins suspended new grant proposals for biomedical research with chimpanzees and requested that the NIH Council of Councils develop a working group to provide guidelines for implementing the IOM's recommendations (National Institutes of Health, 2011).

In January 2013, the Council of Councils issued its report on the use of chimpanzees in NIH-supported research and made several important recommendations that (when implemented) will dramatically improve ape welfare and promote a shift away from laboratory environments for genomic, behavioral, and cognitive research. First, the report advises that any chimpanzees housed in captivity should reside in ethologically appropriate physical and social environments, defined as social groups of at least seven individuals with year round access to a large natural outdoor environment, vertical climbing structures at least 20 feet tall, and materials to construct new sleeping nests on a daily basis. Second, the report recommended that the majority of NIH-owned chimpanzees be retired to a federal sanctuary system. Third, the Council advised that NIH should not continue to breed chimpanzees. Thus, in addition to retiring the current population of apes, no new individuals will be introduced to the system, effectively ending the era of publicly funded laboratory research with great apes.

Lastly, the Council's report recommended that NIH should review its funding priorities for behavioral, cognitive, and genomic research with chimpanzees and should consider funding projects that can be completed at a low cost and in nontraditional research settings that maintain ethologically appropriate environments. As we have summarized above, African sanctuaries meet all these requirements by providing apes with ethologically relevant physical and social environments and prioritizing animal welfare while simultaneously accommodating state-of-the-art research. Therefore, as the era of biomedical research with captive chimpanzees comes to a close, the new era of collaborative research with African sanctuaries is only just beginning.

LABORATORY ALTERNATIVES TO RESEARCH WITH DOMESTIC DOGS

The Dog's Cognitive Claim to Fame

As the first domesticated species, dogs have always played a special role in human societies. In the last 20 years, however, dogs have also become one of the most intensively studied species in comparative cognition. This surge of interest in dog cognition was spurred by two publications in the late 1990s documenting social-cognitive skills in dogs that appeared to be more human-like than those of humans' closest living primate relatives (Hare et al., 1998; Miklósi et al., 1998). Since these initial discoveries, scientists have uncovered remarkable cognitive flexibility in dogs, including processes analogous to those through which human children acquire language (Kaminski et al., 2004; Pilley & Reid, 2011). These remarkable similarities with humans have led to new hypotheses about how and why human cognition evolved (Hare et al., 2002; Hare & Tomasello, 2005) and have spurred increased scientific interest in dogs more broadly (Bensky et al., 2013). Most recently, scientists have begun functional brain imaging in awake and unrestrained dogs–procedures that require restraint and/or sedation in other species but are feasible in dogs due to their domesticated temperament and the ease with which dog behaviors can be trained using positive reinforcement (Andics et al., 2014; Berns et al., 2012; Jia et al., 2014). All these accomplishments were possible because scientists developed alternative research models for working with dogs that do not rely on laboratory-housed research populations. Below, we review four laboratory alternatives for research with domestic dogs and highlight how these models promote both animal welfare and cutting-edge research.

Campus Centers for Behavioral Research with Dogs

By far, the most common alternative to keeping a laboratory population of dogs is to recruit pet dogs for participation in behavioral studies at campus-based research centers. In review of the dog cognition literature, Bensky et al. (2013) reported that of 285 publications on dog cognition, 72% of studies were conducted with pet dogs, whereas only 19% of studies used dogs bred or raised specifically for research. Campus-based research centers for the study of pet dogs follow a similar research model to that in developmental psychology, in which participants are members of the community who are volunteered for research by their parents or caregivers. As with child research, these studies rely on voluntary participation from animal subjects. Dogs who are fearful, anxious, or merely uninterested in participating in behavioral games are not coerced to do so. Therefore, the success of any experiment relies entirely on devising clever ways to ask research questions that are perceived as fun opportunities for the dog to obtain food, toys, or social rewards. Recruitment for these studies also follows the model in developmental psychology in which interested participants register their child or dog to be selected for study participation. Due to the prevalence of dog ownership in the U.S., these participant databases can easily include thousands of research participants. Consequently, these demographically diverse subject pools allow scientists to design studies with a degree of flexibility that is not possible when working with laboratory animals. For example, studies of breed differences can easily target specific breeds of interest, whereas studies of cognitive development or senescence can selectively recruit dogs of specific ages. Moreover, if researchers require dogs that are naïve to test procedures, they can easily recruit first-time visitors, whereas other experiments may benefit from enrolling seasoned and regular participants from previous studies. This ability to flexibly construct samples based on a study's optimal design is a luxury in animal research but one that is easily afforded by this research model.

Importantly, the scientific possibilities for working with pet dogs are not limited to strictly behavioral measures. For instance, the pioneering studies in dog functional magnetic resonance imaging (fMRI) were conducted with pet dog populations that were trained using positive reinforcement to remain motionless while unrestrained inside the scanner (Andics et al., 2014; Berns et al., 2012). Moreover, because dogs learn socially from both humans and conspecifics, researchers have been able to incorporate social learning as well as traditional operant techniques when training dogs to participate in these activities. For example, Andics et al. (2014) allowed novice dogs to observe experienced dogs being rewarded for performing the requisite behaviors in order to facilitate learning in an ethologically-relevant context.

In addition to these scientific benefits, this approach places a premium on dog welfare by selectively working with animals who live in their natural ecological environment, which for many dogs is a human family. Visits to campus-based research centers provide a fun outing both for dog owners and their canine companions, and can be used as a practical exercise for socializing a dog or visiting novel environments. Lastly, because these centers are not sequestered inside large biomedical facilities, they provide an ideal environment for humane education with school groups that visit to observe humane animal research in action. These visits provide an exceptional opportunity both to stimulate children's interest in scientific research and to illustrate the compassionate approach with which animal research should be conducted.

Shelters and Dog Daycare Centers

Research at animal shelters and daycare facilities shares many of the strengths of working with pet dogs at dedicated research centers, but also provides unique opportunities to promote animal welfare. From the researcher's perspective, these settings again create exceptional opportunities by allowing access to hundreds of animals that are not under the primary care or financial responsibility of the scientist. Most shelters and daycares have extra rooms typically used for visitation purposes, or outdoor play areas, which can easily accommodate behavioral research. Thus, like campus-based research centers, these facilities can support the vast majority of cognitive and behavioral research being done with domestic dogs.

However, behavioral research at shelters and daycare facilities comes with the added advantage that dogs receive supplemental social interaction and enrichment opportunities through their participation in science. These opportunities may be especially important in shelter settings, where overburdened staff struggle to provide animals with the level of attention they deserve. Through these collaborations, researchers receive access to animals and testing facilities in exchange for providing these animals with enriching social and problem-solving experiences (i.e., cognitive enrichment) that are vital to health and wellbeing (Clark, 2011; Clark & Smith, 2013; Herrelko et al., 2012; Manteuffel et al., 2009; Meehan & Mench, 2007; Yamanashi & Hayashi, 2011; Zebunke et al., 2013).

Lastly, cognitive research at animal shelters provides a window into the mental lives of these animals and has the potential to identify individuals at risk of affective or behavioral problems that may prevent successful rehoming. For example, in a test of cognitive bias, shelter dogs with separation-related problem behaviors exhibited a "pessimistic" bias compared to dogs without separation-related problems, potentially indicating more generalized negative affect (Mendl et al., 2010). Thus, in addition to their basic research value, cognitive and behavioral studies conducted at animal shelters have the potential to lead to a better understanding of how these environments impact psychological wellbeing and how to identify animals that may benefit from targeted interventions.

Collaboration with Working Dog Organizations

A third alternative strategy for research with dogs involves collaboration with working dog organizations who breed and train dogs for roles ranging from assisting individuals with disabilities to searching for explosives. Like research with shelters and daycares, conducting research with working dog populations accommodates studies where neither the subjects nor the testing facilities are on university campuses, reducing the logistical, financial, and welfare challenges of maintaining a dedicated research colony. Although working dogs are less commonly used in cognitive studies than pet dogs (Bensky et al., 2013), these populations offer several unique opportunities for cognitive and behavioral research (Bray et al., In press). First, unlike pet and shelter populations, working dog populations tend to be relatively homogenous due to the use of a limited number of breeds and selective breeding for a target phenotype within these breeds. In many research applications, this homogeneity is desirable because it reduces extraneous biological variation, permitting research designs with smaller sample sizes. Second, many working dog organizations have extensive veterinary facilities that can support the collection and processing of biological samples. Thus, in addition to behavioral research, collaborations with working dog organizations can accommodate a wide range of studies that may not be possible with pet or shelter dogs (e.g., MacLean, Gesquiere, Gee, et al., 2017; MacLean, Gesquiere, Gruen, et al., 2017). Third, due to their important roles in society, there are a variety of funding mechanisms available to support research with working dogs, ranging from major federal organizations (e.g., NIH, DoD) to private foundations (McCune et al., 2020). Similarly to collaborations with shelters, these sponsored projects have an element of mutualism in which researchers gain access to animals and can collect data on basic research questions while simultaneously generating data that can improve the practices through which working dogs are bred, trained, cared for, and selected for vocational roles. For example, in our research group, we have active collaborations with assistance and military working dog organizations to study individual differences in canine cognition. With respect to basic research, we are interested in the dimensions of variance underlying individual differences in dog psychology and whether individual differences in dogs resemble those in humans. At the applied level, we use data on individual differences to help predict which dogs will be successful as assistance or military working dogs (Bray et al., 2019; MacLean & Hare, 2018).

Canine Citizen Science

A final alterative to laboratory research with dogs is to engage the public in data collection, a process known as "citizen science" (Bonney et al., 2009; Cohn, 2008). In recent years, citizen science has led to major advances in fields ranging from ecology to astronomy by enlisting the public to record their observations of the natural world (Lintott et al., 2008; Silvertown, 2009). More recently, the citizen science approach has been expanded to projects in animal behavior (Hecht & Cooper, 2014), including multiple projects with domestic dogs. For example, "Project: Play With Your Dog" (Horowitz Dog Cognition Lab, Barnard College) draws on user-submitted videos of interspecific play to better understand the nature of human-animal interactions.

Citizen science can also include experimental research, including studies of dog cognition. For instance, the Dognition® platform allows dog owners to test their own dogs in short problem-solving tasks similar to those conducted by comparative psychologists. Users receive a web-based tutorial on how to conduct each task and enter their data in real-time through the site's user interface. Upon completion of the tasks–which are designed as games for animal participants–users discover their dog's unique strengths represented through one of nine possible cognitive profiles. Users can also navigate the website to compare their dog to others that have been tested, filtering results by factors such as age and breed group.

Data collection through citizen science has both strengths and weaknesses compared to a traditional approach. The primary weakness of citizen science is that the resulting data are more likely to contain errors than data collected by scientists themselves. However, this weakness can be mitigated through data screening procedures that assess inter-observer reliability or algorithms that flag questionable data for further review. Additionally, comparisons of data collected by citizen scientists have replicated many findings from conventional studies, supporting the validity of this approach (Stewart et al., 2015). With regard to strengths, citizen science allows researchers to collect data at a scale and pace that is impossible using traditional approaches. For example, in a study of breed differences, citizen scientists can provide data on hundreds of dogs of various breeds in a matter of weeks, whereas these data would take years to obtain through traditional methods (Gnanadesikan, Hare, Snyder-Mackler, & MacLean, 2020; Horschler et al., 2019; MacLean, Snyder-Mackler, vonHoldt, & Serpell, 2019; Watowich et al., In press). Consequently, findings from citizen science can play an important role in exploratory research by revealing trends in data that can subsequently be tested in more rigorous ways. Given the unique strengths and weakness of citizen science, we expect that this approach will provide an important complement, not replacement, to traditional research methods.

CHALLENGES FOR NON-TRADITIONAL RESEARCH MODELS

In this chapter, we have summarized a variety of approaches for conducting humane research with animals in non-traditional settings. While the benefits of these research models are vast–including significant advantages for animal welfare, the financial costs of research, and the quality and quantity of data that can be collected–alternative research models come with unique challenges that the researcher should be prepared to face. First, current regulatory systems (i.e., Institutional Animal Care and Use Committees [IACUCs]) were designed primarily for the oversight of research using animals owned by the scientist and maintained in research colonies on campus. One common element in all the approaches described above is that the researcher neither owns nor provides daily care for the animals she or he studies. At the same time, however, these research models involve experimental approaches precluding classification as a "field study" (which does not require IACUC oversight). Therefore, depending on whether research is conducted on campus or at a collaborating institution, research activities may be classified as "field research" or regulated as traditional laboratory studies. In all cases, because the animals are neither wild nor owned by the scientist, researchers should expect to develop memorandums of understanding (MOUs) between all collaborating parties, as well as informed consent procedures for individuals who volunteer their animals for research. Many challenges with respect to oversight may simply result from the novelty of these research arrangements, which do not fall neatly into extant regulatory categories. However, in our experience, IACUC representatives have been helpful in accommodating a wide range of approaches, and we expect these research models to become increasingly common with a future generation of scientists dedicated to humane research.

Second, conducting research with animals that the scientist does not own requires one to embrace the perspective that access to animals is a privilege, not a right. Although this perspective is universally important in work with animals, research conditions can be especially unpredictable in non-traditional settings. For example, changes in social group composition, veterinary appointments, and adoptions can all disrupt an ongoing study at inopportune moments. Researchers must be prepared to accept these minor setbacks, recognizing that they are considerably outweighed by the ultimate benefits of these research models.

Lastly, all the models we have discussed are based in a culture of mutualism, in which collaborating parties have unique but complementary interests, and each brings valuable resources to the collaboration. Therefore, researchers should expect to *give* as much as they *take* as a part of these arrangements. For example, in return for access to animals and testing facilities, researchers may be able to help their collaborators by donating excess medical equipment, analyzing data, or giving a public presentation. Ultimately, successful research collaborations depend not only on parties mutually interested in humane research but also in their desire to help one another more broadly.

CONCLUDING REMARKS

Throughout this chapter we have highlighted ways in which researchers can engage in humane research by stepping outside the traditional laboratory model. Although the examples we present focus specifically on strategies for research with great apes and domestic dogs, it is important to note that similar approaches can be adopted with many other species. Therefore, as comparative psychologists continue to broaden their taxonomic focus (MacLean et al., 2012; MacLean et al., 2014), we urge researchers to "think outside the lab" (Woods & Hare, 2010) when deciding how best to study a species. Ultimately, the best research models will be ones that prioritize not only high-quality science but also the welfare of the animals being studied.

References

Altevogt, B. M., Pankevich, D. E., Shelton-Davenport, M. K., & Kahn, J. P. (2011). *Chimpanzees in biomedical and behavioral research: Assessing the necessity.* National Academies Press.

Andics, A., Gácsi, M., Faragó, T., Kis, A., & Miklósi, Á. (2014). Voice-sensitive regions in the dog and human brain are revealed by comparative fMRI. *Current Biology, 24*(5), 574-578.

Andre, C., Kamate, C., Mabonzo, P., Morel, D., & Hare, B. (2008). The conservation value of Lola ya Bonobo sanctuary. In I. Takesi & J. Thompson (Eds.), *Bonobos revisited: Ecology, behavior, genetics, and conservation* (pp. 303-322). New York: Springer.

Baumans, V., Coke, C., Green, J., Moreau, E., Morton, D., Patterson-Kane, E., et al. (2007). *Making lives easier for animals in research labs.* Washington, DC: Animal Welfare Institute.

Beauchamp, T. L., & DeGrazia, D. (2019). *Principles of animal research ethics*: Oxford University Press.

Beck, B., Walkup, K., Rodrigues, M., Unwin, S., Travis, D., & Stoinski, T. (2007). *Best practice guidelines for the re-introduction of great apes.* Gland, Sweden: SSC PrimateSpecialist Group of the World Conservation Union.

Bensky, M. K., Gosling, S. D., & Sinn, D. L. (2013). The world from a dog's point of view: A review and synthesis of dog cognition research. *Advances in the Study of Behavior, 45,* 209-406.

Berns, G. S., Brooks, A. M., & Spivak, M. (2012). Functional MRI in awake unrestrained dogs. *PloS one, 7*(5), e38027.

Bonney, R., Cooper, C. B., Dickinson, J., Kelling, S., Phillips, T., Rosenberg, K. V., et al. (2009). Citizen science: A developing tool for expanding science knowledge and scientific literacy. *BioScience, 59*(11), 977-984.

Bowie, A., Krupenye, C., Mbonzo, P., Minesi, F., & Hare, B. (2020). Implicit measures help demonstrate the value of conservation education in the democratic republic of the congo. *Frontiers in psychology, 11,* 386.

Bray, E. E., Gruen, M., Gnanadesikan, G., Horschler, D. J., Levy, K., Kennedy, B. S., et al. (In press). Cognitive characteristics of 8-to-10-week-old assistance dog puppies. *Animal Behaviour.*

Bray, E. E., Levy, K. M., Kennedy, B. S., Duffy, D. L., Serpell, J. A., & MacLean, E. L. (2019). Predictive models of assistance dog training outcomes using the canine behavioral assessment and research questionnaire and a standardized temperament evaluation. *Frontiers in veterinary science, 6,* 49.

Calisi, R. M., & Bentley, G. E. (2009). Lab and field experiments: Are they the same animal? *Hormones and Behavior, 56*(1), 1-10.

Clark, F. E. (2011). Great ape cognition and captive care: Can cognitive challenges enhance well-being? *Applied Animal Behaviour Science, 135*(1), 1-12.

Clark, F. E., & Smith, L. J. (2013). Effect of a cognitive challenge device containing food and non-food rewards on chimpanzee well-being. *American journal of primatology, 75*(8), 807-816.

Clay, Z., Pika, S., Gruber, T., & Zuberbühler, K. (2011). Female bonobos use copulation calls as social signals. *Biology letters*, rsbl20101227.

Cohn, J. P. (2008). Citizen science: Can volunteers do real research? *BioScience, 58*(3), 192-197.

Farmer, K. H. (2002). Pan-African Sanctuary Alliance: Status and range of activities for great ape conservation. *American Journal of Primatology, 58*(3), 117-132.

Fischer, A., Prüfer, K., Good, J. M., Halbwax, M., Wiebe, V., André, C., et al. (2011). Bonobos fall within the genomic variation of chimpanzees. *PLoS One, 6*(6), e21605.

Fritz, J., Nash, L., Alford, P., & Bowen, J. (1992). Abnormal behaviors, with a special focus on rocking, and reproductive competence in a large sample of captive chimpanzees (pan troglodytes). *American Journal of Primatology, 27*(3), 161-176.

Gagneux, P., Moore, J. J., & Varki, A. (2005). The ethics of research on great apes. *Nature, 437*(7055), 27-29.

Gamble, K. C., Moyse, J. A., Lovstad, J. N., Ober, C. B., & Thompson, E. E. (2011). Blood groups in the Species Survival Plan®, European Endangered Species Program, and managed in situ populations of bonobo (pan paniscus), common chimpanzee (pan troglodytes), gorilla (gorilla ssp.), and orangutan (pongo pygmaeus ssp.). *Zoo biology, 30*(4), 427-444.

Garner, J. P., & Mason, G. J. (2002). Evidence for a relationship between cage stereotypies and behavioural disinhibition in laboratory rodents. *Behavioural Brain Research, 136*(1), 83-92.

Gnanadesikan, G. E., Hare, B., Snyder-Mackler, N., & MacLean, E. L. (2020). Estimating the heritability of cognitive traits across dog breeds reveals highly heritable inhibitory control and communication factors. *Animal Cognition*, 1-12.

Goldberg, T. L., Gillespie, T. R., Rwego, I. B., Wheeler, E., Estoff, E. L., & Chapman, C. A. (2007). Patterns of gastrointestinal bacterial exchange between chimpanzees and humans involved in research and tourism in western Uganda. *Biological Conservation, 135*(4), 511-517.

Goodall, J. (1986). *The chimpanzees of Gombe: Patterns of behavior*. Cambridge, Mass.: Belknap Press of Harvard University Press.

Goodall, J., Lonsdorf, E. V., Ross, S. R., & Matsuzawa, T. (2010). *The mind of the chimpanzee: Ecological and experimental perspectives*: University of Chicago Press.

Goossens, B., Setchell, J., Tchidongo, E., Dilambaka, E., Vidal, C., Ancrenaz, M., et al. (2005). Survival, interactions with conspecifics and reproduction in 37 chimpanzees released into the wild. *Biological conservation, 123*(4), 461-475.

Grimm, D. (2016). Chimpanzee sanctuaries open door to more research. *Science, 353*(6298), 433-434.

Gruber, T., Clay, Z., & Zuberbühler, K. (2010). A comparison of bonobo and chimpanzee tool use: Evidence for a female bias in the *pan* lineage. *Animal Behaviour, 80*(6), 1023-1033.

Hare, B. (2011). Improving animal housing and welfare. *ILAR Journal, 52*(Supplement), 463-467.

Hare, B., Brown, M., Williamson, C., & Tomasello, M. (2002). The domestication of social cognition in dogs. *Science, 298*(5598), 1634-1636.

Hare, B., Call, J., & Tomasello, M. (1998). Communication of food location between human and dog (*canis familiaris*). *Evolution of Communication, 2*(1), 137-159.

Hare, B., Melis, A. P., Woods, V., Hastings, S., & Wrangham, R. (2007). Tolerance allows bonobos to outperform chimpanzees on a cooperative task. *Current Biology, 17*(7), 619-623.

Hare, B., & Tomasello, M. (2005). Human-like social skills in dogs? *Trends in Cognitive Sciences, 9*(9), 439-444.

Hare, B., & Yamamoto, S. (2017). *Bonobos: Unique in mind, brain, and behavior*: Oxford University Press.

Hecht, J., & Cooper, C. B. (2014). Tribute to tinbergen: Public engagement in ethology. *Ethology, 120*(3), 207-214.

Herrelko, E. S., Vick, S. J., & Buchanan-Smith, H. M. (2012). Cognitive research in zoo-housed chimpanzees: Influence of personality and impact on welfare. *American journal of primatology, 74*(9), 828-840.

Herrmann, E., Call, J., Hernandez-Lloreda, M. V., Hare, B., & Tomasello, M. (2007). Humans have evolved specialized skills of social cognition: The cultural intelligence hypothesis. *Science, 317*(5843), 1360-1366.

Herrmann, E., Hare, B., Call, J., & Tomasello, M. (2010). Differences in the cognitive skills of bonobos and chimpanzees. *Plos One, 5*(8).

Herrmann, E., Hernandez-Lloreda, M. V., Call, J., Hare, B., & Tomasello, M. (2010). The structure of individual differences in the cognitive abilities of children and chimpanzees. *Psychological Science, 21*(1), 102-110.

Herrmann, E., Wobber, V., & Call, J. (2008). Great apes' (*pan troglodytes, pan paniscus, gorilla gorilla, pongo pygmaeus*) understanding of tool functional properties after limited experience. *Journal of Comparative Psychology, 122*(2), 220.

Horschler, D., Hare, B., Call, J., Kaminski, J., Miklósi, Á., & MacLean, E. (2019). Absolute brain size predicts dog breed differences in executive function and social cognition. *Animal Cognition, 22*(2), 187-198.

Idani, G. i., & Hirata, S. (2007). Studies at the Great Ape Research Institute, Hayashibara.

Jia, H., Pustovyy, O. M., Waggoner, P., Beyers, R. J., Schumacher, J., Wildey, C., et al. (2014). Functional MRI of the olfactory system in conscious dogs. *PloS one, 9*(1), e86362.

Jones, P., Cordonnier, N., Mahamba, C., Burt, F., Rakotovao, F., Swanepoel, R., et al. (2011). Encephalomyocarditis virus mortality in semi-wild bonobos (*pan panicus*). *Journal of medical primatology, 40*(3), 157-163.

Kaminski, J., Call, J., & Fischer, J. (2004). Word learning in a domestic dog: Evidence for "fast mapping". *Science, 304*(5677), 1682-1683.

Kano, T. (1992). *The last ape : Pygmy chimpanzee behavior and ecology.* Stanford: Stanford University Press.

Krief, S., Escalante, A. A., Pacheco, M. A., Mugisha, L., André, C., Halbwax, M., et al. (2010). On the diversity of malaria parasites in African apes and the origin of plasmodium falciparum from bonobos. *PLoS pathogens, 6*(2), e1000765.

Lintott, C. J., Schawinski, K., Slosar, A., Land, K., Bamford, S., Thomas, D., et al. (2008). Galaxy zoo: Morphologies derived from visual inspection of galaxies from the sloan digital sky survey. *Monthly Notices of the Royal Astronomical Society, 389*(3), 1179-1189.

Lopresti-Goodman, S. M., Kameka, M., & Dube, A. (2012). Stereotypical behaviors in chimpanzees rescued from the African bushmeat and pet trade. *Behavioral Sciences, 3*(1), 1-20.

Lucca, K., MacLean, E. L., & Hare, B. (2017). The development and flexibility of gaze alternations in bonobos and chimpanzees. *Developmental Science.*

MacLean, E., & Hare, B. (2013). Spontaneous triadic engagement in bonobos (pan paniscus) and chimpanzees (pan troglodytes). *Journal of Comparative Psychology.*

MacLean, E., Snyder-Mackler, N., vonHoldt, B., & Serpell, J. (2019). Highly heritable and functionally relevant breed differences in dog behavior. *Proceedings of the Royal Society B: Biological Sciences.*

MacLean, E. L. (2016). Unraveling the evolution of uniquely human cognition. *Proceedings of the National Academy of Sciences, 113*(23), 6348-6354.

MacLean, E. L., Gesquiere, L. R., Gee, N. R., Levy, K., Martin, W. L., & Carter, C. S. (2017). Effects of affiliative human-animal interaction on dog salivary and plasma oxytocin and vasopressin. *Frontiers in Psychology, 8*, 1606.

MacLean, E. L., Gesquiere, L. R., Gruen, M. E., Sherman, B. L., Martin, W. L., & Carter, C. S. (2017). Endogenous oxytocin, vasopressin, and aggression in domestic dogs. *Frontiers in Psychology, 8*, 1613.

MacLean, E. L., & Hare, B. (2012). Bonobos and chimpanzees infer the target of another's attention. *Animal Behaviour, 83*(2), 345-353.

MacLean, E. L., & Hare, B. (2018). Enhanced selection of assistance and explosive detection dogs using cognitive measures. *Frontiers in Veterinary Science, 5*, 236.

MacLean, E. L., Hare, B., Nunn, C. L., Addessi, E., Amici, F., Anderson, R. C., et al. (2014). The evolution of self-control. *Proceedings of the National Academy of Sciences*, E2140-E2148.

MacLean, E. L., Herrmann, E., Suchindran, S., & Hare, B. (2017). Individual differences in cooperative communicative skills are more similar between dogs and humans than chimpanzees. *Animal Behaviour, 126*, 41-51.

MacLean, E. L., Matthews, L., Hare, B., Nunn, C., Anderson, R., Aureli, F., et al. (2012). How does cognition evolve? Phylogenetic comparative psychology. *Animal Cognition, 15*(2), 223-238.

MacLean, E. L., Prior, S. R., Platt, M. L., & Brannon, E. M. (2009). Primate location preference in a double-tier cage: The effects of illumination and cage height. *Journal of Applied Animal Welfare Science, 12*(1), 73 - 81.

Manteuffel, G., Langbein, J., & Puppe, B. (2009). From operant learning to cognitive enrichment in farm animal housing: Bases and applicability. *Animal Welfare, 18*(1), 87-95.

Mason, G. J., Cooper, J., & Clarebrough, C. (2001). Frustrations of fur-farmed mink. *Nature, 410*(6824), 35-36.

Matsuzawa, T., Tomonaga, M., & Tanaka, M. (2006). *Cognitive development in chimpanzees*: Springer.

McCune, S., McCardle, P., Griffin, J., Esposito, L., Hurley, K., Bures, R., et al. (2020). Editorial: Human-animal interaction (HAI) research: A decade of progress. *Human-Animal Interaction (HAI) Research: A Decade of Progress.*

McIntyre, M. H., Herrmann, E., Wobber, V., Halbwax, M., Mohamba, C., de Sousa, N., et al. (2009). Bonobos have a more human-like second-to-fourth finger length ratio (2d:4d) than chimpanzees: A hypothesized indication of lower prenatal androgens. [Article]. *Journal of Human Evolution, 56*(4), 361-365.

Meehan, C. L., & Mench, J. A. (2007). The challenge of challenge: Can problem-solving opportunities enhance animal welfare? *Applied Animal Behaviour Science, 102*(3), 246-261.

Mendl, M., Brooks, J., Basse, C., Burman, O., Paul, E., Blackwell, E., et al. (2010). Dogs showing separation-related behaviour exhibit a 'pessimistic' cognitive bias. *Current Biology, 20*(19), R839-R840.

Miklósi, Á., Polgárdi, R., Topál, J., & Csányi, V. (1998). Use of experimenter-given cues in dogs. *Animal Cognition, 1*(2), 113-121.

Morimura, N., Idani, G. i., & Matsuzawa, T. (2011). The first chimpanzee sanctuary in Japan: An attempt to care for the "surplus" of biomedical research. *American Journal of Primatology, 73*(3), 226-232.

National Institutes of Health. (2011). Statement by NIH director Dr. Francis Collins on the Institute of Medicine report addressing the scientific need for the use of chimpanzees in research. From http://www.nih.gov/news/health/dec2011/od-15.htm

Nishida, T., Kano, T., Goodall, J., McGrew, W. C., & Nakamura, M. (1999). Ethogram and ethnography of Mahale chimpanzees. [Review]. *Anthropological Science, 107*(2), 141-188.

Nunn, C. L., & Hare, B. (2012). Pathogen flow: What we need to know. *American Journal of Primatology, 74*(12), 1084-1087.

Office of the Federal Register – National Archives and Records Administration. (2013). Announcement of agency decision: Recommendations on the use of chimpanzees in NIH-supported research. *Federal Register, 78*(127), 39741-39757.

Olsson, I. A. S., Nevison, C. M., Patterson-Kane, E. G., Sherwin, C. M., Van de Weerd, H. A., & Würbel, H. (2003). Understanding behaviour: The relevance of ethological approaches in laboratory animal science. *Applied Animal Behaviour Science, 81*(3), 245-264.

Ongman, L., Colin, C., Raballand, E., & Humle, T. (2013). The "super chimpanzee": The ecological dimensions of rehabilitation of orphan chimpanzees in Guinea, West Africa. *Animals, 3*(1), 109-126.

Peterson, D. (2003). *Eating apes* (Vol. 6): Univ of California Press.

Pilley, J. W., & Reid, A. K. (2011). Border collie comprehends object names as verbal referents. *Behavioural Processes, 86*(2), 184-195.

Pritchard, D. J., Hurly, T. A., Tello-Ramos, M. C., & Healy, S. D. (2016). Why study cognition in the wild (and how to test it)? *Journal of the Experimental Analysis of Behavior, 105*(1), 41-55.

Prüfer, K., Munch, K., Hellmann, I., Akagi, K., Miller, J. R., Walenz, B., et al. (2012). The bonobo genome compared with the chimpanzee and human genomes. *Nature, 486*(7404), 527-531.

Rosati, A. G., & Hare, B. (2011). Chimpanzees and bonobos distinguish between risk and ambiguity. *Biology Letters, 7*(1), 15-18.

Rosati, A. G., & Hare, B. (2012). Chimpanzees and bonobos exhibit divergent spatial memory development. *Developmental science, 15*(6), 840-853.

Rosati, A. G., Herrmann, E., Kaminski, J., Krupenye, C., Melis, A. P., Schroepfer, K., et al. (2013). Assessing the psychological health of captive and wild apes: A response to Ferdowsian et al.(2011).

Rose, A. (1998). Growing commerce in bushmeat destroys great apes and threatens humanity. *African Primates, 3*(1), 2.

Ross, S. R., Schapiro, S. J., Hau, J., & Lukas, K. E. (2009). Space use as an indicator of enclosure appropriateness: A novel measure of captive animal welfare. *Applied Animal Behaviour Science, 121*(1), 42-50.

Rowan, A. N. (1990). Refinement of animal research technique and validity of research data. *Fundamental and Applied Toxicology, 15*(1), 25-32.

Shutt, K., Heistermann, M., Kasim, A., Todd, A., Kalousova, B., Profosouva, I., et al. (2014). Effects of habituation, research and ecotourism on faecal glucocorticoid metabolites in wild western lowland gorillas: Implications for conservation management. *Biological Conservation, 172*, 72-79.

Silvertown, J. (2009). A new dawn for citizen science. *Trends in Ecology & Evolution, 24*(9), 467-471.

Stewart, L., MacLean, E. L., Ivy, D., Woods, V., Cohen, E., Rodriguez, K., et al. (2015). Citizen science as a new tool in dog cognition research. *PloS one, 10*(9), e0135176.

Stokes, R., Tully, G., & Rosati, A. (2018). Pan African sanctuary alliance: Securing a future for the African great apes. *International Zoo Yearbook, 52*(1), 173-181.

Tan, J., & Hare, B. (2013). Bonobos share with strangers. *PloS one, 8*(1), e51922.

Trayford, H. R., & Farmer, K. H. (2013). Putting the spotlight on internally displaced animals (IDAs): A survey of primate sanctuaries in Africa, Asia, and the Americas. *American Journal of Primatology, 75*(2), 116-134.

Wallis, L. J., Virányi, Z., Müller, C. A., Serisier, S., Huber, L., & Range, F. (2016). Aging effects on discrimination learning, logical reasoning and memory in pet dogs. *Age, 38*(1), 6.

Watowich, M., MacLean, E. L., Hare, B. A., Call, J., Kaminski, J., Miklósi, Á., et al. (In press). Age influences domestic dog cognitive performance independent of average breed lifespan. *Animal Cognition*.

Westin, J. L. (2017). Habituation to tourists: Protective or harmful. *Ethnoprimatology: A practical guide to research at the human-nonhuman interface*, 15-28.

Wobber, V., Hare, B., Lipson, S., Wrangham, R., & Ellison, P. (2013). Different ontogenetic patterns of testosterone production reflect divergent male reproductive strategies in chimpanzees and bonobos. *Physiology & Behavior, 116-117*, 44-53.

Wobber, V., Hare, B., Maboto, J., Lipson, S., Wrangham, R., & Ellison, P. T. (2010). Differential changes in steroid hormones before competition in bonobos and chimpanzees. *Proceedings of the National Academy of Sciences, 107*(28), 12457-12462.

Wobber, V., & Herrmann, E. (2014). The influence of testosterone on cognitive performance in bonobos and chimpanzees.

Wobber, V., Herrmann, E., Hare, B., Wrangham, R., & Tomasello, M. (2013). Differences in the early cognitive development of children and great apes. *Developmental Psychobiology, 56*(3), 547-573.

Wobber, V. T., & Hare, B. (2011). Psychological health of orphan bonobos and chimpanzees in african sanctuaries. *Plos One, 6*(6), e17147.

Woods, V., & Hare, B. (2010). Think outside the lab: African sanctuaries as a new resource for non-invasive research on great apes. In D. Mills (Ed.), *Encyclopedia of animal behavior and welfare*: CABI publishing.

Yamanashi, Y., & Hayashi, M. (2011). Assessing the effects of cognitive experiments on the welfare of captive chimpanzees (pan troglodytes) by direct comparison of activity budget between wild and captive chimpanzees. *American Journal of Primatology, 73*(12), 1231-1238.

Zebunke, M., Puppe, B., & Langbein, J. (2013). Effects of cognitive enrichment on behavioural and physiological reactions of pigs. *Physiology & Behavior, 118*, 70-79.

Figure 1. Bonobos at Lola ya Bonobo, Kinshasa, Democratic Republic of Congo. Large forested enclosures at African sanctuaries allow apes to forage and socialize under naturalistic conditions

.

CHAPTER ELEVEN

ANIMALS, PUBLIC POLICY AND HIGHER EDUCATION: A NEW FOCUS

Andrew N. Rowan, WellBeing International

The development of academic interest in animal protection, animal welfare, and what is now commonly referred to as the human-animal bond (HAB) is relatively recent, dating back to the 1970s in Europe and a little later in the U.S. Three groups of academics have played the dominant role in promoting and advancing these topics: animal behavior specialists (particularly those studying farm animal behavior), psychiatrists, and veterinarians. Of course, the interest in animal issues among university academics has arisen in part because of the growth of the animal protection movement and its increased political clout (see Figure 1).

UNIVERSITY CENTERS FOR ANIMAL STUDIES

As research into this topic has grown, a number of centers have sprung up at universities around the world, mostly at veterinary schools. Academic veterinary medicine has, together with farm animal welfare experts, played a major role in the development of the animal studies area, although many of the individuals who are currently leaders in the field (in terms of academic publications) are not veterinarians. The information in Table 1 illustrates the importance of the veterinary community in the early academic examination and promotion of the HAB.

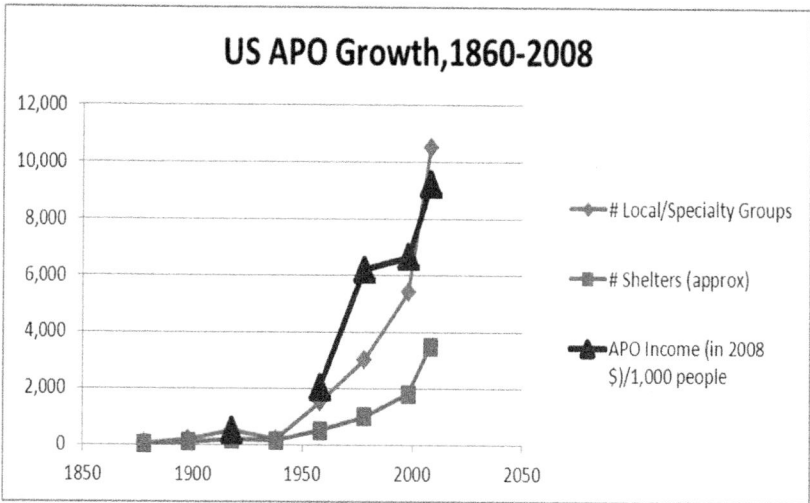

Figure 1. Increased size and support for animal protection issues (United States).

Curriculum offerings on the HAB appeared in the late 1970s and early 1980s in veterinary schools in Minnesota, Washington, and Pennsylvania, and the University of Edinburgh offered courses in animal welfare science. Yet such offerings were not that well-received by traditionalists. According to Hines (2003), when Leo Bustad started the People-Pet Partnership at Washington State and began his Reverence for Life class at the veterinary school, many faculty members disapproved because the field was peripheral to veterinary medicine. Elsewhere in the world, veterinary schools in Australia (Melbourne, Perth, and Queensland), the Netherlands (Utrecht), the United Kingdom (Glasgow and Cambridge), and the Swedish University of Agricultural Sciences (Uppsala) included animal behavior and people-pet relations in their core curricula.

However, despite the interest in HAB by some veterinarians and veterinary schools, most of academic veterinary medicine (and most students) did not perceive HAB as important enough to include in the formal curriculum. The Pew Veterinary Education program (in the early 1990s) required all the U.S. veterinary schools to undertake a strategic planning exercise. Of the 27 schools, only six referred to animal issues in their written strategic plans and, of these, three saw the topic of animal welfare solely as a threat. In other words, only 10% of the veterinary schools saw the possible opportunities (for them and their students) of engaging the topic of animal welfare and human-animal interactions. Pew subsequently funded a project at Tufts to develop a curriculum on the HAB, but less than half the schools viewed the subject as important enough to send a faculty member to a 1994 workshop at Tufts that described and delivered copies of a pre-packaged curriculum on HAB for veterinary students.

Table 1: Some Early Milestones in Animal Studies

YEAR	ORGANIZATION, CENTER or EVENT
1964	Ruth Harrison book, Animal Machines
1968	First Human-Animal Bond Conference, UK
1971	First book on Animal Ethics (Eds, Godlovitch, Godlovitch and Harris)
1974	Joint Advisory Committee on Pets in Society (JACOPIS, UK)
1976	Association Francaise d'Information et de Recherche sur l'Animal de Compagnie (AFIRAC, France)
1977	Institute for Interdisciplinary Research on the Human Pet Relationship (IEMT, Austria)
	Center on Interaction of Animals and Society, University of Pennsylvania
1979	Society for Companion Animal Studies, United Kingdom
1979	People-Pet Partnership, Washington State University
1980	Joint Advisory Committee on Pets in Society (JACOPIS, Australia)
1981	AVMA Task Force on the Human-Animal Bond.
	Institute for the Human-Companion Animal Bond, AMC, New York City
	Center to Study Human-Animal Relationships and Environments (CENSHARE, Univ. of Minnesota)
	First Farm Animal Welfare conference, Amsterdam – followed by significant EU funding of farm animal welfare studies
1982	Center for Applied Ethology and Human-Animal Interactions, Purdue University
1983	Center for Animals and Public Policy, Tufts University, MA
1984	Center for Animals and Society, UC Davis, CA

Note: Adapted from "Historical perspectives on the human-animal bond," by L. M. Hines, 2003, American Behavior Scientist, 47, p. 7-15.

Today, there are important animal studies programs at numerous universities and colleges (see Table 2 for a partial list).

Table 2: University Degree Programs on Animal Studies

University/College	Country	Degree/Topic	Comments
Brock University	Canada	Critical Animal Studies	
Canisius	USA	Anthrozoology	MS
Colorado State Univ	USA	Animality Studies	
Drury Univ	USA	Animal Studies	
Eastern Kentucky Univ	USA	Animal Studies	
Edinburgh Univ	UK	Animal Welfare	
Massey Univ	New Zealand	Animal Welfare	
Michigan State Univ	USA	Ecology & Culture	
New York Univ	USA	Animal Studies	
Tufts Univ	USA	Animals & Public Policy	MSc
Univ of Brit Columbia	Canada	Animal Welfare	MSc & PhD
Univ of Canterbury	New Zealand	Animal Studies	
Univ of Vienna	Austria	Animal Studies	
Univ of Wales	UK	Anthrozoology	
Uppsala University	Sweden	Animal Studies	
Wurzburg Univ	Germany	Literary Animal Studies	

PUBLISHING IN ANIMAL STUDIES

Degree programs are not the only index of the growth of academic interest in animal studies. Academic journals and publications are also important. Table 3 lists most of the academic journals that specialize in animal studies, together with their founding dates. Neither of the two journals that were established first survived, but the later journals are all still publishing, and a number (*Anthrozoos, Animals & Society,* and *Journal of Applied Animal Welfare Science and Animal Welfare*) are experiencing growing pains while general publications (like the Public Library of Science journals) are also publishing more papers in the field.

Table 3: Academic Journals Covering Animal Studies

Journal	Founding Date
Animal Regulation Studies, Elsevier (lasted 4 years)	1979
International Journal for the Study of Animal Problems (lasted 4 years)	1979
Agriculture & Human Values	1983
Between the Species	1983
Anthrozoos (Delta Society)	1987
Agriculture & Animal Ethics	1988
Animal Welfare (UFAW)	1992
Society & Animals (PsyETA)	1993
Journal of Applied Animal Welfare Science (PsyETA)	1998
Journal of Critical Animal Studies	2003
Antennae	2007
Humanimalia	2009
Animal Ethics	2011
Animals	2011

The number of academic books appearing in the field of animal studies has also exploded since 1970. Several publishers have produced successful series on animal studies such as the Reaktion Books series (featuring single word titles like *Tiger, Cockroach,* and so on). When I took on editing *Anthrozoos,* which the Delta Society journal launched in 1987, I was able to cover the entire field of animal studies and read most of the new and relevant books. Today, that is no longer remotely possible (see Figure 2).

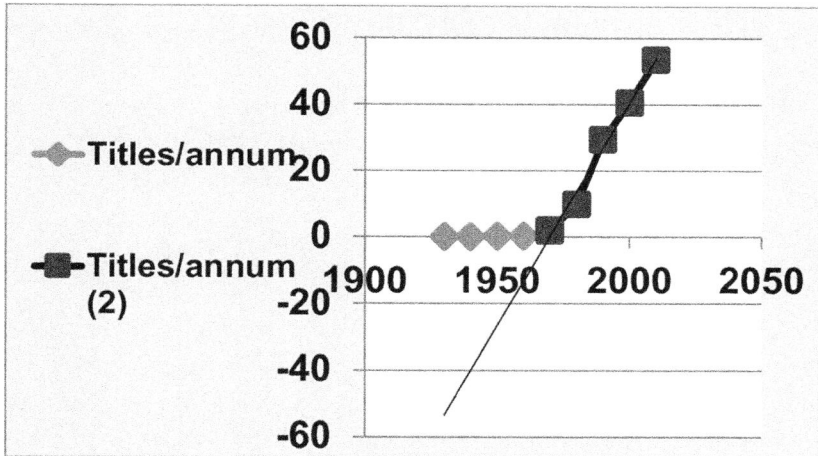

Figure 2. Number of academic books on animal studies appearing annually. The equation describing the trend line of the graph from 1970 to 2010 is $Y=1.342x - 2643.6$.

FUNDING FOR ANIMAL STUDIES

The majority of funding to establish and advance the field of animal studies has historically come from foundations and the pet food industry. Important early foundation donors were the Geraldine Dodge Foundation and the Island Foundation. Each provided hundreds of thousands of dollars to the University of Pennsylvania to establish their center and to Pennsylvania State University to support Dan Lago's studies on animal-assisted therapy, respectively. The pet industry also provided several million dollars during and around the 1980s to support human-animal bond research, a significant proportion of which ended up in the various veterinary school centers. But, by the mid-1990s, much of the corporate funding had disappeared. Mars has recently teamed up with the National Institute of Child Health and Development to provide several million dollars to support research on child-animal interactions.

Currently, there are five main sources of funding for the various university centers, but the total amounts available are relatively small by comparison with other successful academic centers. The five sources are the following:

- University/veterinary school support for faculty associated with animal studies (e.g., the Purdue University center)
- Foundation support (e.g., the Sir James Dunn center at the University of Prince Edward Island)
- Industry (e.g., animal protection, pet food, pet product, breed registration groups, and assistance animal programs) support
- Individual donors and bequests (e.g., the Animal Medical Center in New York City)
- Tuition income (e.g., Tufts University).

These sources do not include the major supporter of university health research: federal and state funds. At this time, I estimate that one probably needs a minimum of around $100,000 a year (in salary support and program funding) to maintain anything close to an active academic center. The more productive centers have "hard" money (departmental salaries, funds for equipment) and "soft" grant income of at least $250,000 a year. Overall, the various North American centers probably draw in a total of about $5 million a year in institutional and external support. When one considers that the U.S. companion animal market amounts to around $41 billion a year (Brady & Palmieri, 2007), the amount spent by the above centers on animal studies projects is tiny.

THE NEXT CHALLENGE:
DEVELOPING A HUMANE UNIVERSITY

Universities are important centers supporting innovation and expanding human understanding of the world around us. However, they are more than purveyors of education and supporters of research. They also contribute to the development of culture and a society's moral core. Many scholars, including Humboldt, Newman (19th century), and Robbins (1960s) all examined the role of universities and commented on their various roles in society. These roles include the following:

a) Teaching and research
b) Shaping national cultures and underpinning a national identity
c) Transmission of knowledge and the search for original truth
d) Serving economic innovation and growth

For a university or college to aspire to being a center for "humane" values and behaviors, it would need to establish an ethos and implement programs that value/embody the following:

- Individual growth, autonomy, and moral thinking
- Such growth should not be at the expense of/or in conflict with an enriching community
- A healthy and sustainable environment (sustainable energy, consumption, waste management, etc.)
- A recognition that the "community" includes more than just human inhabitants (building harmonious human-animal interactions)
- An understanding that the community extends not just to the immediate neighborhood, but to encompass the state, nation, and ultimately global health

The factors above, if incorporated into values and behaviors of the staff and students, will mean that such a university would need to do far more than pay attention to environmental sustainability and its energy footprint. Food choices and policy would have to be an essential component, as would the manner in which biomedical research is supported and conducted.

Conclusion

It is remarkable how much interest in human-animal issues has grown in the past 30 years. It is not beyond the bounds of possibility that a modern university could embrace an overall "humane" approach. Certainly, there are indications that there is sufficient student interest to sustain a "humane" university. Funding may be a challenge, but there are indications that there are donors who would enthusiastically support such a university. May this book inspire more conversations about humane universities and support the development of courses, departments, and campus policies and structures.

References

Brady, D., & Palmeri, C. (2007). The pet economy. *Business Week*. Retrieved from http://www.businessweek.com/magazine/content/07_32/b4045001.htm?campaign_id=nws_insdr_jul28&link_position=link1

Hines, L. M. (2003). Historical perspectives on the human-animal bond. *American Behavioral Scientist, 47*, 7-15.

PART FOUR
COURSE DESIGN AND SYLLABUS SAMPLES

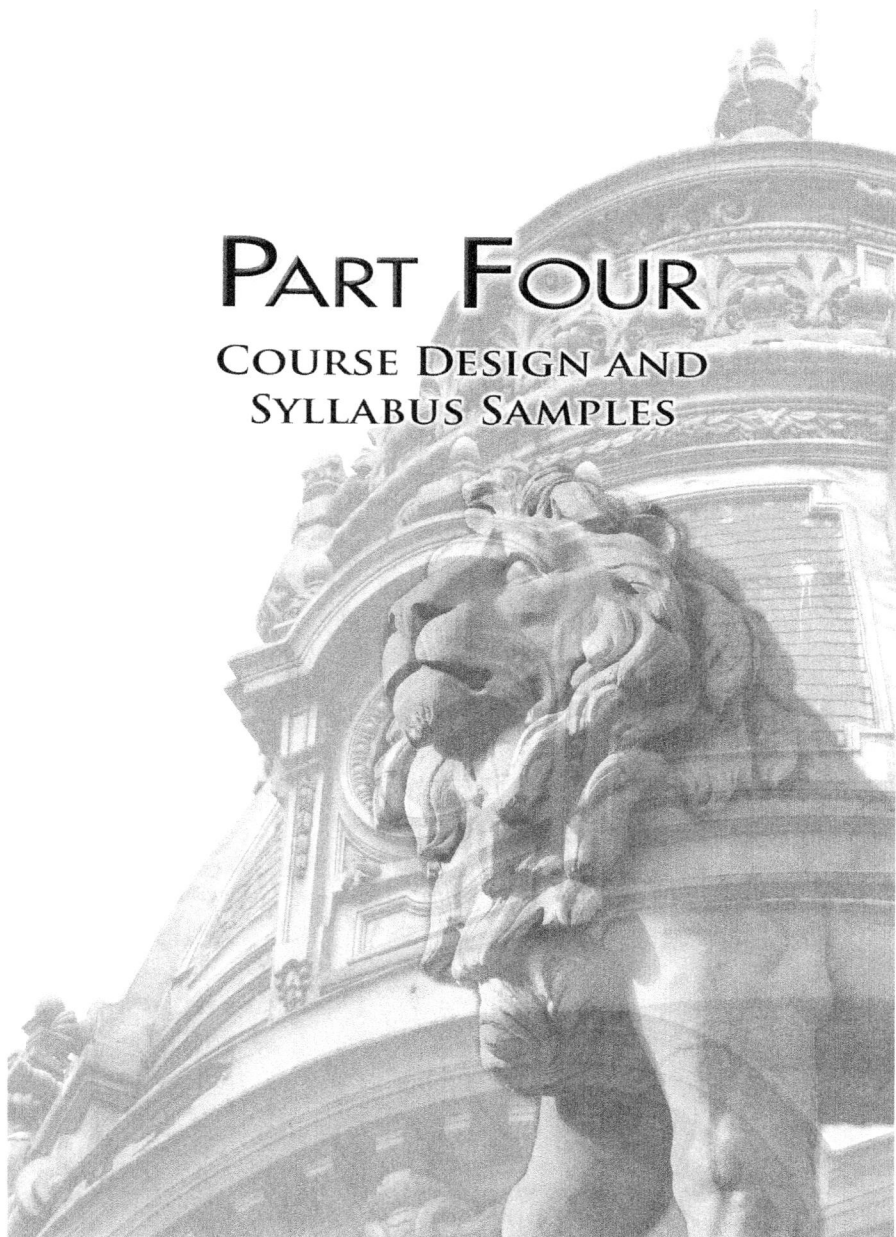

After reading this book, it is our hope that you are interested in offering a new course or thinking about infusing inclusive humane concepts into an existing one. This last section presents sample course overviews, syllabi, and service-learning development templates from a variety of inclusive humane education courses taught at the collegiate level.

Honors Seminar
University of Texas at San Antonio

Honors Seminar Online Humane Education, *Stephanie Itle-Clark*

This humane education course was taught to undergraduate learners through the Honors College at the University of Texas in San Antonio. The goal of the class was to help students learn about inclusive humane education, relate the ways humane education connects to other prosocial frameworks, recognize ways to introduce humane education content into various careers and programs, and to complete a service-learning project with a local charity. The class partnered with San Antonio Youth (SA Youth). SA Youth empowers San Antonio's high-risk youth and young adults to achieve their full potential by providing quality educational programming in a safe environment. The class and SA Youth staff worked together to create a humane education summer camp that was piloted by SA Youth the summer of 2018. The curriculums were written to help youth ages 6 to 13 learn about animal safety, animal care, and the human-animal bond. Each curriculum is a three-hour, week-long camp with extensions that can provide up to two additional hours of material. However, the individual learning activities in each lesson can be stand-alone lessons or projects. The full set of curriculums can be found at https://www.prosocialacademy.org/resources.

Due to this being an Honors Seminar class, the student population included mixed majors. When students worked in groups to create the summer camp materials, the instructor ensured that each group had an education major present.

HON-3233-005-Spring-2018-
HonSem: Online Humane
Education Term: Spring 2018

Faculty Information:

Instructor: Stephanie Itle-Clark

Course Meeting Time: M 6-8:45 PM CT (See each lesson to determine if there is a live meeting, we will not meet live every week)

Office hours: Wednesday and Thursday 3:30-6:30 PM CT (4:30 -7:30 PM ET); Available by phone for scheduled appointments at other times

Will respond to emails and discussion posts within 24 hours – If you need me, reach out and we will make time!

Course Site: Blackboard

Live Meetings: Log in and choose your audio (phone or computer) and turn on your camera

Course Description: Do you want to help shape the future? Interested in promoting empathy and compassion for animals? Learn about humane education (the teaching of empathy and perspective to support compassion for people, animals, and the environment) and help us develop the first UTSA Summer Animal Camp for kids! In this class, we will focus specifically on animal welfare education and humane education activities that support development of positive behaviors. Discover how stories, role-play, and experiential learning activities can help children develop an understanding of other people and animals, critical thinking skills, and prosocial behaviors–and then put this knowledge to use by working as a team to create a summer camp curriculum. Students will begin the course by discussing child development and appropriate content as it relates to moral development and critical thinking strategies for our targeted camp age group. Students will also research various animal welfare issues that can be taught during the camp. Using the knowledge gained in the first portion of the class, students will create a final project of an age-appropriate activity which will be used during the camp.

We will try to arrange site visits to practice a lesson from the curriculum with our partner later in the term. This will be arranged as the partner is available. The last half of the course will have more flexibility to make that happen.

Students who completed Humane Education (part 1 - Fall 2017) and this course, Humane Education (Part 2 - Spring 2018) are eligible to earn Certified Humane Education Specialist (CHES) credentials from the Academy of Prosocial Learning. If you take both courses, you will work with the instructor at the end of this term to complete the credential paperwork.

Student Learning Outcomes:

Students will be able to:

- Relate the ways humane education connects to other prosocial frameworks and recognize ways to introduce humane education content into curriculum.
- Describe, discuss, and analyze the way stories and questions build perspective and critical thinking.
- Distinguish between higher-order thinking questions and lower-order or leading questions.
- Compose a unit of study and teaching strategies that provide opportunity for age-appropriate humane pedagogy and prosocial learning focused on animal welfare education. (Specifically companion animal care and welfare issues.)
- Apply principles, skills, and strategies gained to instruction and personal humane pedagogy.

Grading and Assignments:

Class Participation
This is an online, instructor-mediated course in which you are expected to "attend" class by participating in the live meetings and by logging into the course and making substantive postings and/or completing assignments as outlined in the syllabus. Lessons will begin Mondays. Class participation will be measured in several ways.

First, your attendance will be recognized through your contributions to the postings. For each discussion forum, please post a minimum of two times. One post should be original and one a response to class-mates. Second, the quality of your postings will shape your participation grade. To fully benefit from and contribute to the course, you should raise questions that stimulate discussion about aspects of the readings or the comments of the instructor or classmates. You should actively share thoughts based on your ideas and experiences. More details on netiquette and appropriate postings will be provided as necessary.

For each discussion week, you will be able to earn 12 points. See attached Discussion Post Rubric for details. Briefly, posts will be graded on a scale from 3 to 0 as follows:

1. 3 points – an excellent post is analytical, integrates reading, and furthers discussion
2. 2 points – a good post shows familiarity with topic and responds to instructor or classmate's questions or comments on the week's topic
3. 1 point – a poor post does not show familiarity with reading beyond classmate's comments or is off-topic.

Students who do not make substantive posts will receive a reduced score for each missing post. Students are encouraged to make more than two posts per week. For grading, the instructor will look at the combined strength of the posts among a student's discussion board contributions.

Course assignments are the additional components of course grad-ing. Each lesson will contain a quiz or assignment. If the assignment is a larger one, then it will be marked as receiving a higher weight and this will be noted in the course platform.

If you face difficulties in during a particular week (e.g. family emer-gencies, illness), please inform me immediately. Accommodations may be made for you to complete a comparable assignment. However, I urge students to make every effort to participate regularly in class.

Writing Expectations:

Students are to reference course material in their discussions, as well as outside resources they know of or find during each lesson. All writing is to be completed using the APA format. The Purdue OWL Writing Lab is the best source for up-to-date APA style information https://owl.english.purdue.edu/owl/section/2/10. If you have trouble, please contact me prior to submitting assignments.

Grade Distribution:

Five Lessons – 56%
Presentation – 10%
Participation/Reflection – 12%
Quizzes and Assignments – 22%

NOTE: There is an optional site visit to San Antonio Youth on either 1/23, 1/24, 1/25. You may sign up for one of the days. Carpooling is encouraged and if transportation is an issue, a university vehicle will be attending. You may sign up for any day, sign up will be done in Blackboard and we need to know when you are attending by 1/17/2018.

LESSON ONE: (1/08/2018-1/14/2018) WHAT IS HUMANE EDUCATION? AND LET'S GET OUR PROJECT STARTED!

Activities and Readings:
Live class meeting: 1/08/2018 6:00-8:45 PM CT

Agenda:

1. Introductions and Housekeeping
2. Lecture and Discussion – What is humane education?
3. Presentation – Who is our partner organization? What animal welfare issues are most common in their population?
4. Discussion – Optional Site Visit 1/23, 1/24, 1/25 from 5:00 PM – 6:00 PM CT
5. Introduce the structure of our final project and choose groups (you will choose ONE group, groups are first-come, first-filled) Five-day flexible curriculum and a pre-/post-test based on your chosen topic.

Review the following items in the Blackboard platform between

1/08/2018 and 1/14/2018:

1. Download Syllabus
2. Complete Lecture Element–Welcome (and corresponding SA Youth goal link)
3. Complete Lecture Element–Humane Education and Humane Pedagogy Overview
4. Read–Humane Education: A Way to Empower Youth, Enhance Humane Behaviors, and Promote Animal Welfare
5. Complete Lecture Element–Knowing What is Age-Appropriate Content and Making Lessons that Create Change
6. Read–Developmentally Appropriate Activities, Piaget's Cognitive Development Theory, and Stages of Development Reading (3 items)
7. Complete Assignment Element

Assignments:
Complete the following assignments:

1. Assignment #1 – Choose your group; group sign-up sheets are in Blackboard You may have up to four student members per group and groups are first-come, first-filled
2. Assignment #2 – Discussion Forum: We selected our groups this week! These are the topics about which you will write your one-week curriculum and pre-and post-test. What do you think will be the most difficult part of making this topic fit the age group outlined by our partner organization? Why? Incorporate course references as well as outside materials and use APA style to cite references. (Original response due by 11:59 PM CT 1/12/2018; response to a classmate extending the conversation due by 11:59 PM CT 1/14/2018.)

Assignment #1 is due by 11:59 PM CT 1/14/2018 or a group will be assigned to you; Assignment #2 first post is due by 11:59 PM CT 1/12/2018 and the second post is due by the end of Lesson One 11:59 PM CT 1/14/2018.

Lesson Two: (1/15/2018-2/04/2018) Research Your Topic, Interview the Experts, and Present Your Findings

Activities and Readings:
No live meeting

Agenda:

Review the following items in the Blackboard platform between 1/15/2018 and 2/04/2018:

1. Complete Lecture Element – Researching Your Group Topic and Creating a Presentation
2. Read – Group Appropriate Resource Sheet (Found on Your Group Page and Main Course Site)
3. Complete Element – Writing Unit Learning Outcomes (the main learning goal for all five lessons combined)
4. Optional Read- Culturally Competent Educators file:///G:/Cuturally%20Competent%20educators.pdf (This may be repeat if you took last term's class, but it is important for those who did not take last term's class to think about as you prepare lessons for a varied audience.)

Assignments:
Complete the following assignments:

1. Assignment #1 – quiz on content from Lesson One and Two
2. Assignment #2 – Learning Goals: In your group, create the main learning outcomes or goals you wish to teach in your curriculum. These are the goals for your overall unit of study, not for each lesson. We will work on those in later weeks. Aim for one or two big goals. I will help you in your group forum, make sure the group starts thinking about it early, so we can go back and forth on ideas before the end of the lesson.
3. Assignment #3 – Prepare your Group Presentation (Complete research using the Group Resource Sheet and by interviewing your expert contact. Your goal for Lesson Two is to become our class experts and share a presentation on 2/05/2018 in our live class

meeting. In your presentation, it is expected that all group members will contribute in some way. See the rubric in Blackboard for grading specifics and requirements.)

4. Assignment #4 – Private Journal: In the journal folder title your submission "Lesson Two __Your Name__ Journal" and answer the following question. (Question: What has been the most surprising thing that you learned about your topic?)

Assignments #1, #2, and, #4 are due at the end of Lesson Two, 11:59 PM CT 2/04/2018; Assignment #3 is due 2/05/2018 in live meeting.

LESSON THREE (2/05/2018-2/11/2018) THE POWER OF A GOOD STORY, STANDARDS, AND PUTTING YOUR CURRICULUM TOPICS IN ORDER

Activities and Readings:
Live class meeting: 2/05/2018 6:00-8:45 PM CT

Agenda:

1. Groups present overview of their topic and their learning outcome(s) for the unit
2. Lecture and Discussion – picking your story and designing your curriculum overview

Review the following items in the Blackboard platform between 2/05/2018 and 2/11/2018:

1. Complete Lecture Element – The Power of Story in Creating Affective and Behavior Change
2. Complete Lecture Element – Scaffolding Knowledge
3. Complete Lecture Element – Standards and the 40 Developmental Assets

Assignments:
Complete the following assignments:

1. Assignment #1 – Develop your lesson topic ideas for the full week (five days). As a group, agree on and create five topics, in a sequential order, scaffold the ideas so they connect. Along with your ideas for the five days, include the story you think you can include. These will be worked on and then submitted in your group forum for the assignment.
2. Assignment #2 – Discussion Forum: In the full class discussion forum (located in Lesson Three folder), answer the question about stories and why they are powerful. Incorporate course references, as well as outside materials, and use APA style to cite references. (Original response due by 11:59 PM CT 2/09/2018; response to a classmate extending the conversation due by 11:59 PM CT 2/11/2018.)
3. Assignment #3 – Private Journal: In the journal folder title your submission "Lesson Three __Your Name__ Journal" and answer the following question. (Question: Why did your group choose the five topics they did? Was there another topic your group wanted to include, but was not sure how to do so?)

Assignments #1 and #3 are due at the end of Lesson Three; Assignment #2 first post is due by 11:59 PM CT 2/09/2018 and the second post is due by the end of Lesson Three.

LESSON FOUR (2/12/2018-2/25/2018) LESSON ONE DRAFT AND GOOD QUESTIONS

Activities and Readings:
Live class meeting: 2/12/2018 6:00-8:45 PM CT

Agenda:

1. This is an optional meeting where I will be online to answer any questions or to help groups put ideas together.

Review the following items in the Digital Chalk platform:

1. Complete Lecture Element – Questions that Extend Thinking
2. Complete Lecture Element – Cognitive, Affective, Psychomotor, and Conation
3. Read – Helping Learners Care: Conation as An Important Factor of Mind http://www.edpsycinteractive.org/topics/conation/conation.html
4. Complete Lecture Element – Putting Lesson One Together (Learning Outcomes; How Is it Written; Curriculum Template)
5. Read – Types of Questions

Assignments:
Complete the following assignments:

Agenda:

1. Assignment #1 – Draft of Lesson One

Your submission must include the following (scoring of each section is noted):
a. Title of the lesson: /3
b. The learning objective (goal) of your lesson: /12
c. Grade level: /3
d. Subjects included: /6
e. Opening: /12
f. Lesson Body: /30 (Lesson Body and Closure will include the questions verbatim and show where they are to be asked. The questions are part of the score.)
g. Closure: /17
h. Extension: /17
i. Possible standards (TEKS): BONUS /+10

Complete the Lesson One draft as a group and submit in the Blackboard folder called Lesson Four Assignment #1. Due at the end of Lesson Four (2/25/2018). You may use the private group forum called "Lesson One" to share ideas.

2. Assignment #2 – Discussion Forum: In this lesson we learned about the way questions help connect the affective domain to conation, or

the desire to act. Describe a time when you learned about an issue and knew you wanted to do something to take action. What made you move beyond having a feeling about the topic and helped you to get active? Incorporate course references as well as outside materials and use APA style to cite references. (Original response due by 11:59 PM CT 2/20/2018; response to a classmate extending the conversation due by 11:59 PM CT 2/25/2018.)

3. Assignment #3 – quiz on content from Lesson Three and Lesson Four (in Blackboard platform)

Assignments #1 and #3 are due at the end of Lesson Four; Assignment #2 first post is due by 11:59 PM CT 2/20/2018 and the second post is due by the end of Lesson Four.

Lesson Five (2/26/2018-3/11/2018)
Lesson Two and Pre-Test

Activities and Readings:
No live meeting

Agenda:

Review the following items in the Blackboard platform between 10/16/2017 and 10/30/2017:

1. Complete Lecture Element-Student-Centered Learning Revisited
2. Read – Student Centered Learning: It Starts with the Teacher https://www.edutopia.org/blog/student-centered-learning-starts-with-teacher-john-mccarthy and 1 PDF in course
3. Complete Lecture Element – Starting the Pre-and Post-Tests: Why and How Ours Will Look
4. Read – Pre-Test – Post-test Design and Measurement of Change http://cehd.gmu.edu/assets/docs/faculty_publications/dimitrov/file5.pdf
5. Download – Pre-Test/Post-Test Template

Assignments:
Complete the following assignments:

1. Assignment #1 – Draft of Lesson Two

Your submission must include the following (scoring of each section is noted):

a. Title of the lesson: /3
b. The learning objective (goal) of your lesson: /10
c. Grade level: /3
d. Subjects included: /5
e. Possible standards (TEKS): /14
f. Opening: /10
g. Lesson Body: /30 (Lesson Body and Closure will include the questions verbatim and show where they are to be asked. The questions are part of the score.)
h. Closure: /15
i. Extension: /15

Complete the Lesson Two draft as a group and submit in the Blackboard folder called Lesson Five Assignment #1. Due at the end of Lesson Five (11:59 PM CT 3/11/2018). You may use the private group forum called "Lesson Two" to share ideas.

2. Assignment #2 – Private Journal: In the journal folder title your submission "Lesson Five __Your Name__ Journal" and answer the following question. (Question: How is the lesson writing process going? What is going well/less well?)

3. Assignment #3 – Pre-Test/Post-Test: Use the course template to begin your pre-test and post-test for the first two lessons. Use the lesson learning objectives as your guide. More detail will be provided in the Lesson Five Assignment #3 folder. This item is due at the end of Lesson Six (11:59 PM CT 3/25/2018).

Assignment #1 and #2 are due at the end of Lesson Five. Assignment #3 is due 3/25/2018.

Lesson Six (3/12/2018-3/25/2018) Lesson Three

Activities and Readings:
No live meeting

Agenda:

Review the following items in the Blackboard platform:

1. Complete Lecture Element – Refresher on Keeping Bias Out of the Lessons
2. Read – The Influence of Teaching http://www.agi.harvard.edu/projects/TeachingandAgency.pdf
3. Complete Lecture Element – Setting up a Site Visit (to test lesson one!) – do between 3/19-4/20

Assignments:
Complete the following assignments:

1. Assignment #1- Draft of Lesson Three

Your submission must include the following (scoring of each section is noted):
a. Title of the lesson: /3
b. The learning objective (goal) of your lesson: /10
c. Grade level: /3
d. Subjects included: /5
e. Possible standards (TEKS): /14
f. Opening: /10
g. Lesson Body: /30 (Lesson Body and Closure will include the questions verbatim and show where they are to be asked. The questions are part of the score.)
h. Closure: /15
i. Extension: /15

Complete the Lesson Three draft as a group and submit in the Blackboard folder called Lesson Five Assignment #1. Due at the end of Lesson Six (3/25/2018). You may use the private group forum called "Lesson Three" to share ideas.

2. Assignment #2 – Private Journal: In the journal folder title your submission "Lesson Six __Your Name__ Journal" and answer the following question. (Question: What has been the hardest part about keeping the unit lessons age appropriate? In what ways have

you realized that a teacher has more influence on a learner than that of pure knowledge imparted?)
3. Assignment #3 – Pre-Test/Post-Test (started in Lesson Five): Use the course template to begin your pre-test and post-test for the first two lessons. Use the lesson learning objectives as your guide. Submit in the Lesson Five Assignment #3 folder. This item is due at the end of Lesson Six (3/25/2018).

Assignment #1, #2, and #3 are due at the end of Lesson Six (3/25/2018).
NOTE: We will be contacting San Antonio Youth to arrange a visit and time to pilot one lesson.

Lesson Seven (3/26/2018-4/08/2018) Lesson Four

Activities and Readings:
No live meeting

Agenda:

1. Complete Lecture Element – Testing Your Lesson (pre-test, teach, post-test)
2. Complete Lecture Element – Managing the Pre- and Post-Test to Reduce Educator Influence
3. Complete Lecture Element – Classroom Management
4. Read – Classroom Management Tips

Assignments:

1. Assignment #1- Draft of Lesson Four

Your submission must include the following (scoring of each section is noted):
a. Title of the lesson: /3
b. The learning objective (goal) of your lesson: /10
c. Grade level: /3
d. Subjects included: /5
e. Possible standards (TEKS): /14

f. Opening: /10
g. Lesson Body: /30 (Lesson Body and Closure will include the questions verbatim and show where they are to be asked. The questions are part of the score.)
h. Closure: /15
i. Extension: /15

Complete the Lesson Four draft as a group and submit in the Blackboard folder called Lesson Four Assignment #1. Due at the end of Lesson Seven (4/08/2018). You may use the private group forum called "Lesson Four" to share ideas.

2. Assignment #2 - quiz on content from Lesson Six and Lesson Seven (in Blackboard platform)

LESSON EIGHT (4/09/2018-4/22/2018) LESSON FIVE

Activities and Readings:
Live class meeting: 4/09/2018 6:00-8:45 PM CT

Agenda:

1. Group discussion and review of the five lessons and preparing the final copy!!

Review the following items in the Blackboard platform:

1. No recorded content this lesson. Focus on completing Lesson Five and preparing the whole curriculum, making all edits as needed (as a group) and getting it into format for final submission in Lesson Nine.

Assignments:
Complete the following assignments:

1. Assignment #1 – Draft of Lesson Five

Your submission must include the following (scoring of each section

is noted):
a. Title of the lesson: /3
b. The learning objective (goal) of your lesson: /10
c. Grade level: /3
d. Subjects included: /5
e. Possible standards (TEKS): /14
f. Opening: /10
g. Lesson Body: /30 (Lesson Body and Closure will include the questions verbatim and show where they are to be asked. The questions are part of the score.)
h. Closure: /15
i. Extension: /15

Complete the Lesson Five draft as a group and submit in the Blackboard folder called Lesson Five Assignment #1. Due at the end of Lesson Eight (4/08/2018). You may use the private group forum called "Lesson Five" to share ideas.

2. Assignment #2 –Submit overview of Pre- and Post-test results from site visit
3. Assignment #3: Private Journal: In the journal folder title your submission "Lesson Eight __Your Name__ Journal" and answer the following question. (Question: Describe the process of visiting the site to test an hour of your first lesson. Detail who attended, who led which part of the lesson, etc. Also, describe how the students responded. What went well? What would you do differently next time?)

Assignments #1, #2, and #3 are due at the end of Lesson Eight 11:59 PM CT 4/22/2018.

LESSON NINE (4/23/2018-5/4/2018) FINAL PRODUCTS IN EDITED FORM AND REFLECTIONS DUE

Activities and Readings:
No live meeting

Agenda:

1. Complete Lecture Element – Final curriculum presentation overview

Assignments:
Complete the following assignments:

1. Assignment #1 – Final edited version of the curriculum submission (submit in Word format via Blackboard in the provided forum.) Due at the end of Lesson Nine by 11:59 PM CT 5/4/2018. Curriculums must include five lessons in the required template (one of which is designed around a book or story.) See rubric in Lesson Nine for details of scoring, etc.
2. Assignment #3 – Pre- and Post-Test for the group in final edited version (submit in Word format via Blackboard in the provided forum.) Due at the end of Lesson Nine by 11:59 PM CT 5/4/2018. See Lesson Nine Assignment #3 folder for details of scoring.
3. Assignment #3 – Private Journal: Personal reflections on the process. May be written, in video, or in audio. These presentations will be submitted in Blackboard in the Lesson Nine Reflection Forum. Specifics will be provided in the Lesson Nine Assignment #3 Course Folder.

Assignments #1, #2, and #3 are due at the end of Lesson Nine 11:59 PM 5/04/2018.

Required Texts

No text is required for this class.
Links for selected readings and resources will be provided as applicable to the content each lesson.

SERVICE-LEARNING IN HIGHER EDUCATION INSTITUTIONS—FOSTERING HUMAN-ANIMAL INTERACTIONS THROUGH SERVICE-LEARNING BABE-BOLYAI UNIVERSITY

Animal Psychology
Alina Simona Rusu

Institutions of higher education often include service-learning as a means to support learning and personal growth related to civic and social issues. Service-learning tasks students to work as a team, to communicate, and to acquire and practice new skills.

An overview of the course Animal Psychology was presented at the Service-Learning in Higher Education conference in 2020, organized as a dissemination event within the SLIHE Erasmus project (www.slihe.eu). SLIHE project is co-funded by the European Union under the Erasmus+ Program and is designed to foster the third mission of universities and promote civic engagement of students. The template below was provided to attendees at SLIHE and can be utilized by institutions and educators as they develop core components of course content and build partnerships.

The Day of Human-Animal Interaction event (i.e. ZIOA in Romanian language) is a community-oriented event/service-learning program organized twice per year by the School of Psychology and Sciences of Education (Babe-Bolyai University, Cluj-Napoca) and the School of Veterinary Medicine (University of Agricultural and Veterinary Sciences, Cluj-Napoca), in collaboration with several local agencies in the field of animal-assisted activities, animal rescue and inclusive services for persons with special needs, as well as student organizations. Each ZIOA edition gathers together more than 100 student participants and more than 500 community members (with or without their companion animals). The spring edition of ZIOA is organized indoors at the Museum of Zoology and the Vivarium of Babes-Bolyai University on the day marking the start of Animal Psychology class for undergraduate students in Psychology. The summer edition of ZIOA is organized outdoors at the School of Veterinary Sciences (a short walking distance from the Central Park of Cluj-Napoca) on the June 1 and it marks the International Day of Children.

The main goal of this SL program is to engage the students in promoting the responsible ownership and to facilitate the development of favorable attitudes toward animals and nature, by involving the community members in a series of activities, such as: free counseling on the management of human-animal interactions, dog dancing, free therapeutic interactions with dogs and horses, free riding lessons for children, educational workshops on adoption and rehabilitation of animals, sensorial exercises with animals, meaningful and thematic face-painting, parade of the animals (including animals with disabilities), agility exercises, free educational visits of the Zoology Museum with service dogs, and workshops on the needs of companion animals (including exotic pets). Entrance to the event is free. ZIOA is highly mediatized (TV, radio, written media) and it is considered a brand of community-oriented events of Cluj-Napoca city. Students are expected to:

- learn how to communicate with community partners
- advocate for animal rights as sentient beings
- design awareness campaigns and materials for promoting responsible ownership and optimal human-animal and human-nature interactions.

[See charts next page.]

Co-funded by the
Erasmus+ Programme
of the European Union

Develop a structure of recommendation and unified structure for collecting examples of good practice

Babeș-Bolyai University

Template for examples of good practice of courses with SL component

Institutional Data *(Where is the example taking place? With what kind of support in place?)*	**University/Faculty/Department** **(name, short/basic info, web)**	Babeș-Bolyai University/ School of Psychology and Sciences of Education/ Department of Psychology https://psiedu.ubbcluj.ro
	Study Programme / Level **(undergraduate/graduate/postgraduate)**	Undergraduate/ Psychology, second year
	Community Partner(s) **(name, short/basic info, web)**	Romanian Association of Psychology Students – ASPR Student Organization for Nature – OsPN Local and regional NGOs in the area of animal protection, wildlife conservation and human-animal interactions in education and therapy: iCare, NUCA, Arca lui Noe, Angel Dog, SOR, Zoological Museum, Viarium of Babes-Bolyai University, Animal Society, Angel Dogs Satu-Mare, WWF Romania, Descoperă Natura. Dog training schools: Pet Joy Sports Cluj-Napoca

		Pet owners from the community of Cluj-Napoca
		The social media link for the program can be found here: https://www.facebook.com/Ziua-Interactiunii-Om-Animal-Day-of-Human-Animal-Interactions-527797154073739/
	Scope of the practice/engagement (local/regional/national/global)	Local and regional
	Support resources at the institutional/organisational (community partners') level	Approval and support from the universitary consortium in the field of human-animal interactions (Babeș-Bolyai University and University of Agricultural Sciences and Veterinary Medicine). Approval for the location of the SL program by the currator of Zoological Museum of Babes-Bolyai University and the executive director of the Vivarium BBU. Collaboration contracts in the field of education and placement of students for internships and field education with most of the NGOs involved.
	Type of the university/professor - organisation/partner relationship (formal/non-formal/contracts signed?)	Formal and non-formal
Good practice/ course data	**Course/project name (title)**	**Animal Psychology**/ Day of Human-Animal Interactions (in Romanian language: Ziua Interacțiunii Om-Animal #ZIOA)

	ECTS credit points (if applicable)	4 ECTS
(Who is engaged and how? How is their engagement/cont ribution evaluated? Where/at what places did the learning take place?)	Year(s) of previous implementation // Starting for the first time?	7 years
	Teacher's/professor's years of experience in SL	7 years
	Short summary of the course/project	The Day of Human-Animal Interaction event (i.e. ZIOA in Romanian language) is a community-oriented event/ Service-Learning program organized twice per year by the School of Psychology and Sciences of Education (Babeș-Bolyai University, Cluj-Napoca) and the School of Veterinary Medicine (University of Agricultural and Veterinary Sciences, Cluj-Napoca), in collaboration with several local agencies in the field of animal-assisted activities, animal rescue and inclusive services for persons with special needs, as well as student organizations. Each ZIOA edition gathers together more than 100 student participants and more than 500 community members (with or without their companion animals). The spring edition of ZIOA is organized indoors at the Museum of Zoology and the Vivarium of Babes-Bolyai University on the day marking the start of Animal Psychology class for undergraduate students in Psychology. The summer edition of ZIOA is organized outdoor at the School of Veterinary Sciences (at short walking distance from the Central Park of Cluj-

Napoca) on June 1 and it marks the International Day of Children.

The **main goal** of this SL program is to engage the students in promoting responsible ownership and to facilitate the development of favorable attitudes toward animals and nature by involving community members in a series of activities, such as: free counseling on the management of human-animal interactions, dog dancing, free therapeutic interactions with dogs and horses, free riding lessons for children, educational workshops on adoption and rehabilitation of animals, sensorial exercises with animals, meaningful and thematic face-painting, parade of the animals (including animals with disabilities), agility exercises, free educational visits of the Zoology Museum with service dogs, and workshops on the needs of companion animals (including exotic pets). The entrance to the event is free. ZIOA is

Main course goals / learning outcomes
highly mediatized (TV, radio, written media) and it is considered a brand of community-oriented events of Cluj-Napoca city. Students are expected to: learn how to communicate with community partners, advocate for animal rights as sentient beings and design awareness campaigns and materials for promoting responsible ownership and optimal human-animal and human-nature interactions.

Methods of engaging students
Working directly with users and community members.

Methods of assessing students' engagement	Reflective questions on prosocial and civic attitudes related to involvement in the SL program, presentations of individual activities (blogs, educational video materials, posters).
Scope of community partners' engagement	Connection of community partners with students and academic staff, visibility of NGOs activity and of their offers to students based on the identified needs (e.g.,, work at the shelter, awareness campaigns, part- or full-time employement opportunities).
Methods of evaluating/assessing community partners' engagement	Positive responses in terms of participation to each edition of the Day of Human-Animal Interactions and diversification of the activities involving the students.
Technology enhanced SL course/project?	
YES/NO – using online management tools, portfolio systems etc.?	no

	Follow-up on the SL course/project – **what has happened later with the** **course? Students? Community partners?** **Any new collaboration(s) as a result?** **new projects? Was it one-time only** **collaboration or sustained one?**	The SL project had become a brand of the community-oriented activities of students in Cluj-Napoca city, but also an example of SL good practice at national level. Invitations have been issued by national HEIs and other NGOs to organize in partnership this type of program in their own locations.

Several students continue their involvement in working with the community partners after the closure of the Day of Human-Animal Interactions.

The project has now reached the 19th edition, so it is a sustained one. |
| **"Livestream"** **data** **(What do those** **engaged have to** **say about it?** **What data is** **available for** **interested** **public?)** | **Students' statements** | Students reported to be highly motivated by making a difference in the community.

In the assessment questionnaire of the SL project, most of the students indicated that they felt that the activity was meaningful and connected with the curricular content. |
| | **Teachers' statements** | |

Community members' statements	The community partners are looking forward to participating and collaborating with the new generations of students in each edition of the Day of Human-Animal Interactions. Some students have founded their own NGOs in the field of animal protection after the participation to this community-oriented project.
University management statements	The project is fully supported by the University and it is included in the official annual reports as one of the programs fostering the community engagement of students.
Photos & Videos (if available)	http://clujescu.ro/2019/05/31/zioa-ziua-interactiunii-om-animal https://ilikecluj.ro/28-februarie-ziua-interactiunii-om-animal https://cluj.com/articole/1-martie-cluj-ziua-interactiunii-om-animal https://www.usamvcluj.ro/index.php/galerie-foto/16-galerie-foto/806-zioa-2017-2 https://www.facebook.com/Ziua-Interactiunii-Om-Animal-Day-of-Human-Animal-Interactions-527797154073739 https://www.youtube.com/watch?v=d3_rPHubvf4&t=171s
Social Networks (if available)	https://www.facebook.com/Ziua-Interactiunii-Om-Animal-Day-of-Human-Animal-Interactions-527797154073739

Available data/references – e.g., any available data related with the SL course/project on national language and/or English language? Was case-study already published?

Service learning in higher education 2017-1-SK01-KA203-035352

This project is co-funded by the European Union

Criminal Justice and Sociology
Iona College

Species Justice: Animals and Criminal Justice
Kimberly Spanjol

This undergraduate course is currently part of the studies at Iona College and it examines the animal protection socio-political movement, including global issues impacting animals and justice for them, as well as definitions, causes, and extent of animal suffering and exploitation, with a focus on solutions. We will explore theoretical orientations that explain the psychological, social, political, cultural, spiritual and economic forces that drive our relationships with non-human animals as well as the legislation and legal frameworks that criminalize practices that harm animals and their enforcement—or unfortunately, don't. The course also encourages students to grapple with, and determine, their own ethics regarding non-human animals and examines ways in which humans, animals, and ecosystems can be protected for the good of all while developing techniques for learning and teaching about complex issues in a positive manner that invites dialogue and positive change.

IONA
COLLEGE
School of Arts & Science

Species Justice: Animals and Criminal Justice
CRJ 342A
Fulfills department major/general elective

Semester/Year: Spring 2020
Meeting Days & Times: Tuesday, Thursday and Friday, 11-11:52 am
Location: Murphy Center 132
Instructor's Name: Dr. Kimberly Spanjol

Course Description:

This course examines the animal protection socio-political movement, including global issues impacting animals and justice for them, as well as definitions, causes, and extent of animal suffering and exploitation with a focus on solutions. We will explore theoretical orientations that explain the psychological, social, political, cultural, spiritual and economic forces that drive our relationships with non-human animals, as well as the legislation and legal frameworks that criminalize practices that harm animals and their enforcement—or don't.

We will use case studies to critically analyze problems and enforcement methods and you will take direct action through a project centered on a topic of your choice. We will focus on solution-oriented approaches, balancing the study of species justice and its challenges with action toward creating sustainable and restorative systems that benefit non-human animals, humans, and the earth. We will seek multiple solutions for these complex challenges, and aim to build your capacity for critical thinking and advocating for change. Discussions of issues impacting non-human animal issues will include agribusiness, poaching, experimentation, hunting and trapping, companion animal concerns, and more. The course explores different philosophies regarding the treatment of sentient beings, exploring rights, responsibility, care and liberation.

The course also encourages students to grapple with, and determine, their own ethics regarding non-human animals and examines ways in which humans, animals, and ecosystems can be protected for the good of all while developing techniques for learning and teaching about complex issues in a positive manner that invites dialogue and positive change.

Consider these quotes as we move through the course:

"The greatness of a nation and its moral progress can be judged by the way its animals are treated" – Mahatma Gandhi

"We should have respect for animals because it makes better human beings of us all" – Jane Goodall

"We need another and a wiser and perhaps a more mystical concept of animals ... For the animals shall not be measured by man. In a world older and more complete than ours, they move finished and complete, gifted with extensions of the senses we have lost or never attained, living by voices we shall never hear. They are not brethren, they are not underlings; they

are other nations, caught with ourselves in the net of life and time, fellow prisoners of the splendour and travail of the earth." – Henry Beston, The Outermost House

"The reason I dedicate myself to helping animals so much is that there are already so many people dedicated to hurting them." – unknown

Course Student Learning Outcomes (SLOs):

Upon successful completion of this course, students are expected to...

Course SLO Narrative	Department SLO	Method(s) of Course SLO Assessment
• Demonstrate critical thinking skills in regard to philosophical foundations and theories regarding the treatment of non-human animals	• critical thinking skills (i.e.; the ability to apply logic to any problem) • problem-solving skills (the ability to analyze and seek a solution to any problem) • commitment to ethical decision making • commitment to the principles of justice and fairness • commitment to integrity and professionalism	Weekly readings and written responses Class discussions Service project and presentation Final paper
• To be able to explain process and procedures regarding the treatment and protection of non-human animals related to social issues and the criminal justice system.	• effective communication skills (both oral and written) • critical thinking skills (i.e., the ability to apply logic to any problem) • problem-solving skills (the ability to analyze and seek a solution to any problem)	Weekly readings and written responses Class discussions Service project and presentation Final paper
• Evaluate and critique our relationships with non-human animals in society, including the criminal justice system, and protecting non-human animals from harm	• effective communication skills (both oral and written) • critical thinking skills (i.e., the ability to apply logic to any problem) • problem-solving skills (the ability to analyze and seek a solution to any problem) • knowledge/understanding of criminal law and procedure associated with the operations and practices (related to non-human animals) • commitment to ethical decision making • commitment to the principles of justice and fairness • commitment to integrity and professionalism	Weekly readings and written responses Class discussions Service project and presentation Final paper

Required Texts/Source Materials:

1) Cusack, C.M.. (2015). Animals and criminal justice. New Brunswick (U.S.A.) and London (U.K.): Transaction Publishers.
2) Additional assigned readings will be posted to Blackboard

Grading Criteria & Assessment Information:

*****Weekly Reading Responses (30%):** Prior to each class week by Tuesday 11am, you will submit a short response paper on Blackboard (300-500 words) that briefly discusses your reaction to ALL of the assigned weekly readings. You will be graded Pass/Fail at the end of the semester. You should also have access to your response in class so you can draw on it during the discussion that day.

*****Attendance/Participation:** ATTENDANCE AND PARTICIPATION MATTERS IN THIS CLASS! Be prepared for in-class discussions with TWO questions and TWO comments for EACH Assigned Reading (you will be called on to share randomly). Please see item #4 under Instructor's Course Policies & Procedures section below for more details on how your attendance and participation grade will be calculated.

Extra Credit Opportunities: All extra credit opportunities will require a written assignment to be completed and handed in UNLESS OTHERWISE NOTED. Extra credit assignment guidelines are posted on Blackboard under the "assignments" tab. Any Animal Welfare Coalition Club event can be attended and written up for extra credit for this course.

There will also be a number of extra credit opportunities that will not require a written assignment, but you will need to sign an attendance sheet, pay attention (not be on your phone, etc.) and stay the ENTIRE TIME for credit These opportunities will be posted and updated in Blackboard under a separate "Extra Credit" tab.

Please mark your calendars for extra credit opportunities available to you and take advantage of them–they can make a big difference for your final grade. After I total your final course grade, I will look at the number of extra credits you have completed–however, extra credit is EXTRA and will not substitute for fulfilling course requirements.

Course Outline – subject to change. Updates to the course outline will be made and posted on Blackboard.

Please note: We will likely focus on some topics more than others depending on class interest and we may fall behind the syllabus in our class discussions–continue to complete your weekly readings and responses assignment on Blackboard as listed on the syllabus, regardless of where we may be in class discussions.

REMEMBER: Be sure to read the assigned materials and complete your assignments prior to the week they are assigned! You must be prepared with at least two discussion questions AND two excerpts of each reading to comment on in class as part of your participation grade requirements.

Week of	Topic	READING/ASSIGNMENT DUE
		IMPORTANT:
		1) If a link I provide you for the reading no longer works, simply Google the article name and author to find it online!
		2) There will be a number of speakers visiting us this semester. You will be required to complete and post a speaker reflection on Blackboard for each. IT IS EXTREMELY IMPORANT TO ATTEND CLASS ON ALL DAYS, BUT PARTICULARLY WHEN WE HAVE A SPEAKER! Speaker schedule will be posted and updated as needed on Blackboard.
		3) Please note that the Cusack Textbook chapter readings are typically short. Assigned page numbers for your readings are roughly the same week to week.
Week 1 JAN. 21, 23, 24	Course Introduction Review syllabus, Assignments, Course content	**READ:** 1) Cusack Chapter 1: Introduction to Animals in Human Society 2) NY Times Opinion: What does it mean to be human? Don't ask: https://www.nytimes.com/2018/08/20/opinion/what-does-it-mean-to-be-human-dont-ask.html (Posted in Blackboard under course content) **DO:** 1) Buy textbook

	Criminal Justice/ Speciesism and Interspecies Ethics	3) Complete first MOGO questionnaire and Animal Attitude Assessment posted on Blackboard under "Assignments." Please email to me. Note: You must copy and email me your answers submitted to the Animal Attitudes Questionnaire. **DUE Tuesday, Jan. 28 by 11am.**
Week 2 **JAN. 28, 30, 31**	Animals and Criminal Justice/ Speciesism and Interspecies Ethics (continued)	**Tuesday, Jan. 28 last day to add/drop/swap classes** READ: 1) Is there such a thing as prejudice toward animals? By Scott Prous pp. 509-525 https://secure.understandingprejudice.org/pdf/animals.pdf (posted under Course Content in Blackboard) 2) Animals, Equality and Democracy Ch. 2 – The politics of being a non-human animal pp. 25-36 (posted under Course Content in Blackboard) **DO**: 1) Post 300-500 word weekly reading reaction on Blackboard
Week 3 **FEB. 4, 6,7**	Speciesism (cont.) Expanding Empathy Toward Non-Human Animals	**READ:** All also posted under Course Content in Blackboard): 1) Yancy, G. and Singer, P. (2015). Peter Singer: On racism, Animal Rights and Human Rights. New York Times. Retrieved from: https://opinionator.blogs.nytimes.com/2015/05/27/peter-singer-on-speciesism-and-racism/ 2) How to Be a Good Creature (posted in Blackboard under Course Content) – Ch. 4 Clarabelle pp. 62-79 3) Empathy article: https://www.nytimes.com/2015/07/12/opinion/sunday/empathy-is-actually-a-choice.html **DO**: 1) Post 300-500 word weekly reading reaction on Blackboard
Week 4 **FEB 11, 13, 14**	Animal Control/ Historical Treatment of Animals in Criminal Justice/ Animals and the Law	**READ:** 1) Cusack – Chapter 9, 13 2) https://www.forbes.com/sites/andreamorris/2018/11/19/judge-grants-historic-case-on-whether-an-elephant-is-a-person/#7513f590cda2 3) https://newrepublic.com/article/146870/law-recognizes-animals-people 4) https://www.cnn.com/2019/11/09/world/sandra-orangutan-florida-home-trnd/index.html **DO:** 1) Post 300-500 word weekly reading reaction on Blackboard **WATCH:** In-class viewing and discussion of *Unlocking the Cage* (Required viewing for your film assignment)

Week 5 **FEB. 18, 20, 21**	Animal Mistreatment and LINK Violence	**No class meeting TUESDAY, FEB 18, CLASSES FOLLOW MONDAY SCHEDULE**

No class meeting Thursday, Feb 20 Your readings are heavier because no class Feb 20.

READ: 1) Cusack Chapter 7, 12, and 16

2) National Link Coalition. What is the link? Retrieved from: http://nationallinkcoalition.org/what-is-the-link

3) Animal Cruelty as a Gateway Crime pp. 1-19 (Posted under in Course Content in Blackboard)

DO: 1) Post 300-500 word weekly reading reaction on Blackboard

Week 6 **FEB 25, 27, 28**	Animal Mistreatment and LINK Violence (cont.)	**READ**:

1) Murdering Animals by Piers Bierne pp. 21-38 and 197-203 (Posted under course content in Blackboard)

2) https://www.aspca.org/animal-protection/nypd-partnership

3) Explore the Animal Legal Defense Fund website and state rankings of animal cruelty laws https://aldf.org/
https://aldf.org/how_we_work/criminal-justice/
https://aldf.org/project/2018-us-state-rankings/

DO: 1) Post 300-500 word weekly reading reaction on Blackboard–note where your home state ranks on ALDF's website

Week 7 **MARCH 3, 5, 6**	Multiple Animals	**READ**:1) Cusack – Chapter 17

2) ASPCA (2017). A closer look at puppy mills. Retrieved from https://www.aspca.org/animal-cruelty/puppy-mills/closer-look-puppy-mills

DO: 1) Post 300-500 word weekly reading reaction on Blackboard

WATCH: In-class viewing of Oprah Winfrey Puppy Mill Episode (Required for your short film assignment)
https://www.youtube.com/watch?v=yMK4dpMfc5c (45:20).

Week 8 **MARCH 10,12,13**	Crimes Against Wildlife	**DUE:** Friday, March 15: **Submit one-page proposal (hard copy, in class) on CHOICE OF SERVICE PROJECT for presentation/final paper. See Blackboard for assignment guidelines. Daily points off final project for late submissions.**

READ:1) Following the Weapons: Rhino Poaching
https://www.nytimes.com/2018/12/25/us/politics/rhinos-poachers-south-africa-czub.html

2) Explore the Conflict Awareness Project website and include in your weekly reaction:

https://www.conflictawareness.org

3) They're like the Mafia: The supergangs behind Africa's poaching crisis
https://www.theguardian.com/environment/2017/aug/19/super-gangs-africa-poaching-crisis

4) The psychology and thrill of trophy hunting: Is it criminal?
https://www.psychologytoday.com/us/blog/animal-emotions/201510/the-psychology-and-thrill-trophy-hunting-is-it-criminal

5) Optional for extra credit: National Geographic: Dark World of the Rhino Horn Trade:
https://www.nationalgeographic.com/magazine/2016/10/dark-world-of-the-rhino-horn-trade/

DO: 1) Post 300-500 word weekly reading reaction on Blackboard

WATCH: In-class viewing of An Apology to Elephants (HBO)

Week 9 **MARCH 17, 19, 20**		**NO CLASSES, SPRING BREAK, MONDAY MARCH 16-FRIDAY MARCH 20**

Week 10 **MARCH 24, 26, 27**		**NO CLASSES March 24, 26, 27** – No classroom meetings. I will be presenting at the Academy of Criminal Justice Sciences Annual Conference this week. **READ:**

1) Palm oil is destroying rainforests. But try to go a day without it. https://www.msn.com/en-gb/lifestyle/spotlight/palm-oil-is-destroying-rainforests-but-try-going-a-day-without-it/ar-BBQXgz2?ocid=sf

DO: 1) Post 150-300 word weekly reading reaction on Blackboard (shorter this week as you only have one article assigned and have a paper due)

WATCH: 1) VICE (2016). Indonesia's palm bomb – required (VICE on HBO: Season 3, Episode 6) Retrieved from: https://www.youtube.com/watch?v=7xOPKI169SU . Watch from 14:00 to 28:46 (Required for short film paper)
   2) Watch the Film Earthlings and write reflection paper. Details are posted in Blackboard under "Assignments"– due Tuesday, March 31

Available for free: http://www.nationearth.com (1hr 35 min)

Week 11 **MARCH 31,** **APRIL 2,3**	Farmed Animals/Animal Agriculture/Agribusiness	**READ:** 1) DeMello, M. (2012). Animals and Society. Ch. 7 – The making and consumption of meat – pp. 132-144 ONLY. Posted in Blackboard under course content.

2) Robbins, J. (2010). The pig farmer. John's Blog. Retrieved from: https://www.johnrobbins.info/the-pig-farmer

3) Kaye, R. (2017). Gatsby's rescue from a dog meat farm changed my life. CNN. Retrieved from: https://www.cnn.com/2017/06/23/opinions/how-rescuing-gatsby-from-dog-meat-farm-changed-my-life-opinion-kaye/index.html
4) McWilliams, M. (2013). Why fish no longer escape our conscience. Free From Harm. Retrieved from https://freefromharm.org/?s=why+we+have+no+compassion+for+fish

DO: 1) Post 300-500 word weekly reading reaction on Blackboard

DUE: Tuesday March 31 – email me Earthlings reflection paper by 11am

WATCH: In-class viewings of:

Joy, M. (2015). The Secret Reason We Eat Meat (18:03).
(required for short film paper)
https://www.youtube.com/watch?v=ao2GL3NAWQU
Mercy for Animals (2016). Farm to Fridge
https://mercyforanimals.org/farm-to-fridge-changing-lives-helping-animals (15:29).

Week 12	Violence as Entertainment	**NO CLASS Thursday, April 9 Holy Thursday or Friday, April 10 Good Friday**
APRIL 7,9,10		**Tuesday, April 7 Service Project Topics and presentation schedule will be finalized**

READ: 1) Cusack Chapter 2

2) The NYC circus ban is just the beginning:

https://www.huffingtonpost.com/entry/the-nyc-circus-ban-is-just-the-beginning_us_594b4c39e4b092ed90588bb

DO: 1) Post 300-500 word weekly reading reaction on Blackboard

Week 13	Marine Animals	**Wednesday, April 15 is last day to withdraw from classes with a "W" grade**
APRIL 14,16,17		

READ:

1) How to Be a Good Creature (posted in Blackboard under Course Content) – Ch. 9 Octavia pp. 141-161

2) Pages 6-26 only of Bondaroff, T, van der Werf, W. & Reitano, T. (2015). The illegal fishing and organized crime nexus: Illegal fishing as transnational organized crime. The Global Initiative Against Transnational Organized Crime and The Black Fish. https://www.unodc.org/documents/congress/background-information/NGO/GIATOC-Blackfish/Fishing_Crime.pdf

DO: 1) Post 300-500 word weekly reading reaction on Blackboard

Week 14	Lab Animals/Animal Testing/ Animals Used for Clothing	**READ**:
APRIL 21,23,24		

1) DeMello, M. (2012). Animals and Society. Ch. 9 – Animals and Science, pp. 171-192. Posted in Blackboard under course content.
2) PETA: Animals Used for Experimentation. https://www.peta.org/issues/animals-used-for-experimentation
3) Animals in Science Policy Institute. Greer, C. Human organs on chips: A promising future for health care without animal testing. https://www.animalsinscience.org/blog/human-organs-on-chips-a-promising-future-for-healthcare-without-animal-testing/
4) PETA: Animals Used for Clothing. https://www.peta.org/issues/animals-used-for-clothing/
5) Roberts, A. (2018). Confused about cruelty: The Canada Goose story. https://www.huffpost.com/entry/confused-about-cruelty-th_b_14421002

DO: 1) Post 300-500 word weekly reading reaction on Blackboard

Week 15 APRIL 28, 30 MAY 1	Animal Welfare and Animal Rights/ Animal Activism	**READ**: 1) Cusack Chapter 10 2) DeMello, M. (2012). Animals and Society. Ch. 19 – The Animal Protection Movement, **pp. 407-417 ONLY.** Posted in Blackboard under course content. 3) Animal activists face a possible 60-year prison sentence for "open rescue" of piglets Retrieved from: https://meaww.com/animal-activists-direct-action-everywhere-the-smithfield-five-felony-charges **DO:** 1) Post 300-500 word weekly reading reaction on Blackboard **WATCH:** in class Animal People (2019) https://www.imdb.com/title/tt2337280 (Required for film paper)
Week 16 MAY 5, 7, 8	Canine Officers/ Service Animals in the CJS/ Animals in Corrections and Rehabilitation	**Thursday, May 7:** **Final Paper DUE – POINTS OFF FOR LATE SUBMISSION** **Friday, May 8 Last Day of Classes** **READ**: Cusack Ch. 4, 6, 8 **DO:** 1) Post 300-500 word weekly reading reaction on Blackboard **FINAL EXAM: No in-class final exam. Your last assignments due by the date and time of the final exam to be emailed to me are:** 1) **Final film paper and** 2) **Final MOGO questionnaire and online animal attitudes survey (I need a copy of your survey questions)** **Final exam date TBA – Day Final Exams Begin Monday, May 11 and end Friday, May 15**

Department Mission Statement

The Department of Criminal Justice is dedicated to nurturing ethical and skilled decision makers, developing problem solvers who embrace diversity and are committed to providing quality service to all segments of the community, and producing independent thinkers for whom the goals of justice and fairness are paramount. These hallmarks of a criminal justice education at Iona will be achieved through a program that considers critical issues in the field from an interdisciplinary perspective in a true liberal arts tradition. In furtherance of this mandate, the Department of Criminal Justice will ensure that our graduates:

- Section A: are not only familiar with all components of the criminal justice system, from both a theoretical and practical perspective, but have been taught to question existing practices and procedures in search of more effective and viable alternatives
- Section B: have a thorough appreciation of the nature and causes of crime, recognizing in particular how strong families, stable communities, effective schools, and reductions in violence and poverty are integral to any crime prevention initiatives and programs
- Section C: have an appreciation for the myriad social, political, legal and ethical concerns embedded in complex criminal justice issues
- Section D: not only have a complete understanding of criminal law (both substantive and procedural) but also appreciate how fair and equal treatment under the law is essential to the American system of criminal justice
- Section E: consider themselves professionals whose integrity is beyond reproach and who are committed to treating both victims and offenders with respect and dignity
- Section F: are equipped with excellent communication skills, both oral and written, as well as the technological expertise necessary to access, analyze and utilize information.

Success in our mission will ensure that Iona criminal justice graduates are well positioned for many diverse careers in the field.

Department Goals

Consistent with this stated mission, the Department has identified an array of specific learning goals that must be achieved by our students.

These include:

- effective communication skills (both oral and written)
- critical thinking skills (i.e., the ability to apply logic to any problem)
- problem-solving skills (the ability to analyze and seek a solution to any problem)

- technological skills necessary to access, analyze and utilize information
- knowledge/understanding of substantive criminal law
- knowledge/understanding of criminal procedure and constitutional legal issues associated with the operations and practices of the criminal justice system
- knowledge/understanding of the criminal justice system and its processes, both in theory and in practice
- knowledge/understanding of the nature and causes of crime
- knowledge of effective crime prevention and control measures
- commitment to ethical decision making
- commitment to the principles of justice and fairness
- commitment to integrity and professionalism.

AUTHOR BIOGRAPHIES

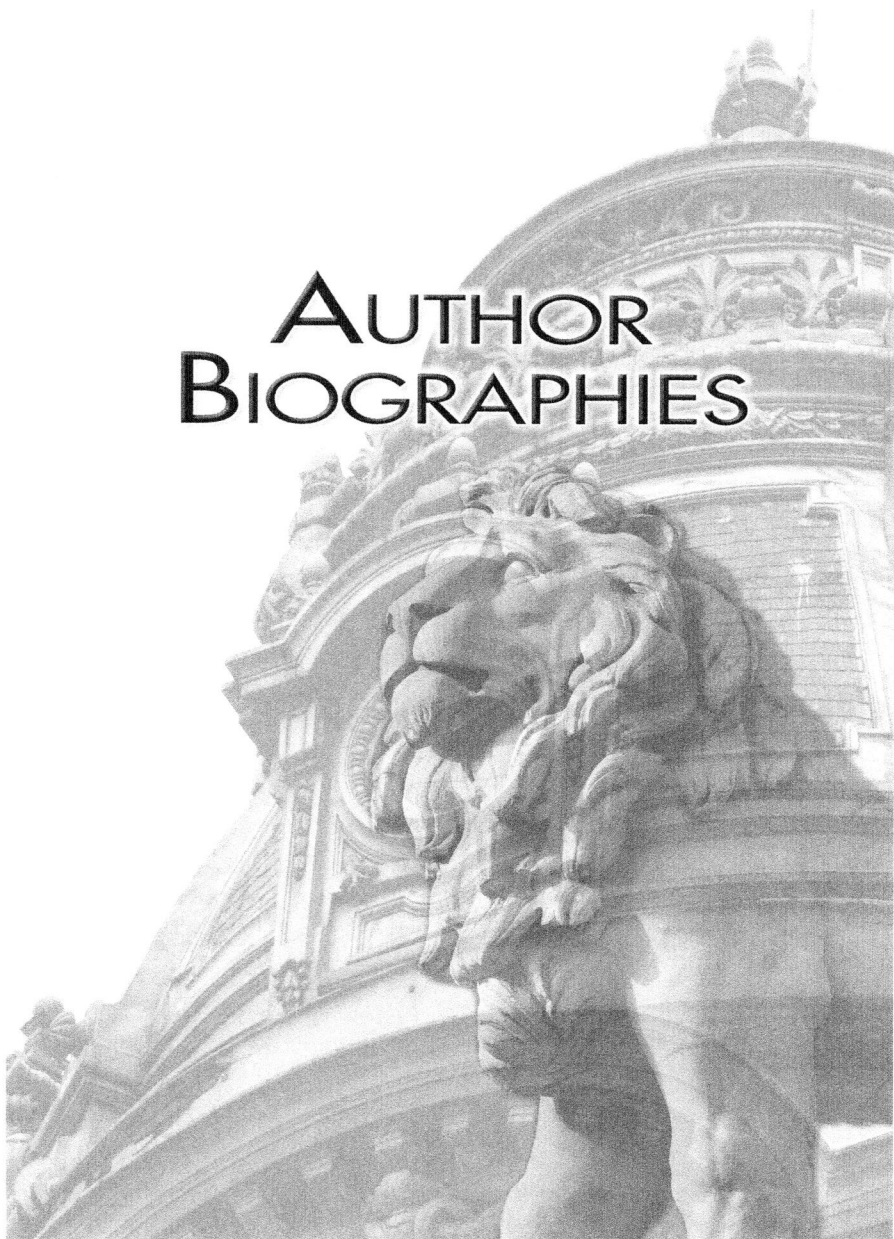

Jonathan Balcombe is a biologist with a PhD in ethology, the study of animal behavior. His books include Pleasurable Kingdom, Second Nature, The Exultant Ark, and New York Times best-seller *What a Fish Knows.* His next book, all about flies, will be published later this year by Penguin Books. In addition to writing books, Jonathan does professional editing for aspiring and established authors, and he has taught a course in animal sentience for the Viridis Graduate Institute. Formerly Director of Animal Sentience with the Humane Society Institute for Science and Policy, and Department Chair for Animal Studies with Humane Society University, in Washington, DC, Jonathan has also served as Associate Editor of the journal Animal Sentience. He lives in Belleville, Ontario, where in his spare time he enjoys biking, baking, birding, Bach, and trying to understand the neighborhood squirrels.

Cini Bretzlaff-Holstein, DSW, LSW, FOCAE, is the Bachelor of Social Work (BSW) Program Director, Social Work Department Chair, and an Associate Professor of Social Work at Trinity Christian College in Palos Heights, IL. Additionally, she is a licensed social worker in the state of Illinois. Bretzlaff-Holstein completed her Master of Social Work (MSW) degree at Baylor University Diana R. Garland School of Social Work in Waco, TX, and her Doctor of Social Work (DSW) degree at St. Catherine University-University of St. Thomas School of Social Work in St. Paul, MN. She completed a banded dissertation (three publishable articles: one research-based, two conceptual) for the doctoral program titled *The Case for Humane Education in Social Work Education.* One of her conceptual articles was published in the international journal *Social Work Education.* Bretzlaff-Holstein's scholarly interests include food justice, vegan studies, environmental and ecological justice, social work education and humane education, and the human-animal bond in social work. Furthermore, she is currently exploring vegetarianism and veganism as presented in young adult fiction with a colleague in Trinity's education department, as well as veganism, vegan studies, and the professoriate as a research project. Since October 2018, Bretzlaff-Holstein has been a Fellow of The Ferrater Mora Oxford Centre for Animal Ethics, Oxford, England.

Erin Comaskey, EdD, CHES, is an educator who has built a career around developing teaching and learning strategies focused on access, equity, and excellence. She began as a classroom teacher in New Jersey's Abbott district schools after graduating with a BS in Early Childhood Education from The College of New Jersey. Following a move to Montreal, Canada, Erin completed a Master's degree in Educational Psychology from McGill University where her research focused on a free web-based literacy tool to improve reading outcomes. Her subsequent position at the Center for the Study of Learning and Performance continued this effort to bring free evidence-based tools to children across Canada. More recently, Erin has dedicated her work to helping to promote humane pedagogical practices. In her work with The Humane Society of the United States, the Academy of Prosocial Learning, and as a founding board member at The Humane Education Coalition, Erin has worked with educators and students to expand social justice issues to include planetary and non-human animal perspectives. Erin received her Doctor of Education degree from Johns Hopkins University, where she developed a culturally relative framework for humane education programs. She currently lives in Amsterdam, Netherlands.

Andrew Domzalski, PhD, has been a full-time faculty member at Madonna University, Livonia, Michigan, since 1999, currently in the rank of professor and serving as the chair of the Department of Humanities. He has taught human-animal studies since 2005, engaging students in creative, humane service-learning projects in collaboration with the Detroit Zoo. In 2012, he and his colleagues co-created a Master of Science in Humane Studies, now Humane Leadership program, which he has co-directed since. Among his other administrative duties, he also serves as the director of the Center for Humane Studies at Madonna University. To his teaching and scholarship, Domzalski brings a varied background in psychology, reading education, linguistics, and theology. He has published and presented in the areas of Humane Education and Human- Animal Studies, in addition to his work in the field of Teaching English to Speakers of Other Languages. His current research interests revolve around religious conceptualizations of animals in both Western and Eastern traditions, with a focus on Christian and Buddhist views. Most recently, those interests include views on animal souls and afterlife.

He holds a PhD from Oakland University and master's degrees from Marygrove College and Warsaw University. Beyond the academe, he has been involved in cat rescue.

Boguslawa Gatarek holds a PhD in Educational Studies, with specialty in Cognition and Learning, from the University of Windsor, Windsor, Ontario, Canada, and a master's degree in Clinical Psychology from Warsaw University, Warsaw, Poland. Over the last two decades she has taught a variety of graduate and undergraduate courses in research methodology, human development, and related areas at Madonna University, Livonia, Michigan. In 2012, together with her colleagues, she co-created a Master of Science in Humane Studies, now Humane Leadership program, at Madonna University, which she currently co-directs. Since that time, she has taught courses in Humane Education and Human-Animal Studies. Her research interests span a vast spectrum of topics, from research methodology in education and social sciences to humane education to animal ethics. Gatarek has published and presented at regional, national, and international conferences in areas related to those interests. She volunteers for Community Cats Toronto, where she regularly conducts TNR workshops for the colony cats' caretakers. This work has led to her most recent interest in different ways community cats are perceived as either feral pets, invasive species, or wildlife. She lives with her husband and their rescued felines.

Brian Hare, PhD, is a core member of the Center of Cognitive Neuroscience, a Professor in Evolutionary Anthropology, and Psychology and Neuroscience at Duke University. He received his PhD from Harvard University, founded the Hominoid Psychology Research Group while at the Max Planck Institute for Evolutionary Anthropology in Germany, and subsequently created the Duke Canine Cognition Center when arriving at Duke. He has co-authored three books and published over 100 scientific papers including in *Science, Nature* and *PNAS*. His research on dozens of different animal species including dogs, wolves, bonobos, chimpanzees, and humans has taken him everywhere from Siberia to the Congo Basin.

Stephanie Itle-Clark, EdD, CHES, is the Founder and Chief Academic Officer of the Academy of Prosocial Learning. She received her BS in Education from Indiana University of Pennsylvania, MEd in Educational Curriculum and Development from Wilkes University, and EdD in Educational Leadership from Fielding Graduate University, where she focused on the impact of humane education professional development for teachers. She also holds Certified Humane Education Specialist credentials. Prior to founding the Academy of Prosocial Learning, she taught in both private and public education sectors and was the Director of Learning at The Humane Society of the United States. She specializes in humane pedagogy and supporting educators as they develop lessons that infuse inclusive humane and prosocial education into the standards-based curriculum in order to increase learner growth in the cognitive, affective, and behavioral domains. Stephanie is the editor of the *International Journal of Humane Education,* a past board president of the Association of Professional Humane Educators, and a current board member of the Humane Education Coalition and the United Federation of Teachers Humane Education Committee. She is also the author of humane education picture books, including the Early Empathy Series built around early reader sight words and themes of compassion and acceptance.

Mary Lee Jensvold, PhD, currently is the Primate Communication Scientist and Associate Director at Fauna Foundation in Carignan, Quebec. She is former director of the Chimpanzee & Human Communication Institute and is a Senior Lecturer in the Primate Behavior and Ecology Program and Anthropology Department at Central Washington University. She has over 30 years of experience working in chimpanzee sanctuaries in care, management, and design. Her expertise is in behavior and communication, including American Sign Language in chimpanzees and other apes. Her research includes conversational behaviors between chimpanzees and humans, private signing, phrase development, chimpanzee-to-chimpanzee conversation, and imaginary play. Other research includes caregiving practices, zoo visitor effects, and public education about chimpanzees. Jensvold is a member of the board of directors of the Animal Welfare Institute, Fauna Foundation, and Friends of Washoe. She is an alternate on the North American Primate Sanctuary Alliance steering committee. She is past Sigma Xi distinguished lecturer and has numerous journal article and book chapter publications. She wrote the book *Chimpanzee Behaviour: Recent Understandings from Captivity and the Forest.*

Kerrie Anne Loyd, PhD, is a wildlife biologist and Senior Lecturer at Arizona State University. She strives to incorporate humane activities in all biology labs. Dr. Loyd earned her BS in Wildlife Science from Virginia Tech and her MA in Science Education from the University of Georgia (UGA). She worked in Environmental Education in Atlanta, Georgia, for seven years before returning to graduate school to study wildlife ecology. She completed her education at the UGA in 2012 and moved to Arizona. Dr. Loyd's research has focused on domestic cat impact on wildlife in suburban areas and urban burrowing owl ecology. She has published 12 manuscripts and a book chapter on these topics.

Evan MacLean, PhD, is an Assistant Professor at the University of Arizona, where he holds appointments in Anthropology, Veterinary Medicine, Psychology, and Cognitive Science. He is the founder and Director the Arizona Canine Cognition Center. Dr. MacLean received his doctorate in Evolutionary Anthropology from Duke University in 2012, where he was a James B. Duke Fellow. His research integrates methods from evolutionary biology and comparative psychology to address questions about the mechanisms through which animals represent and reason about the world, and the processes through which cognition evolves. He also conducts applied work investigating how research on dog behavior, cognition, genetics, and neuroendocrinology can improve the processes through which dogs are selected, bred, and trained for roles in society. In addition to his work on animal behavior and cognition, Dr. MacLean studies the biological mechanisms involved in human-animal-interaction, with a focus on the neuropeptides oxytocin and vasopressin. In the last five years, Dr. MacLean has led diverse projects on these topics, which have been supported by the National Institutes of Health, Office of Naval Research, the AKC Canine Health Foundation, and the Waltham Center for Pet Nutrition. In 2015, he was awarded a Next Generation Canine Research Fellowship from the Stanton Foundation, and his work has been highlighted in media outlets including The New

York Times, National Public Radio, the BBC, and National Geographic.

Brian Ogle, EdD is an Associate Professor of Anthrozoology at Beacon College with specialties in zoo studies, applied animal management, and humane education. He holds a doctorate in curriculum and instruction, as well as a master's degree in anthrozoology. His research interest spans both the application of anthrozoological themes in zoological institutions and the examination of college science teaching practices. Throughout his career, he has actively been involved in professional organizations dedicated to furthering the field of humane education.

Andrew Rowan, DPhil, is the President and Chief Program Officer for WellBeing International (Potomac, Maryland). He has served in numerous board, advisory, and consultative roles for government bodies, private corporations and non-profits. Before WellBeing International, Andrew was the Chief Scientific Officer of the Humane Society of the United States and CEO of Humane Society International. He was the founder and director of the Tufts University Center for Animals and Public Policy (1983) and started the first graduate degree program in animal policy (1995). He was the founding editor of Anthrozoos (1987). He is the recipient of a Rhodes Scholarship (1968), the Russell and Burch award (1996) for his advancement of alternatives to animal testing, and a number of other awards. Dr. Rowan has authored and co-authored many books and articles on animal research, wildlife conservation, and companion animal management. He was born in Zimbabwe and raised in Cape Town, South Africa. He received a BSc (1968) from Cape Town University and an MA (oxon) and DPhil (1975, biochemistry) from Oxford University.

Alina S. Rusu, PhD, CHES (biologist and psychologist), is currently Associate Professor in the Department of Special Education, School of Psychology and Sciences of Education, Babes-Bolyai University, Cluj-Napoca, Romania, and Fulbright Ambassador for the Romanian Academic Environment Her professional and research interests are humane education, interdisciplinary curricular development, applied values of human-animal interactions and the multidimensional study of community-oriented volunteering. She teaches "Animal Psychology" (undergraduate level), and "Animal-Assisted Therapy" and "Positive Psychology in Inclusive Institutions" (master level). Dr. Rusu received her PhD in Natural Sciences (Animal Behavior) from University of Zurich in 2004. Since 2004, she was the director of several research grants funded by national and international agencies, most of them based on interdisciplinary approaches, i.e. applied animal behavior, evolutionary psychology, and animal-assisted therapy targeting the socio-emotional development of ASD children. The outcomes of these research projects, including those resulted from the successful coordination of several PhD theses in psychology, are reflected in her publications in peer-reviewed journals, book chapters and conference proceedings. In 2017, Dr. Rusu was a Fulbright Senior Scholar at School of Social Work, Rutgers University, New Brunswick, US. Her Fulbright project had the objective of developing an interdisciplinary curriculum in collaboration with social work academics, i.e., "*Service-Learning for civic responsibility through positive human-animal interactions*".

Kimberly Spanjol, PhD, BCBA-D, LMHC, CHES, is a Doctoral Level Board Certified Behavior Analyst, Licensed Mental Health Counselor and Certified Humane Education Specialist. She received her PhD in Criminal Justice with a specialization in Forensic Psychology in 2005 from the City University of New York and holds a Master's Degree in Mental Health Counseling as well as multiple certifications in Behavior Analysis, Animals and Human Health, Humane Education and Teaching Mindfulness to Youth. She serves as an educator, researcher, consultant and clinician. As an Assistant Professor of Criminal Justice and Sociology at Iona College in New Rochelle, New York, and an adjunct professor in the Sustainability and Environmental Justice program at John Jay College of Criminal Justice, Dr. Spanjol teaches social justice in Corrections, Criminology, Environmental Crime, Environmental Justice, Gender, Species Justice and more. Her clinical work focuses on children, teens and young adults with a variety of behavioral, developmental and mental health issues, as well as their families in private practice, educational and correctional settings. Her areas of specialization are Animal-Assisted Therapy, Animals and Criminal Justice, Animal Protection, Behavior Modification, Cognitive Behavioral Therapy, Environmental Criminology, Humane Education, The Human-Animal Bond, Intersectionality and Social Justice, and Social Emotional Learning.

Bernard Unti, PhD, is Senior Policy Advisor at the Humane Society of the United States and has represented the organization and its affiliates in a range of domestic and global campaigns and initiatives. His interests include the evolution of human attitudes toward animals, the history and sociology of the animal protection movement, the development of petkeeping, animal sheltering and the kindness-to-animals ethic, the humane education of children, and the place of animal protection within American philanthropy. He is the author of *Protecting All Animals: A Fifty-Year History of The Humane Society of the United States* (2004) and other works on animal protection as an historical and contemporary concern.

About WCY Humane Press

The WCY Humane Press Imprint is Dedicated to Publication of Academic Texts Advancing Humane Pedagogy in the Classroom

Who Chains You Books, a publisher of animal-related titles based in Virginia, has unveiled a new imprint serving the postsecondary community. WCY Humane Press will feature titles that provide new and emerging texts related to academic efforts in animal welfare and humane education classrooms at the college level.

We hope you'll visit our website and join us on this adventure we call animal advocacy publishing. We're currently accepting scholarly queries. We welcome you.

Learn more at wcyhumanepress.com.

BOOKS FOR THE EARLY EDUCATION CLASSROOM FROM AUTHOR STEPHANIE ITLE-CLARK AND WCY BOOKS

Tiffany Rolls On

Flock of Friends

Oliver's Big Problem

Out of the Dog House

ABOUT THE EDITOR

⌒━━◆━━⌒

STEPHANIE ITLE-CLARK, EdD, CHES, is the Founder of the Academy of Prosocial Learning. She received her BS in Education from Indiana University of Pennsylvania, MEd in Educational Curriculum and Development from Wilkes University, and EdD in Educational Leadership from Fielding Graduate University. She specializes in humane pedagogy and supporting educators as they develop lessons that infuse inclusive humane and prosocial education into the standards-based curriculum in order to increase learner growth in the cognitive, affective, and behavioral domains.

Stephanie is the editor of the International Journal of Humane Education, a past board president of the Association of Professional Humane Educators, and a current board member of the Humane Education Coalition and the United Federation of Teachers Humane Education Committee. She is also the author of humane education picture books, including the Early Empathy Series built around early reader sight words and themes of compassion and acceptance.

Books for Classroom Case Study Use

IT WENT TO THE DOGS: HOW MICHAEL VICK'S DOGFIGHTING COMPOUND BECAME A HAVEN FOR RESCUE PUPS, BY TAMIRA THAYNE

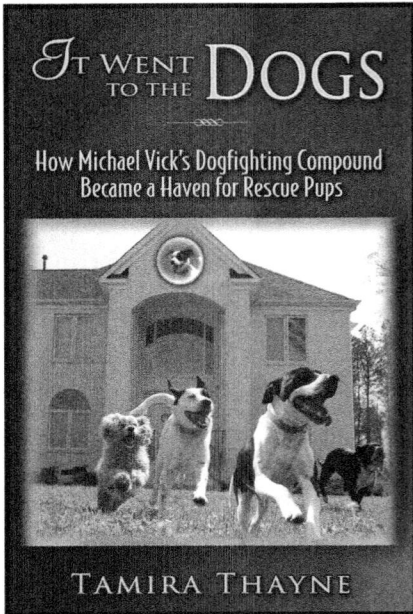

The house sat empty, an eerie white sentinel against the flat winter landscape, now guarding only whispers of the past. A six-foot white metal fence with entry gate lined the country road, abandoning its purpose at the property line and allowing passage to all with the temerity and curiosity to walk around.

The bullet hole in the front window went unnoticed...

Tamira Thayne was early for her appointment with the Hampton Roads, Virginia realtor. She was to tour Michael Vick's former dogfighting compound, something she'd never imagined nor particularly wanted to do. The decision Tamira would make that fateful day in February 2011 would lead not only to a home for her nonprofit's rescue dogs, but also to the most turbulent four years of her life.

Turns out there was a reason Michael Vick felt he could get away with dogfighting in Surry, Virginia...*Read more and order from whochainsyou.com, Amazon, and other outlets.*

Books for Classroom Case Study Use

I Once Was Lost, But Now I'm Found: Daisy and the Olympic Animal Sanctuary Rescue by Laura Koerber

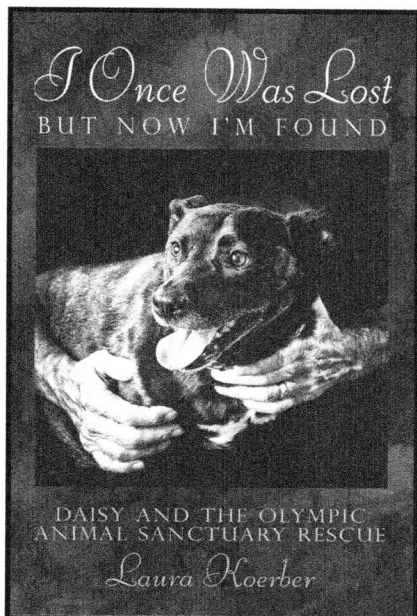

On the far side of the Olympic Peninsula in Washington State, halfway between the mountains and the ocean, stands the little town of Forks. In that town, in a quiet neighborhood of modest homes and shabby businesses, there remains a dilapidated pink warehouse.

Packed inside that warehouse, living in deplorable conditions, were once over 120 dogs. In one of the crates was a black dog named Daisy. This is her story.

It is also the story of the rescue of one hundred and twenty-four dogs—and one snake—from the Olympic Animal Sanctuary. The OAS rescue was an epic narrative that extended over several years and featured small town politics, protests, assault, lawsuits, arrests, and a midnight escape, all played out to a nationwide audience.

...Read more and order from whochainsyou.com, Amazon, and other outlets.

Printed in Great Britain
by Amazon

74193410R00163